REPETITION

AND

PHILOSOPHICAL CRUMBS

SØREN AABYE KIERKEGAARD (1813–1855) was born in Copenhagen, Denmark's main trading port. He was a defining figure in Denmark's 'Golden Age', when its art and literature rivalled the best from Paris or Berlin. He earned the equivalent of a doctorate in 1841 with a dissertation on *The Concept of Irony, with Constant Reference to Socrates*. A substantial inheritance freed him to write full time and sidestep the compromises of an academic career. Though he went through an abortive engagement, he never married and was freed from the distractions of family life. He published *Either/Or*, *Fear and Trembling*, *Repetition*, and *Philosophical Crumbs* in 1843–4, and several other works in a variety of innovative genres thereafter. His writing career was to end with the massive *Concluding Unscientific Postscript* (1846), intended to be, indeed, his concluding statement, after which he would lead the simple life of a pastor. But by nature incurably polemical, a bitter dispute with a popular Copenhagen weekly kept him in the public eye. His critiques of the popular press, mass politics, and 'social club religion' were to have a profound influence on twentieth-century existentialist, Marxist, and religious commentary on bourgeois society. As philosophers and social critics Heidegger, Arendt, Camus, and Sartre relied heavily on him, while his dazzling insights and literary skills were to influence the writers Ibsen, Rilke, and Kafka, Auden and Dinesen, as well as such theologians as Tillich, Barth, Buber, Bonhoeffer, and Levinas.

M. G. PIETY is an Associate Professor of Philosophy at Drexel University. She was a Visiting Scholar at the Department of Søren Kierkegaard Research at the University of Copenhagen from 1990 to 1998, and has published articles on Kierkegaard and on the philosophy of religion.

EDWARD F. MOONEY is Professor of Philosophy and Religion at Syracuse University. He is the author of *On Søren Kierkegaard: Dialogue, Polemics, Lost Intimacy and Time* (2007), as well as two other books on Kierkegaard and articles on Kierkegaard and moral philosophy.

OXFORD WORLD'S CLASSICS

*For over 100 years Oxford World's Classics have brought
readers closer to the world's great literature. Now with over 700
titles — from the 4,000-year-old myths of Mesopotamia to the
twentieth century's greatest novels — the series makes available
lesser-known as well as celebrated writing.*

*The pocket-sized hardbacks of the early years contained
introductions by Virginia Woolf, T. S. Eliot, Graham Greene,
and other literary figures which enriched the experience of reading.
Today the series is recognized for its fine scholarship and
reliability in texts that span world literature, drama and poetry,
religion, philosophy, and politics. Each edition includes perceptive
commentary and essential background information to meet the
changing needs of readers.*

OXFORD WORLD'S CLASSICS

═══

SØREN KIERKEGAARD

Repetition
and
Philosophical Crumbs

═══

Translated by
M. G. PIETY

With an Introduction by
EDWARD F. MOONEY

and Notes by
EDWARD F. MOONEY and M. G. PIETY

OXFORD
UNIVERSITY PRESS

OXFORD
UNIVERSITY PRESS

Great Clarendon Street, Oxford ox2 6DP

Oxford University Press is a department of the University of Oxford.
It furthers the University's objective of excellence in research, scholarship,
and education by publishing worldwide in

Oxford New York

Auckland Cape Town Dar es Salaam Hong Kong Karachi
Kuala Lumpur Madrid Melbourne Mexico City Nairobi
New Delhi Shanghai Taipei Toronto

With offices in

Argentina Austria Brazil Chile Czech Republic France Greece
Guatemala Hungary Italy Japan Poland Portugal Singapore
South Korea Switzerland Thailand Turkey Ukraine Vietnam

Oxford is a registered trade mark of Oxford University Press
in the UK and in certain other countries

Published in the United States
by Oxford University Press Inc., New York

British Library Cataloguing in Publication Data

Data available

Library of Congress Cataloging in Publication Data

Library of Congress Control Number: 2008943927

Typeset by Cepha Imaging Private Ltd., Bangalore, India
Printed in Great Britain
on acid-free paper by
Clays Ltd, Elcograf S.p.A.

ISBN 978-0-19-921419-8

CONTENTS

INTRODUCTION

In 1843, a few months before the publication of *Repetition* and about
a year before that of *Philosophical Crumbs*, Kierkegaard published
Either/Or in two volumes; the first ('Either') evokes a fragment of life
from the angle of an aesthetic existence, the second ('Or'), from an
'ethical' standpoint. The compilation of papers evoking an aesthetic
way of life includes poetic musings, music criticism, and reflections
on tragedy. A mood of somewhat sinister dissipation and manipula-
tion permeates the psychological intrigues of 'The Seducer's Diary', a
small novelette that has often been published separately. The second
volume, also a compilation, includes letters addressed to the aesthete of
Volume 1. They come from the pen of one 'Judge Wilhelm', a worthy
citizen who gives a rather long-winded defence of an ethical way of
life. There is a tension, then, between the *Either* and the *Or* that invites
readers to weigh the aesthetic and ethical dimensions of their own
orientations in life. Just to complicate matters, a short religious tract
is inserted in the final pages. Beyond the life of a poet or a judge is the
life of a pastor or priest. The pastor's contribution to this 'fragment of
life' is a severe, accusatory sermon on our being 'always in the wrong'
as against God. Thus, in Volume 2 we have a critique not only of the
self-indulgent 'aesthete' but also of the self-satisfied Judge.

Either/Or, like *Crumbs* and *Repetition*, seeks to map the subtle ways
that suffering is imposed and self-imposed, and to suggest paths of
relief. We are aware that the book holds up a troubling mirror to our
lives, and we see that as readers we have a role to play in negotiating
the tensions between the ethical and the aesthetic, for instance. The
book's use of pseudonyms, and complex dramatic stagings, are characteristic. While *Either/Or* is but a small fraction of Kierkegaard's
total literary, philosophical output, *Repetition* and *Crumbs* represent
an even smaller fraction, but their small size and lavish detail make
them marvellous doors into Kierkegaard's worlds.

Repetition marks the end of Kierkegaard's initial, and in many ways
richest, year of publication, 1843. *Philosophical Crumbs* comes a few
months later. The *Concluding Unscientific Postscript*, a 500-page sequel
appearing in 1846, is a tragi-comic treatise that stages Kierkegaardian
subjectivity and objectivity, the roles of knowledge and passion in

orienting a self, and the face-off between Reason and Faith. Front and centre is a self radically distinct from any social mass or group membership. Singular individuals struggle to make sense of things, to find a basis for life-shaping decisions, to find insight to ease the ubiquity of affliction, not least one's own. *Repetition* and *Philosophical Crumbs* open these themes, and display the artistry and wit of Kierkegaard's infinitely restless moral and religious imagination.

REPETITION

At times *Repetition* reads like a short novel, full of puzzles and twists of fate. At other times it reads like a technical disquisition on a quasi-metaphysical concept called 'repetition'. In the first half of the book Kierkegaard's narrator, Constantine Constantius, introduces the contrast between 'repetition' and the ancient Platonic concept of recollection. Plato's idea is that we already possess the rudiments of all the knowledge we need. It is part of the inherited structure of our minds. Once we begin thinking, we have a glimmer of the ideas that 2 plus 2 equal 4, and that we should always do what is good, for instance. All we have to do is remember these truths, and a teacher like Socrates can prompt us. The royal road to knowledge, for Plato, is through prompted remembering or recollection. But Constantine says that the modern age needs a new concept, and that he will provide it. He calls the alternative royal road to insight 'repetition'. Repetition means getting our cognitive and moral bearings not through prompted remembering, but quite unexpectedly as a gift from the unknown, as a revelation from the future. Repetition is epiphany that sometimes grants the old again, as new, and sometimes grants something radically new.

The second half of this strange and innovative book is a series of letters between Constantine and a lovesick, overwrought young man. This nameless young man seeks a 'revelation' that will remove, or at least ease, his sorrow. He seeks out Constantine as a mentor, wise in the ways of breaking-up, of love lost, and perhaps wise in erasing the false promise of love altogether. He needs stable footing. Perhaps he needs to make peace with the fact that he has jilted his sweetheart, or perhaps he needs to keep the flame of that love alive. He seems excessively happy, at the end, to learn that she has released him by marrying another man. But that may be false bravado; we don't really know.

In any case, he needs the return of a viable life, a 'repetition' that will end his heartache.

Constantine's response is jaded. His friend's *angst* is 'an interesting issue'. It's doubtful that he has any sympathy for the young man. He suggests a cruel stratagem to destroy any lingering attachment the girl might still have. He is cynical about love. Is the young man hopelessly lost? In the best case, repetition would be the hope that he will regain love. In a less than ideal case, the hope would be that he will 'get over' his attachment and thereby regain a guiltless outlook. The broad question *Repetition* poses is how a sense of meaning and direction in life can be regained as we suffer its absence.

Loss and Restoration

Abraham (in *Fear and Trembling*), Job (in the 'Job Discourse'), and the young man in *Repetition* are afflicted or threatened by great loss. The first is about to lose his son—by his own hand, no less. The second has lost his wealth, children, health, even his friends—for no fathomable reason. The third loses his sweetheart—though it is hard to grasp why he dropped her in the first place, and why, as his letters continue, he nevertheless imagines himself in the role of her husband. Behind this writing on loss and redemption is Kierkegaard's broken engagement to the young Regine Olsen. He was a melancholy 27; she an innocent 16. Perhaps he believed his gloom would poison her brightness; perhaps he thought that domestic life would derail his vocation as a writer. In any case, as he broke off the engagement he wrote books that take up themes of inexplicable loss and the dream of requital.

Kierkegaard wonders painfully if he is made with sufficient strength to wrest meaning from loss. Socrates and Hegel bet that human wit and will are sufficient to expel despair. Looking at Job and Abraham and his own ill fortune, Kierkegaard has doubts. Both *Repetition* and *Crumbs* are preoccupied with the question of whether we are built with sufficient resources to expel despair on our own—or instead, are radically insufficient to the task.

More often than not, especially in the first five years of his authorship, Kierkegaard publishes under pseudonyms. *Philosophical Crumbs* is by Johannes Climacus (John the Climber), *Repetition* by Constantine Constantius, *Fear and Trembling* by Johannes de silentio, and so on. Pseudonyms leave a subtle air of mystery—though everyone in

Copenhagen knew who invented them. They also convey a more sophisticated point. A book takes a particular angle on life, and as that angle changes from book to book, so, in a way, does the author doing the writing. *Fear and Trembling* is signed 'Johannes de silentio' in part because the horror of the story reduces *that* author (and Kierkegaard) to silence. Constantine Constantius is constantly looking for constancy. The flesh-and-blood author 'Søren Kierkegaard' is of little interest relative to the Constantine or the Johannes involved in writing *this* title or *that* one. The complex standpoint of a singular book is what matters, and that standpoint is just a small fragment of the amazing range of Kierkegaard's attunements to life, of the full range of the writer.

Although it often makes sense to distinguish the stance of a pseudonym from that of the writer behind it, flesh-and-blood Kierkegaard may believe much that a pseudonym brings out. The first order of business, therefore, is not to make hard-and-fast, all-purpose divisions between pseudonyms and 'pure Kierkegaard', but to inhabit a text's singular viewpoint, and to give it the best reading we can. If we hit on a difficulty in interpretation, there is no turning to the Copenhagen writer for sure-fire rescue; pausing over the pseudo-author's name *might* help. Does Johannes Climacus provide us with a ladder to climb out of the cellar? Constantine might offer a stable centre around which renewal revolves. Or he might hint that even the constant holds motion in store. Mr Constant is Constant-Constant.

The wit that dances on nearly every page keeps us from simple answers. It works also as self-protection. Kierkegaard knows he has massive intelligence and talent, and knows he must resist the hubris of taking those gifts too far. After crowing proudly, he will efface himself. He undersells *Repetition* by calling it, in his *Journal*, 'insignificant, without any philosophical pretension, a droll little book, dashed off as an oddity'. Yet he opens it by suggesting that western metaphysics ought to set Platonic recollection aside and embrace *his* concept, repetition. So Constantine's 'oddity' aims to accomplish in just a few pages a revolution on the scale achieved by Heidegger or Wittgenstein. He would change the world with sly words, a love story, and a wink.

Choice and Reception of Meaning

Many commentators assume that Kierkegaard is a source for the view, promoted by Jean-Paul Sartre, that ethical values and standpoints are a matter of radical choice. Moderns are aware of a primordial freedom that leaves them in the lurch to choose both their own selves and their own values. Sartre seems to lift this view from the ethical Judge Wilhelm. But this is not fair to the text of *Either/Or* or to Kierkegaard's considered view. The self that the judge enjoins the aesthete to choose is embedded socially and historically, encumbered by a deep sense of humanity. It is not a site for unconstrained choice.

In addition, the judge enters a counter-proposal to the theme of self-choice. Rather than self-choice, self-reception becomes the operative term. We find this elaborated in *Repetition* and in 'the Job Discourse', the sixth of his *Eighteen Upbuilding Discourses* of 1843. Job waits through his suffering with *nothing* to choose. He is only dust and ashes. Out of nowhere a storm appears, singing the rebirth of his world. Through the Wind's poetry he is given seas, great birds, infinite stars, the glory of dawn: 'the shape of things is changed by it—they stand forth, as if clothed in ornament' (Job 38: 12, 14). The moral is that when caught in despair there is, at the limit, no 'autonomous choice' by which one lurches out of the muck. One is remade and saved (if one is) by an intervention of the other, as it were. One is offered a call or vision not of one's choice or making: the birds of the air, an assembly of true friends (not Job's mockers), an icon, a Saviour. One does not *create* Truth *ex nihilo*. It jolts one awake, strikes one dumb, steals one's heart.

Reversing the usual flow of meaning-carrying passions will undo a false valorization of choice and unqualified autonomy. The dominant modern image has meaning flow outward, projected from a source in the autonomous self to adhere to others and the world. 'You are what I make you to be, or as I construe you!' The inversion of that image gives a pre-modern or non-modern picture. Meaning arrives in an incoming flow from a source 'without', from the other, the world, the divine. 'I acknowledge and accept who you are; what you are shapes my responsiveness.' Meaning installs itself, breaching autonomy. Under the dominant model of modernity, the 'self-sufficiency model' that Kierkegaard calls 'Socratic' (for us it is the Nietzschean model), selves are autonomous projects, constructors of manifold institutions, practices, even character traits that are then owned or disowned. Under the 'insufficiency' non-Socratic model (a biblical model), selves are passions or souls bequeathed, seated to receive life, making acknowledgement of interdependence inescapable.

Yielding and Dependence

Autonomy is an antidote to servility, while any breach of autonomy is typically assimilated to slavishness—what Kant called heteronomy. To be servile is to be held hostage or intimidated by another, but yielding to another is not always servile. If we are to be loved, we must yield to a passion from another and let responsiveness to that other unfold. But letting oneself be loved, though it requires a yielding will, is not letting oneself be crushed or intimidated. Hearing poetry often means yielding to an image or a sound. Caring for infants (at least some of the time) means listening for their emerging will and desire—not being servile before them. In teamwork, we depend on our coach and each other. In large choral performances, we yield to and are dependent on the spirit of the music, our fellow singers, the wishes of a conductor.

As an autonomous, executive self, Constantine Constantius tries to make repetition happen. This is a satire of true repetition, which is a Job-like yielding to meaning conferred. Constantine tries to induce repetition by retracing his steps in Berlin. It's fine if he longs to have experiences of a former journey come back, but repetition is awaiting the arrival of the new, and welcoming it, if it should arrive. It is precisely *not* scouring the past for the source of its echo. He seeks the excitement of an earlier theatre performance by returning to the spot. In repetition, one faces forward precisely because retracing one's steps won't work. Trying to recover an experience explicitly, as a *project*, is to welcome disaster. If we look up an old flame, the spark *might* reignite, but vibrant happiness can't be *made to happen*, on cue. As the subtitle to *Repetition* tells us, Constantine attempts a 'psychological experiment'. But he is far too detached, as a disinterested observer, for his attempt to be credible. Job is the model for repetition. His world gets restored in his yielding, and in his dependence and acceptance of the wondrous beyond all choice or control. He does not set out on a ridiculous attempt to construct repetition. It happens on its own, in a fresh burst of glory that overtakes and humbles our sense of studied control.

Change and Transition

For Plato, cognitive insight is discovering a changeless past truth that makes the current world of change an illusion. If we need love, we 'think back to' or 'recollect' a reassuring, timeless essence already there to revive us. We have 'known love' all along, but have momentarily forgotten. We try to recall a first love, when all was alive and exciting. Constantine will replace Platonic recollection with repetition. But he has another model to consider. Hegelian 'mediation' also traces the emergence of insight, providing a schema for understanding historical transitions as progressive realizations of insights and co-relative institutions through a conflict of opposites. In the domain of world history, the medieval world, for example, might harbour internal conflicts that give birth to the insightful Renaissance world-view. In the domain of individual history, an adolescent might harbour internal conflicts that give birth to a more insightful young adulthood. Progress is a 'mediation' between an initial state, its opposite, and an emerging resolution. Constantine mocks this '1, 2, 3, three-step' of Hegelian progression (p. 77). To change existentially or religiously is not to be caught up in a mechanical historical advance conceived under the banner of capitalism, socialism, or some cultural or theoretical fad.

Constantine tells us that repetition and recollection are the *same* movement, but in opposite directions. Meaning or value might collect or gather as it is unearthed from the past; but it might also gather as it arises newborn. In repetition, meaning gathers before my front-facing receptivity. Musical meaning is about to peak in a phrase not yet uttered by the cello. Whether it will (or not) is nothing I can control. I await something momentous, gathered as the *future* unveils it toward me. I tilt forward in anticipation, in a hope for the gift of repetition, for I half-know what to expect. Without repetition or recollection, Constantine tells us, 'all of life is dissolved into an empty, meaningless noise' (p. 19). Kierkegaard wants us to feel the allure of true repetition (not Constantine's travesty of it). The overwrought young man's ennui will not fall away as he 'remembers' a pregnant past. He seeks what Job and Abraham found, a transforming cloudburst or the intervention of a sudden angel that instils alertness to future promise. He needs openness to the possibility that a lost world might be regained, whether as marriage or freedom from it.

Faithful Trust

The young man 'awaiting his thunderstorm' is a mild parody of Job. His suffering does not match Job's, nor does he have Job's dignified courage. His plight is a lightly comical anticipation of New Testament apocalypse. He is amidst destruction and awaits a return. He speaks of marriage, yet he also seems to welcome a freedom from marriage. Abraham and Job have no uncertainty about what they want through the office of repetition. One wants the return of a son; the other wants the return of a life. Awaiting repetition is not just a wish but a *faithful trust* in a fulfilling restoration. The young man has only the bare germ of such trust. He *says* he awaits repetition, but his 'despair' can seem like a hysterical affectation, just 'too much drama' to be credible. And what is the restoration he craves? Does he want the girl? Perhaps he just wants to forget her to be rid of guilt and its drag on freedom. Constantine calls him a poet on the *verge* of the religious, but at best he is a religious lightweight, and most likely a *poseur*.

In *Crumbs*, such faithful trust in restoration is spelled out as a non-Socratic possibility. Under the non-Socratic 'insufficiency model', vision or Truth arrives beyond effort or will, and perhaps against them, in great wonder and unlikelihood. The theme of a primitive trust-in-requital, arriving as revelation from a future unknown, travels quietly from *Fear and Trembling* to its explicit treatment in *Repetition* and onto the pages of *Philosophical Crumbs*, when it appears in the contrast between trust that Truth will arrive on its own and trust that it is ready at any time to percolate up from a subject's own resources.

The Suspicion and Need of Metaphysics

Ideas of form and matter, mind and body, substance, consciousness and freedom, passion and reason, and so forth, are Greek metaphysical concepts that have filtered down through the centuries in various articulations. But it is doubtful that they can be joined in a system that gives ultimate knowledge or practical insight. Kierkegaard writes in the wake of Kant, who abandoned the search for knowledge of metaphysical structures. The world is properly studied by natural science, and metaphysics should step aside. Theology evokes virtues of the heart, but will never prove the existence of God. Ethics may appeal to freedom, but freedom cannot be an item of certain knowledge. Although the questions of metaphysics cannot be answered, nevertheless Kant concedes that it is hard to forget them. Metaphysics presented tasks he could neither 'abandon nor carry to completion'. Metaphysical questions are hopeless, but we ask them anyway.

Constantine echoes Kant when he announces a 'new concept', repetition, which is both 'the interest of all metaphysics and [also] the interest upon which metaphysics becomes stranded' (p.19). We are fascinated with the fact that, against all odds, Isaac is returned, or that the world is returned to Job. Fascination grows toward a metaphysical interest. Is there an abstract account of how meaning and truth emerge? We can have a passion for metaphysics, for asking '*why?*', but that does not mean that there are answers to be found. Insofar as Job wonders *why* he has been deprived of a world, he has an *interest* in the quasi-metaphysical concept of repetition. But his faithful trust in restoration does not win him a metaphysical answer. Job gets the *wonder* of a world returned, but he does not learn *why* he suffers. Metaphysical wonder is uncoupled from metaphysical explanation. The reception of a life beyond dust and ashes throws the *need* for an answer aside. In nautical images, we would say that metaphysics (as knowledge, answer, or explanation) founders; its sailing is suspended. For Job, as for the young man, to seek repetition is to ache for a restorative impact.

The consolations of explanation or theory pale beside the shattering wonder of restoration. The impact of such experience overwhelms paltry attempts to *theorize* it. In *Philosophical Crumbs*, Kierkegaard returns in a Kantian vein to the impossibility of metaphysical answers to our deepest questions. Metaphysics is stymied (roughly) because the mind is not designed to answer questions that arise at the deepest level of metaphysical interest. The Socratic position is the optimistic view that, under prompting, we can access truth stored in memory; we are designed that way. The non-Socratic, biblical view is more pessimistic. We are flawed. Our design leaves us irremediably in error, insufficient to acquire truth on our own. For Socrates, limits on knowledge reflect temporary ignorance that can always be cured under proper tutelage. We are innately fitted out to make progress toward infinite knowledge. Inverting this position gives us the biblical position. We are *not* up to the task of acquiring infinite knowledge. Our basic design is flawed. We are in Error (or sin). Nevertheless, we yearn for the infinite.

Philosophy (or metaphysics) is a tragic passion. Metaphysics as an *explanatory system* comes to grief even as metaphysical *interest*, the passion for knowing *why*, continually re-emerges. A biblical revelation responds to a metaphysical 'why' even as it models a Truth that inexplicably 'comes out of nowhere'. The advent of love might relieve metaphysical *angst*, but it does not *explain* anything. The event of repetition only qualifies inexplicable pain, making it sufferable; it remains inexplicable. Repetition provides new and vivid registers of perception. A new world (or love) floats in for us experientially, awaiting poetic articulation. It appears as a site of marvel, praise, and astonishment, and flows healingly, working as a salve. Of course, we must be receptive to such an encounter. In letting go of the drive for *explanation* of hurt, we forgo a striving-to-achieve, forgo the impulse of an autonomous, executive self. This allows receptivity and willingness to supervene. A craving for self-sufficiency subsides. Such is the heart of *Repetition*, and the heart of the Christian option mapped out in *Philosophical Crumbs*.

PHILOSOPHICAL CRUMBS

Philosophical Crumbs reads more like the philosophical first half of *Repetition* than the second. It might be philosophical-theology, although sometimes it sounds like its parody. Like *Repetition*, it unsettles our expectations, starting with the title. A serious heading would be 'Philosophical Reflections' or 'Philosophical Investigations'. At its full length, however, we have the title *Philosophical Crumbs, or a Crumb of Philosophy*. We don't know whether to laugh at this poke at 'serious' philosophy, or to weep at the thought that the only wisdom available is crumbs — or to scowl because the author is pulling our leg. Kierkegaard, or his present pseudonym, Johannes Climacus, is willing to provoke philosophers and theologians who are typically put off by wit and lightheartedness. The Danish word '*Smuler*' means 'bits, scraps, crumbs, or trifles'. For years it has been translated in English as 'fragments'. But 'fragments' is not among a dictionary's favoured options for '*Smuler*', and it guarantees that the nimble irony of that topsy-turvy title is lost.

Kierkegaard loved to satirize all-too-serious ponderous thinkers. Take his *Postscript*. The title signals an addendum to something considerably longer. But *Postscript* is a 500-page sequel to the 100-page *Crumbs*. At full length its title runs: *Concluding Unscientific Postscript to Philosophical Crumbs: a Mimic-Pathetic-Dialectic Compilation: An Existential Intervention*. Seriously hilarious, he takes a poke at stiffness, keeps humour alive and minds alert, mocking the pretension to summon the whole universe or all history — and have it delivered in a three-course meal. He will toss you a crumb.

In the title *Philosophical Crumbs, or a Crumb of Philosophy*, the halves are divided by an 'or' and they mirror each other in a whimsical repetition. Why should philosophy be sombre? '*Smuler*' ('scraps', 'bits', 'crumbs') suggests the remains of a banquet. In the Gospel story Lazarus was content to gather crumbs falling from the rich man's table (Luke 16: 21). Jesus broke bread into bits and scraps. *Philosophical Crumbs* is a parody of books that promise a banquet containing everything.

Reading Kierkegaard requires a rare combination of nimble wit, irreverence, and religious concern. He downplays his own part in the composition, putting forward Johannes Climacus as the author. But 'S. Kierkegaard' is 'responsible for publication'. We are set adrift, left to our own interpretative devices, sharing a raft with a speaker who has only scraps in his sack and who disguises his real name. The original St John Climacus (*c.*570–649) was a Christian monk whose name, meaning John of the Ladder, derives from the title of his treatise on monastic life, *The Ladder of Paradise*. He might have been climbing to heaven. Yet he knows that God knocked down the Tower of Babel, also a ladder. A ladder might be no more than a logo to attract converts. Or it might offer a step up, not to storm heaven but to widen one's horizon for a better survey of common ground. A better vantage on the vagaries of earthly life might improve one's sense of the contrast, which is *religious* virtue or Truth.

Beginning the Text

The motto from Shakespeare at the start of the book, 'Better well hanged than ill wed', can be read as 'I'd rather *be hung on the cross* than bed down with fast talkers selling flashy "truth" in a handful of proposition'. A 'Propositio' follows the preface, but it is not a 'proposition to be defended'. It reveals the writer's lack of self-certainty and direction: 'The question [that motivates the book] is asked in ignorance by one who does not even know what can have led him to ask it.' But this book is not a stumbling accident, so the author's pose as a bungler may be only a pose. Underselling himself shows up brash,

self-important writers who know exactly what they're saying — who
trumpet Truth and Themselves for all comers.

Climacus is not a learned hero or trumpeter or bungling under-
study. He suggests in the Preface that he might be like Archimedes,
the Greek mathematician, who finds a sword over his head after
encircling armies break into the city. Archimedes does not beg for
his life, but for his geometry. His circles, sketched in the sand,
must not be disturbed. Climacus might bequeath gems hidden in
scraps in the sand. He styles himself a bumpkin of little learning
and no opinions, but this masks a clever urbanity. Climacus writes
as a soul at risk. This precludes him from 'having opinions', in this
sense: if one is about to drown, one has not the *luxury* of opinions.
Diogenes appears, rolling his barrel as his city rushes this way and
that preparing for siege. The citizens of Copenhagen are rushing
about *their* business. Is Climacus another Diogenes, aimlessly tossing his crumbs? There follows a more remarkable image. Climacus is
'a nimble dancer in the service of thought', a dancer 'to the honour
of God'. A few sentences later we learn that he dances with no
human partner, for he is wed to another dancer, the nimble 'thought
of death'.

In Chapter I the writer is an assistant professor, a talking head,
pacing at the blackboard charting differences between Socratic
and Christian sites of Truth. Earlier, he's a show-off tossing witty
crumbs at those who couldn't care less. Later he is a poet in the
service of imagination. And in the Preface, he's a dancer with death
before God. This is fluid, polyphonic identity. Each face carries its
own mood. The face of philosophy counters the purveyor of crumbs,
each laughing at or mocking the other. Disruptive wit is steadied by
chapter-by-chapter argument on salvation and history, sin and error,
change and necessity, the reliability of ancient testimony. These
steady arguments respond to the questions on the title page: *Can an
eternal consciousness have a historical point of departure; could such a
thing be of more than historical interest; can one build an eternal happiness on historical knowledge?*

The Historical Jesus and the Christ of Faith

In the decades before and on through Kierkegaard's university and
writing years, a controversy simmered in sophisticated circles about

the relevance of historical scholarship to religious faith. 'The search for the historical Jesus', championed first by German scholars, might be a great boon for Christians: faith might be confirmed through historical fact (with attendant reasoned argument) rather than through revelation or the authority of a priestly institution. On the other hand, the search might also be a fruitless diversion. Archaeological digs and examination of texts might determine the *historical* truths round and about Christianity. One could compile a record of the life of a Jewish prophet, a political agitator, or the Son of God (as the case might be). Perhaps centuries of debate and bloody religious wars would cease, as truth replaced fiction, fact replaced myth. But Climacus never joins this parade. Faith or salvation can't be based on historical records. Just as there will always be gaps between the history of purported egalitarian societies and the egalitarian ideal, so there will always be gaps between the historical Jesus and the Christian ideal. Research won't detect a risen Christ.

Even if one tried, it is not easy to eke out credible narratives about Jesus. The record is scant, transmitted at third- and fourth-hand, and passed down through centuries with little check on accuracy of transmission. There are no 'disinterested' spectators, disciples, reporters, editors, or curators. Even the best-case scenario yields only *the most likely* story. Second, faith seeks immediate assurance and conviction, while historical reports, even reports of revelation, speak from a cautious, narrative-building mind — not from the heart that testifies. Yet again, even if history gave some credence to the fact of a risen Christ, there would be no data confirming a Christ whose *concern endures even to the present*. In *Postscript*, Kierkegaard quotes Lessing's 'leap over an enormous ditch'. From this we get allusions to Kierkegaard's 'leap of faith', pictured as a hero vaulting wildly over a pit of poisonous snakes. But Kierkegaard's 'leap' is closer to the shifts from numbers to values, from the story of good Samaritans to answering a cry for help, or from evidence of atrocities to faith in (or despair of) humanity. To cross over to value or faith or faithful action of any sort, we must leap these sizeable gaps.

The Impact of Truth

Sunsets touch us because we have receptors designed for us to be so touched. We learn simple mathematics so quickly because we are designed to handle arithmetic. We learn by 'remembering how to do it', as it were. That is the Socratic model. Yet Truth can also strike us as utterly strange: *it happened, but I'll never believe it!* And in some cases, it strikes and we are changed in the knowing of it: *I'll never be the same!* Rather than our *doing* something to access truth, through its impact truth accesses *us.* Think of the horrors of battle exposing a soldier to a shattering revelation. It would be non-Socratic, because (a) he had not 'always known' these truths (of brutality, or suffering, or the necessity of doing evil); (b) he is changed through and through by the encounter with them; (c) he can be broken under the impact, showing that he is *not* 'designed' to handle them; (d) he can emerge a new man, as the misfit between who he was before and who he becomes, between his earlier self-sufficiency and his later humbling tremors, resolves itself.

In place of battle-trauma, imagine truth breaking through in soul-shattering conversion-trauma. Christ can make unbelievers Christians 'in the twinkling of an eye'. His Truth fits nothing we were or could know ('Love your enemies!'). Unlike Socrates, a saviour provides a jolting awareness of the heterogeneous. In his technical jargon, Climacus says that Socrates gives us the *occasion* for the arrival of innate Truth, while a saviour gives us the design feature and weakness required as a *condition* of *receiving* Truth. For a Christian, receiving Truth is receiving the saviour who *is* Truth, whose intervention hollows out a space for his own reception. The Socratic models self-realization as becoming what we already 'eternally' are. The Gospel models radical reconstruction, accepting new being with-and-for-others. But this offer will seem exorbitant and offensive in its demands. To accept appears to be participating in one's own extinction.

It is as hard for a human to be Christian as for a fish to sing. A human's design must be totally altered; by nature, it is radically unsuited. 'The god' has to 'create a new being' that after conversion might not look *that* different. But while appearing only to swim, she would be newly fitted to sing, and perhaps do more singing than swimming. Refitting our condition happens in the 'twinkling of an eye', in a poetic 'flash of transforming vision'. Yet the sense of that impact may remain strange. Wonder steps with humble ignorance and fearful unknowing.

Hebraic, Socratic, Christian

The idiom of 'crumbs' mocks professorial chatter. If Climacus is to avoid the appearance of chatter, he must not appear to run on a radically Christian ticket against the Socratic-Hegelian alternative. At most he tenders a case for the *possibility* of a Christian position: if the Socratic stance is incomplete (as the plausibility of transforming truth seems to show), then there is a chance that the alternative is correct — that insight arrives in the fullness of time wherein we are made new. Climacus doesn't worry about all the implications. He assumes the Truth exists; he doesn't consider nihilism, a dismal possibility. And if Truth comes through a revelation that I am powerless to summon, then I may be condemned to endless waiting. At least the Socratic option lets me hunt for a good teacher. Climacus assumes that Truth arrives either from outside or inside the human. But Truth might arise in a negotiation between the other and the familiar. A subject's initiative could be met halfway by an initiative from outside, and vice versa. Additionally, Truth might be non-Socratic and still not quite Christian. It might arrive through Job's Whirlwind — *not* Christ's incarnation.

Repetition's young man is not Christian, nor about to become one. If anything, he is Hebraic. The Socratic model of grasping an innate Truth does not fit the arrival of Job's 'thunderclap' or the return of Isaac. But the advent of a God-man, a *Christian* revelation, is not quite what Job or Abraham undergo, either. Yet the young man of *Repetition* stands closer to Christianity than to Socratic recollection or Hegelian historicism. Neither his sweetheart nor his freedom can be regained through memory or time. An intervening 'thunderclap' is *somewhat* akin to a saviour's advent.

It is remarkable that what starts as a bare outline of a non-Socratic position stealthily acquires the ornaments of Christian theology. Climacus has the teacher become Teacher and Saviour, ignorance become Error and Sin, the Saviour become Atoning Redeemer and Judge, deciding our fate; the Moment becomes Fullness of Time, the beholder Repents, is Converted, becomes a New Creature. These adornments are acquired in only half-a-dozen sentences.

A King and a Maiden

In Chapter II Kierkegaard introduces the fable of a king who finds himself in love with a poor maiden. Differences in class or wealth or power short-circuit understanding, and so short-circuit love. The king's robes and throne hide *him*, for she will see glory and power, not his love. He cannot be generous, showering her with wealth and privilege, for then she would see a bestower of bedazzling goods. To see *him* in his *love*, she can't see his largesse. Seeing his generosity will trigger gratitude, but love in repayment of debt is tainted. The king wants a love that would flow even if he offered nothing but crumbs. If he sheds his glory and power, appearing as only a poor servant, his love still might be hidden. She could pity him as just another beggar looking for leftovers she could spare. The analogy is with God's love. For it to show, God must shed his glory and power. Christian love is love not just of the mighty, but of the least. For the poor and homeless to see God as love rather than might, he must arrive poor and homeless, the equal of those he loves. Yet to appear as a humble servant makes it no easier to show love; the poor can assume he wants company in his affliction. If God is love, he can be neither visible nor invisible.

To break this double bind—love must be seen and not seen—we have to imagine a miracle. The maiden would have to be reborn and refitted in a way that ensured that her love would be blind, at least partially, to wealth, privilege, and power (or their absence)—free from inhibiting gratitude and bedazzlement, yet attuned to the other's love. If the maiden is remade by a transforming revelation (in a Christian reading of the fable), then she may express gratitude (how could she *not!*) and be innocently won over. Yet all the while she is made to see *love as it is*, apart from its worldly disguises: it might arrive as king *or* servant *or* both!

Paradox, Passion, and Reason

Death as salvation, evil forgiven, power as powerlessness—each pair offends reason because each is recalcitrant to it. At a high pitch, this recalcitrance is the offence of Paradox, an incongruity that both stalls and arouses reason. Stalled and aroused, in Chapter III Climacus writes 'a metaphysical caprice' or whimsy. He plays disarmingly with such oddities as a truth that *seeks us*; that unites *temporal and eternal*; a love needing miracles. Running up against such enigmas arouses the passion of reason, making it work that much harder. Then Climacus announces that passion seeks its own *downfall*.

Why? Perhaps love needs to subside in order to reflect back on itself, to measure its strengths. To test a beam's strength, we bring it to its breaking point. To know its strength, the passion of reason must seek its match and its downfall. What better adversary than paradox?

We needn't fault reason for pushing to exhaustion and collapse; that is just the way of any passion. Short of a miracle, neither love nor reason can attain the peace and understanding that it seeks, for several reasons. Each harbours internal conflict: love of others needs self-love, but in ways they are opposites; effective practical reason and would-be imperial reason are mutually opposed. A strong self-love grounds the requirement that we love others as ourselves, yet being-for-others means keeping self-love in check. The more expansive and detached imperial reason becomes, the less it is locally effect-ive. And each faces external conflict: falling in love puts the passion of reason on hold, and the passion of reason can put opportunities for love on hold. But paradox can frustrate reason, with salutary effect. The ever-restless knower-reasoner can be transformed into some-one else—someone humbled, and for a moment, full of wonder. This clears the decks for a 'jolt' of transformation. From Climacus' perspective, the defeat of ever-expanding reason opens space for a God-man's arrival.

Offence

In an 'Addendum' Climacus looks further into the offence to reason as it breaks against paradox. He alludes to an 'acoustical illusion': the ear mishears. It is an illusion if reason hears a death-knell when it is frustrated, for reason can start again elsewhere. Paradox defeats reason, but not every defeat is a humiliation. There is nothing humiliating in reason's discovering its limits. Even the most power-ful passions meet their match, if nowhere else, then in death, and there is no reason to take death as humiliation.

Openness to otherness means suspending the passion of reason. We must be quieted, as Job was, to let the Other speak. Job 'melts away' before the wonder of the Whirlwind and all it delivers. He knows directly the futility of his former questions and stops asking. The intrusion of paradox is coordinate with revelation that raises up life from the ashes of despair. If a person is a nest of self-expanding projects, rooted in desire or thought or imagination, each of these passions or projects can be self-valorizing. When outreachings of the self are halted, time is ripe for refitting. Truth undoes and redoes the receptor to its own specifications. Job is reborn as an ear tuned to the poetry of the world. He is no longer a lawyer demanding *his* turn to speak, *his* turn to interrogate. Climacus takes a lead from the otherness of death; it suspends self-valorization. Death gives a sense to life's dance.

Interlude

Typically, an interlude is a moment of relaxation within a more taxing structure, as a musical interlude is. But Climacus makes the Interlude that follows Chapter IV the most condensed and difficult section in all of *Philosophical Crumbs*. It is worth wrestling with bits of it, though. For a start, he differentiates levels of faith. In ordinary knowing, say in simple historical knowing, faith operates at a familiar and uncontroversial level. We move from hints and possibilities to the assurance that we now *know* what happened, or are pretty sure about it. I may wonder if it is true that a well-known soldier was recently killed by 'friendly fire'. In fits and starts a record accumulates, full of gaps and contradictions. But as facts gather and cover-ups are exposed, a narrative emerges and my doubt subsides. I see that it is really *true* that, in a terrible mix-up, he was shot by his own troops. That occurs, if it does, on the basis of what we can call 'first-level faith', faith as a confidence in some stock of empirical beliefs that grows in scope every day.

A second-level faith is trust in a construal of first-level beliefs. I might construe history as an upward progress (or a slow decline), or construe persons as basically good (or bad, or neither). I might be assured that evil will be punished (or won't). These thoughts about 'the way things are' can be idle musings, or relatively firm beliefs subject to discussion, or indeed, matters of deep and unshakable conviction. A first-level faith brings closure to my belief that there are untold instances of evil-doing. A second-level faith can focus those beliefs into the conviction that 'men are inherently evil'. The 'existential grip' of unshakable conviction transcends what we would expect as a decision reached by discussion. Some might agree that Jesus comforted the poor (a first-level belief), and yet reach no agreement that his is the deepest compassion one could know (a second-level conviction). For Christians, second-level convictions are about the centrality of compassion, but also about rebirth and creation, history and change, the necessity of the past or the indeterminacy of the future. We can subject these convictions to a kind of metaphysical analysis.

Necessity, Change, and History

Whatever undergoes change, Climacus says, already exists. For any change, there is a 'that' that changes. Now a change in being is marked by its invasion by something it is not. A possibility is 'not-being'. Coming into being, then, is the invasion of being by non-being, of a being by what it is not, of actuality by possibility. For someone who earlier was suspicious of metaphysical reason, Climacus seems all too adept at it. It is his chance to show off, but not only that, for he has a metaphysical interest in freedom. If the necessary is a precondition of something coming into existence, then the original necessity cannot itself have come into existence. It is the realm of the unchangeable, where nothing comes or goes. But freedom must enter any account of change, because persons bring things into existence. So Climacus posits a freely acting cause, a basis from which things come into existence. Causes reach bedrock in freedom.

This metaphysical picture is meant to allay two worries. We cannot stomach the anxiety raised by the thought of a universe of *endlessly* receding causal chains. We need to say, '*In the beginning . . .*' Second, we cannot stomach the anxiety raised by the thought of a universe of *nothing but lifeless* causes; there must be room for freedom. To allay both anxieties, Climacus posits a *first* cause (no infinite regress) that is *free* (no exclusion of free agency). This sounds suspiciously like positing God as first cause. Should we cheer Climacus for his brilliance or jeer him from the stage?

Climacus proceeds to differentiate two levels of history. Anything that comes into existence has a past and thus a history. Some things emerge as a matter of physics, chemistry, and physiology. Other things emerge through human choice and become embedded in culture. A natural history (*without* culture) has within itself the possibility of a 'redoubled' coming into existence (history *with* culture and agency). The past isn't necessary, but nevertheless it can't

be changed. Climacus concludes that to know history is to know a
field of freedom. Thus it is *not* a matter of what had to be, or was
fated from eternity.

Resolution and Scepticism

What defeats scepticism, as Climacus sees it, is not so much cognition
as *will*. The greater the contingency of something we would believe
in, the greater the leaps required for conviction. We have three gaps
to leap if we are to be convinced that a child born under a star is a
saviour. The first leap comes when we grant the near certainty that a
particular mother gave birth to a child 2,000 years ago in a particular
land. But another gap must be faced if we think it is important that
this child, as an adult, is compassionate or healing. We need cultural,
not merely biological, knowledge and resolution to believe that Jesus
had compassion for others, or cried in anguish from the cross. And
for some, there will be a third gap to leap. Perhaps this compassionate man is the Saviour, the eternal in time. But a resolution at this
third level will have a radically different structure from the first two
resolutions.

I can bring myself into a cognitive position ready to embrace the
fact that a child came into existence 2,000 years ago, or that Jesus
was compassionate in life and in anguish at death. (I go over the
texts and decide that the evidence *tilts* that way.) But in coming to
believe that Jesus is the Eternal in Time (for instance), I do not *bring
myself into a cognitive position*. Something *displaces* my cognitive position, *obstructs* and *dismantles* it. If I come to believe that the Eternal
entered Time, it is not because I have assumed a position appropriate
for making good cognitive judgements. My best cognitive positions
are roundly dislodged. The eternal disables my expectations and
shuts down reason. If I emerge with a positive Christian conviction,
it is because my receptive equipment has been refitted. Closure at
this third level comes primarily through an unseen initiative that
undoes my preferred cognitive position and simultaneously provides
new angles of orientation—at first unsettling and offensive, at last,
satisfying and saving.

Can this third sort of resolution have any appeal to those who
are not already Christians? Can it appeal—*even to Christians*! There
are severe limits to reason's capacity to exhibit the allure of the

biblical model to the unconvinced, or even to those who think to be a Christian is just to accept one's present social status, for instance. A reader might well stick with the Socratic model, might fail to see why one should acquiesce in having one's will shaped by another. Delineating, as Climacus does, the possibility of a non-Socratic position with regard to Truth may convey to sceptical others some small bit of the allure it holds—generally, and for a believer. But it also may utterly fail. Whether we are persuaded that a revelation of our insufficiency, if it happens, should stick as a plausible description of our condition, or whether we are actually given the sort of revelation he sketches, are matters out of his control, and ours. There is no *forcing* radical transformation.

Closing

The book comes to an end in Chapter V, and a final 'moral of the story'. Climacus discusses the question whether persons who were in close proximity to Jesus have an advantage in grasping the Truth he embodies and speaks over those from later generations and centuries, the 'disciples at second hand'. He answers that those who were in close proximity have 'gaps' to leap every bit as daunting as those faced by persons living centuries later. Being proximate requires faith at three levels, just as being distant would. Being near might even be thought harder, since the templates suitable to assimilate the stark events, refined over centuries of tempering cultural interpretation, would be unavailable. On the other hand, nineteenth-century would-be Christians have to unlearn those accumulated interpretations that make Christianity all-too familiar, a matter of simple socialization from the cradle to the grave. Christianity has to be made strange. But comparing difficulties in understanding across historical eras is a bit like comparing trauma or joy across centuries. For Climacus, the point is that a shattering jolt is inescapable—no one is raised a Christian. It becomes just as impertinent to ask 'whose disruption is greater' as it is to ask 'whose trauma is greater'. A full human response to the witness and writing of Søren Kierkegaard in 1840s Copenhagen is not made less possible by the passage of 170 (or 300) years. Nor is a full human response to the witness and events happening two millennia ago made less possible by the passage of time.

The final 'moral of the story' is concise. We are invited to consider a non-Socratic alternative; and this is clearly the Christian alternative. Climacus avers that to go *beyond* Socrates requires assent to 'a new organ: faith; a new presupposition: the consciousness of sin; a new decision: the moment; and a new teacher: the god in time'. He does not conclude that the Socratic model is erroneous. The admonition is that Copenhagen's so-called Christians, if they are to surpass the Socratic presumption that truth lies within, cannot dodge the requirements: that there is a new organ, a new presupposition, a new decision, a new teacher. To be true to Socrates *and* to Christ, one's Christianity cannot be just another version of the Socratic. Yet as Climacus sees it, that is the radically *un-Christian* style of the philosophy and culture and religion around him.

Kierkegaard confessed late in life that his entire task as a writer had been Socratic. By that he meant, at the least, asking the deepest questions about how one should live, and pursuing them fearlessly. He also meant maintaining a certain irony about the limits of reason. Socrates professed ignorance, in part, to avoid the pretence that there were ready-made answers to deep questions, and to encourage those who listened to resolve these questions on their own, not on his authority. Kierkegaard was true to these features of the Socratic adventure and so characterized his career as Socratic, but he was also unmistakably Christian.

Because *Crumbs* ends with accentuating the *difference* between the Socratic and the Christian, we should note that Kierkegaard finally brings them together. He exploited his Socratic inquisitive challenges to the end of sketching the core of non-Socratic lives — some Christian, some nearly Christian, some anti-Christian, some anti-Socratic, some neither here nor there. He was Socratic in a venture to be Christian, and Christian in a venture to be Socratic. Climacus avers early in *Crumbs* that within the wonder of faith, 'everything is structured Socratically'. Later in his writings we hear Kierkegaard say, in his own voice, 'Socrates has become a Christian'.[1] But to pursue further how one can be both Socratic and Christian brings one to a new wilderness.

---

[1] *The Point of View For My Work as an Author*, trans. Howard V. and Edna H. Hong (Princeton: Princeton University Press, 1998), 54.

The great appeal of Kierkegaard's writing in the twenty-first century and beyond rests on two striking accomplishments. He had an alarmingly powerful capacity to challenge, perplex, and sustain Christian and Socratic intuitions and institutions, not to mention a capacity to provide endless stand-apart aesthetic and ethical insights—challenges, insights, and affirmations that he then quilted into the shapes of a number of partially viable lives. And second, he conducted this venture passionately, poetically, and philosophically in a variety of wonderfully innovative genres, with a style and wit that the best of those who shape culture (poets and novelists, theologians and dramatists, philosophers and painters), have found strange, irresistible, and transforming.

ACKNOWLEDGEMENTS
I would like to thank Rick Furtak and Tony Auuman for their helpful suggestions in the course of writing this Introductions, Bruce Kirmmse for help in historical matters, and Judith Luna for her unwavering tactical intelligence and support.

E.F.M.

NOTE ON THE TRANSLATION

Two very different translation methods have tended to dominate translations of Kierkegaard's works: the semantic method and the faithful method. The former approach allows for a certain creativity on the part of the translator. A faithful translation, on the other hand, strives for absolute fidelity. The difficulty is that the semantic method sometimes results in translations that are too free, and the faithful method often results in translations that are too literal.

Some earlier translators of Kierkegaard were understandably concerned to preserve fidelity to the original text. Precision is crucial in a philosophical translation. There are limits to the degree of precision that is possible, however, due to the nature of translation itself. Unfortunately, a zeal for accuracy can result in a loss of some of the literary quality of the original. Such a loss is particularly lamentable in the case of Kierkegaard because, unlike most philosophers, Kierkegaard was a great prose stylist. Many readers have been attracted to his writings for their literary quality alone.

I have thus, in the translation of these two works, chosen the semantic translation method, but with a keen eye to preserving distinctions that appear important in the original text. I have sometimes departed from the original for aesthetic reasons, as is the case, for example, with several of the poems, where I have made small changes to the wording to render a poem that preserves, as much as possible, both the metre and the rhyme of the original. Aesthetic concerns were also, arguably, behind my decision to translate the Danish *Guden* ('the God') in *Crumbs* sometimes with, and other times without, the definite article. Greek makes much more frequent use of the definite article than does English. Kierkegaard's decision to use the definite article was probably motivated by a desire, clear in other aspects of the work, to emulate the form of the Platonic dialogue. I have omitted the definite article, however, in places that depart, at least to some extent, from the Platonic form to consider more traditional theological questions, such as various proofs for God's existence, and where the inclusion of the article is thus jarring.

It was simple accuracy, however, rather than aesthetic concerns, which lay behind several other decisions. Unlike some earlier translators of Kierkegaard, I have endeavoured, for example, to preserve such important philosophical distinctions as those between 'reality' (*Realitet*), 'actuality' (*Virkelighed*), and 'existence' (*Existents* or *Tilvaerelsen*), and between 'romantic love' (*Elskov*) and what Kierkegaard calls 'the erotic' (*Erotiken* and *Erotisk*).

These translations are based on the texts of *Søren Kierkegaard's Samlede Voerker* (Søren Kierkegaard's Collected Works), ed. A. B. Drachmann, J. L. Heiberg, and H. O. Lange, 2nd edn., vols. 1–15 (Copenhagen: Gyldendal, 1920–36), as well as on *Søren Kierkegaards Skrifter* (Søren Kierkegaard's Writings), the new Danish edition of Kierkegaard's collected works. The former edition was generally considered to be superior both to the first edition of Kierkegaard's collected works, as well as to a later edition produced for popular consumption in the 1960s. This edition is, however, now out of print. As a service to the reader, I have therefore included page correlations in the margins to *Søren Kierkegaards Skrifter*. This edition is, regrettably, prohibitively expensive for anyone but the most dedicated scholars or libraries, but it is freely available online in a searchable edition.

Asterisks in the text indicate an explanatory note at the back of the book. Translations of short foreign words and phrases in Kierkegaard's text are provided as footnotes; other footnotes are by Kierkegaard, and indicated as such.

I would like to acknowledge the help and support I received with this translation from Jeff New and Judith Luna of Oxford University Press, as well as from Ebba Mørkeberg, whose infinitely patient and kind instruction is the foundation of my knowledge of both Danish and German, David Leopold, who kept me amply supplied with earlier translations of Kierkegaard that he came across in his travels, Peter Tudvad, who helped me with translations of passages I found particularly difficult, Eva Thury, who helped with some of the notes, and Brian J. Foley, who kept me sane. Most of all, though, I would like to thank Ed Mooney. If it were not for his generosity, I would not have had the opportunity to do these translations.

M.P.

SELECT BIBLIOGRAPHY

Primary Sources, English and Danish

Kierkegaard's Writings, ed. and trans. Howard V. Hong and Edna H. Hong, *et al.*, 26 vols. (Princeton: Princeton University Press, 1978–2000).

Søren Kierkegaard's Journals and Papers, ed. and trans. Howard V. Hong and Edna H. Hong, 7 vols. (Bloomington, Ind.: Indiana University Press, 1967–78).

Søren Kierkegaards Papirer, ed. P. A. Heiberg, V. Kuhr, and E. Torsting, 16 vols., 2nd edn. N. Thulstrup (Copenhagen: Gyldendal, 1968–78).

Søren Kierkegaards Samlede Værker (Collected Works), ed. A. B. Drachmann, J. L. Heiberg, and H. O. Lange, 14 vols. 1st edn. (Copenhagen: Gyldendal, 1901–6).

Søren Kierkegaards Skrifter, Bind 4, ed. Niels Jørgen Cappelørn, Joakim Garff, Johnny Kondrup, Alastair McKinnon, and Finn Hauberg Mortensen (Copenhagen: G. E. C. Gads Forlag, 1997–).

Biography

Hannay, Alastair, *Kierkegaard: A Biography* (Cambridge, Mass.: Cambridge University Press, 2001).

Kirmmse, Bruce H., *Encounters with Kierkegaard: A Life as Seen by His Contemporaries* (Princeton: Princeton University Press, 1996).

Lowrie, Walter, *A Short Life of Kierkegaard* (Princeton: Princeton University Press, 1942).

Short Introductions

Caputo, John D., *How to Read Kierkegaard* (London: Granta Books, 2007).

Carlisle, Clare, *Kierkegaard: A Guide for the Perplexed* (London: Continuum, 2006).

Pattison, George, *The Philosophy of Kierkegaard* (Chesham: Acumen, 2005).

Background, Interpretation, Critique

Angier, Tom P. S., *Either Kierkegaard/Or Nietzsche: Moral Philosophy in a New Key* (Aldershot: Ashgate, 2006).

Cappelørn, Niels Jørgen, and Deuser, Hermann (eds.), *Kierkegaard Studies*, sponsored by the Søren Kierkegaard Research Center, *Yearbook(s)* (1996–).

Davenport, John, 'What Kierkegaard Adds to Alterity Ethics: How Levinas and Derrida Miss the Eschatological Dimension', in J. Aaron Simmons and David Woods (eds.), *A Conversation between Neighbors:*

Emmanuel Levinas and Søren Kirkegaard in Dialogue (Bloomington, Ind.: Indiana University Press, 2009).

Furtak, Rick Anthony, *Wisdom in Love: Kierkegaard and the Ancient Quest for Emotional Integrity* (Notre Dame, Ind.: University of Notre Dame Press, 2005).

Green, Ronald, *Kierkegaard and Kant: The Hidden Debt* (New York: SUNY Press, 1992).

Hannay, Alastair, *Kierkegaard*, in The Arguments of the Philosophers series, ed. Ted Honderich (London: Routledge, 1982).

—— *Kierkegaard and Philosophy*, Selected Essays (New York: Routledge, 2003).

—— and Marino, Gordon (eds.), *The Cambridge Companion to Kierkegaard* (Cambridge: Cambridge University Press, 1996).

Kirmmse, Bruce H., *Kierkegaard in Golden Age Denmark* (Bloomington, Ind.: Indiana University Press, 1990).

Lippitt, John, *Kierkegaard and Fear and Trembling* (London: Routledge, 2003).

Matustik, Martin J., and Westphal, Merold (eds.), *Kierkegaard in Post/Modernity* (Bloomington, Ind.: Indiana University Press, 1995).

Mooney, Edward F., *On Søren Kierkegaard: Dialogue, Polemic, Lost Intimacy, and Time* (London: Ashgate, 2007).

—— (ed.), *Ethics, Love, and Faith in Kierkegaard: Philosophical Engagements* (Bloomington, Ind.: Indiana University Press, 2008).

Pattison, George, *Anxious Angels, A Retrospective View of Religious Existentialism* (New York, St Martins, 1999).

—— *'Poor Paris!' Kierkegaard's Critique of the Spectacular City*, Kierkegaard Studies: Monograph, Series 2 (Berlin: de Gruyter, 1999).

Perkins, Robert L. (ed.), *International Kierkegaard Commentary*, 19 vols., [keyed to the Princeton edition of *Kierkegaard's Writings*] (Macon, Ga.: Mercer University Press, 1984–).

Rudd, Anthony, ' "Believing All Things": Kierkegaard on Knowledge, Doubt, and Love', in *International Kierkegaard Commentary: Works of Love*, ed. Robert L. Perkins (Macon, Ga.: Mercer University Press, 1999), 121–36.

Stewart, Jon (ed.), *Kierkegaard Research: Sources, Reception, and Resources*, multi-volumes: Vol. 6, *Kierkegaard and his German Contemporaries*, Tome I, *Philosophy*; Tome II, *Theology*; Tome III, *Literature and Aesthetics* (Berlin: de Gruyter, 2007–).

Selected Works on Repetition

Caputo, John D., 'Kierkegaard, Heidegger, and the Foundering of Metaphysics', in Robert L. Perkins (ed.), *International Kierkegaard*

Commentary: 'Fear and Trembling' and 'Repetition' (Macon, Ga.: Mercer University Press, 1993), 201–24.

Carlisle, Clare, *Kierkegaard's Philosophy of Becoming, Movements and Positions* (Albany, NY: SUNY Press, 2005).

Crites, Stephen, ' "The Blissful Security of the Moment": Recollection, Repetition, and Eternal Recurrence', in Robert L. Perkins (ed.), *International Kierkegaard Commentary: 'Fear and Trembling' and 'Repetition'* (Macon, Ga.: Mercer University Press, 1993), 225–46.

Eriksen, Niels, *Kierkegaard's Category of Repetition* (Berlin: De Gruyter, 2000).

Mooney, Edward F., 'Repetition: Getting the World Back', in Alastair Hannay and Gordon Marino (eds.), *The Cambridge Companion to Kierkegaard* (Cambridge: Cambridge University Press, 1998), 282–307.

Pattison, George, 'The Magic Theater: Drama and Existence in Kierkegaard's *Repetition* and Hesse's *Steppenwolf*', in Robert L. Perkins (ed.), *International Kierkegaard Commentary*, '*Fear and Trembling*' and '*Repetition*' (Macon, Ga., Mercer University Press, 1993), 359–77.

Selected Works on Philosophical Crumbs

Evans, C. Stephen, *Passionate Reason: Making Sense of Kierkegaard's Philosophical Fragments* (Bloomington, Ind.: Indiana University Press, 1992).

Furtak, Rick Anthony, 'Believing in Time: Rethinking Faith and History in *Philosophical Fragments, Works of Love, and Repetition*', *Kierkegaard Studies Yearbook 2004*, eds. N. J. Cappelørn, H. Deuser, and J. Stewart (Berlin: De Gruyter, 2004).

Hannay, Alastair, *Kierkegaard, The Arguments of the Philosophers* (London: Routledge, 1982), ch. 4.

Mulhall, Stephen, *Inheritance and Originality, Wittgenstein, Heidegger, Kierkegaard* (Oxford: Oxford University Press, 2001), Part III.

Roberts, Robert, *Faith, Reason, and History: Rethinking Kierkegaard's Philosophical Fragments* (Macon, Ga.: Mercer University Press, 1986).

Rudd, Anthony, 'The Moment and the Teacher: Problems in Kierkegaard's *Philosophical Fragments*', *Kierkegaardiana*, 21 (2000), 92–113.

E.F.M

A CHRONOLOGY OF
SØREN KIERKEGAARD

1813 Søren Aabye Kierkegaard is born 5 May in Copenhagen; Michael Pedersen Kierkegaard, his father, is a wealthy merchant of peasant origin; his mother, Ane Sørensdatter Lund Kierkegaard, had been a household servant; they were married shortly after Michael's first wife's death; his mother is 45, his father 56, at his birth.

1821 Enrolled in the Borgerdyd School; has by now acquired the pet-name 'the fork'.

1830 Enters the University of Copenhagen as a theology student.

1831 Passes exams in Latin, Greek, Hebrew, and history *magna cum laude*, and in physics, mathematics, and philosophy *summa cum laude*.

1834 Begins the journal that will continue throughout his life; his mother dies.

1835 Travels to the rugged seashore at Gilleleie; there he confides to his journal that he seeks 'the idea for which I can live and die'.

1837 In early May, he meets the love of his life, Regine Olsen, then 15; begins teaching Latin.

1838 Drafts a philosophical comedy, 'The Battle between the Old and New Soap-Cellars' (left unpublished); father dies at age 82; publishes *From the Papers of One Still Living, published against his will by S. Kierkegaard*.

1840 Takes comprehensive exams (for his theology degree); proposes to Regine Olsen in September; begins seminary training for the pastorate.

1841 Preaches his first sermon; defends *The Concept of Irony with Constant Reference to Socrates*, his MA thesis (later upgraded to a Ph.D.) in September; breaks his engagement to Regine in October; leaves Copenhagen for Berlin, where he attends Schelling's lectures and begins to sketch out the first few books that establish his lasting reputation.

1842 Returns to Copenhagen in March, writing at rapid pace; begins 'Johannes Climacus, or De omnibus dubitandum est' (left unpublished).

1843 *Either/Or, a Fragment of Life* ('ed. Victor Eremita') appears, 20 Feb.; 16 Oct, *Fear and Trembling* ('by Johannes de silentio'),

Repetition ('by Constantine Constantius'), and *Three Upbuilding Discourses* (including a talk, or discourse, on Job) appear simultaneously; 6 Dec., *Four Upbuilding Discourses* published.

1844 *Philosophical Crumbs, or a Crumb of Philosophy* ('by Johannes Climacus') and *The Concept of Anxiety* ('by Vigilius Haufniensis') appear; also *Prefaces* ('by Nicolaus Notabene') and three sets of *Discourses*.

1845 *Stages on Life's Way* ('edited by Hilarius Bogbinder') is published, and two sets of *Discourses*.

1846 A feud with the *Corsair*, a satirical gossip sheet, begins; considers applying for ordination; *Concluding Unscientific Postscript to Philosophical Crumbs: A Mimic-Pathetic-Dialectic Compilation: An Existential Intervention* ('by Johannes Climacus') appears; then *A Literary Review: Two Ages* ('The Age of Revolution' and 'The Present Age').

1847 Drafts 'The Book on Adler' (left unpublished); publishes *Upbuilding Discourses in Various Spirits*, and *Works of Love*.

1848 *Christian Discourses* and *The Crisis and a Crisis in the Life of an Actress* ('by Inter et Inter') appear; writes *The Point of View of My Work as an Author* (published posthumously in 1859); 'Armed Neutrality' written (left unpublished).

1849 *The Lily of the Field and the Bird of the Air* appears; second edition of *Either/Or*, followed by *The Sickness Unto Death* ('by Anti-Climacus'); three discourses and two minor essays published.

1850 *Practice in Christianity* ('by Anti-Climacus') and a discourse are published; Bishop Mynster, a leading cultural figure and long-time friend of the Kierkegaard family, is provoked into responding to Kierkegaard's charge that the elite of the church seek only a comfortable living.

1851 *On My Work as an Author* appears with two discourses; then, *For Self Examination*.

1852 *Judge for Yourselves!* written (not published until 1876).

1854 Bishop Mynster dies in January, succeeded by H. L. Martensen; Kierkegaard begins a full-scale attack on Martensen and the State Church in the journal *Fædrelandet*.

1855 Continues his attack on the church, widening it to include the clergy, publishing his own broadsheet, *The Moment* [*The Instant*], in ten issues; publishes *This Must be Said; So Let It*

Now Be Said, then *Christ's Judgment on Official Christianity*, and *The Unchangeableness of God: A Discourse*; 25 Sept., last journal entry and last issue of *The Moment*; 2 Oct., collapses and enters Frederiks Hospital; dies 11 Nov.; buried Sunday, 18 Nov.; a disturbance breaks out at the graveside: students who sided with his attack on the church protest loudly that he would object to a church burial

Repetition

An Essay in Experimental Psychology

By

CONSTANTINE CONSTANTIUS

On wild trees the flowers are fragrant, on cultivated trees, the fruits.
(Flavius Philostratus the Elder, *Heroicus*)*

WHEN the Eleatics* denied motion, Diogenes, as everyone knows, [9] came forward in protest, actually came forward, because he did not say a word, but simply walked back and forth a few times, with which gesture he believed he had sufficiently refuted the Eleatic position. When I had been preoccupied for some time, at least when I had the opportunity, with the problem of whether repetition was possible and what it meant, whether a thing wins or loses by being repeated, it suddenly occurred to me: you can go to Berlin, since you were there once before, you could in this way learn whether repetition was possible and what it meant. I had come to a standstill in my attempts to resolve this problem at home. Say what you will, this problem is going to play an important role in modern philosophy because *repetition* is a decisive expression for what '*recollection*' was for the Greeks. Just as they taught that all knowledge is recollection, thus will modern philosophy teach that life itself is a repetition. The only modern philosopher who has had the least intimation of this is Leibniz.* Repetition and recollection are the same movement, just in opposite directions, because what is recollected has already been and is thus repeated backwards, whereas genuine repetition is recollected forwards. Repetition, if it is possible, thus makes a person happy, while recollection makes him unhappy, assuming, of course, that he actually gives himself time to live and does not, immediately upon the hour of his birth hit upon an excuse, such as that he has forgotten something, to sneak back out of life again.

Recollection's love is the only happy love, according to one author.* He is absolutely right about this if one also remembers that it first makes a person unhappy. Repetition's love is in truth the only happy love. Like recollection, it is not disturbed by hope nor by the marvellous anxiety of discovery, neither, however, doesn't have the sorrow of recollection. It has instead the blissful security [10] of the moment. Hope is new attire, stiff and starched and splendid. Still, since it has not yet been tried on, one does not know whether it will suit one, or whether it will fit. Recollection is discarded clothing which, however lovely it might be, no longer suits one because one has outgrown it. Repetition is clothing that never becomes worn, that fits snugly and comfortably, that neither pulls nor hangs too loosely. Hope is a pretty girl, who slips away from one's grasp.

Recollection is a beautiful older woman who never quite suits the
moment. Repetition is a beloved wife of whom one never tires
because it is only the new of which one tires. One never tires of
the old, and when one has it before oneself one is happy, and only
a person who does not delude himself that repetition ought to be
something new, for then he tires of it, is genuinely happy. It requires
youthfulness to hope and youthfulness to recollect, but it requires
courage to will repetition. He who will only hope is cowardly. He
who wants only to recollect is a voluptuary. But he who wills repetition, he is a man, and the more emphatically he has endeavoured to
understand what this means, the deeper he is as a human being. But
he who does not grasp that life is repetition and that this is the beauty
of life, has condemned himself and deserves nothing better than
what will happen to him — death. Hope is an enticing fruit that fails
to satisfy, recollection sorrowful sustenance that fails to satisfy. But
repetition is the daily bread that satisfies through blessing. When one
has circumnavigated existence, then it will become apparent whether
one has the courage to understand that life is repetition and the
desire to look forward to this. He who has not circumnavigated life
before he has begun to live will never really live. He who circumnavigated life but became sated has a poor constitution. He who chooses
repetition, he lives. He does not chase after butterflies like a child,
or stand on tiptoe in order to glimpse the wonders of the world. He
knows them. Neither does he sit like an old woman and spin on the
spinning wheel of recollection. He goes calmly about his life, happy
in repetition. What would life be without repetition? Who would
want to be a tablet on which life wrote something new every moment,
or a memorial to something past? Who would want to be moved by
the fleeting, the new, that is always effeminately diverting the soul?
[11] If God Himself had not willed repetition, there would never have
been a world. He would either have followed the easy plans of hope,
or recalled everything and preserved it in recollection. He did not do
this. This is the reason there is a world. The world consists of repetition. Repetition is actuality and the earnestness of existence. He
who wills repetition is genuinely mature. This is my *Separat-Votum*,[1]
that means in addition that life's earnestness is in no way to sit on
the sofa and pick one's teeth — to be something such as, for example,

---

[1] Private opinion.

a titular counsellor, or to have a dignified walk—and be somebody such as His Reverence, just as little as it is life's earnestness to be the royal riding-master. Such things are in my eyes only jokes, and as such, sometimes bad jokes.

Recollection's love is the only happy love, according to an author who, to the best of my knowledge, is sometimes deceitful, not in such a way, however, that he says one thing and thinks something else, but in that he develops a thought to such an extreme that if it is not grasped with the same energy, it will appear in the next moment to be something else. This claim is presented by him in such a way that one is easily tempted to agree and thus to forget that the claim itself is an expression of the deepest melancholy. Such profound melancholy, condensed in a single remark, could not easily find better expression.

It was about a year ago that I began to take serious notice of a young person with whom I had heretofore often had contact because there was something enticing in his attractive appearance and the determined look in his eye. The way he tossed his head, a certain flippancy in his expressions, convinced me that he was a deep person with many levels to his character, while a certain hesitancy in his tone suggested that he was of that seductive age when the spirit declares its maturity, just as the body does at a much earlier age, by a frequent breaking of the voice. I had, with the help of casual coffee-house acquaintances, already become close to him and persuaded him to see in me a confidant whose talk in many ways succeeded in drawing from him, through occasional convulsions, his melancholy, just as Farinelli* coaxed the miserable king out of his dark hold, which because my friend was still young and malleable was possible to do without the use of pliers. Such was our relationship, when about a year ago, as I said, he came to me quite beside himself. His appearance was more dramatic than usual, his form more beauti- [12] ful, his large, luminous eyes were dilated. In short, he appeared transfigured. When he informed me that he was in love, I could not help but think that to be loved in this way would make any girl happy. He had been in love for a while, he explained, but had con- cealed this from me. Now the object of his passion was within reach. He had confessed his love and found it reciprocated. Despite the fact that I ordinarily have a tendency to relate to other people merely as an observer, it was impossible for me to do this with him. Say what

you will, a love-struck young person is such a beautiful sight that one
cannot help but rejoice in it and thus forget to observe. Deep emotions always disarm the observer in a person. The desire to observe
comes only when there is an emptiness in the place of emotion, or
when emotions are coquettishly concealed. Who could be so inhuman as to wish to observe a person who prayed genuinely with his
whole soul? Who would not rather feel permeated by the flood of
the worshipper's devotion? When, on the other hand, one hears a
priest recite a well-rehearsed sermon in which he repeatedly attests,
independently of any demand on the part of the congregation, in an
artificially worked, even preposterously overworked, passage, that he
expresses a simple faith that knows nothing of flowery speech, but
which gives him through prayer what, according to his own words
and presumably for good reasons, he sought vainly in poetry, art, and
scholarship, then one calmly places the microscope before one's eye,
then one does not allow oneself simply to swallow what was said, but
pulls the blinds and produces the critical apparatus that tests every
sound and every word.

The young person I speak of was deeply, passionately, beautifully,
and self-effacingly in love. It had been a long time since I had been so
happy as I was when I looked at him, because it is often sad to be an
observer. It can be depressing in the same way that it can be depressing to be a police officer, and when an observer genuinely follows his
calling he must be regarded as a police informant who is serving a
higher purpose because the art of observation is to bring forth what
is hidden. The young person talked about the girl he loved. He used
few words. His description was no vapid assessment, as the speeches
of lovers very often are. He exhibited no affectation that would
suggest he felt he was a shrewd fellow for having captured such a girl,
no arrogance — his love was wholesome and pure and uncorrupted.
He confided to me, with an endearing candour, that the reason he
[13] had come to me was that he needed a confidant in whose presence
he could talk to himself out loud, as well as that he feared he might
otherwise spend the whole day with the girl and thus become a nuis-
ance to her. He had already set off for her house many times, but
forced himself to turn around. He asked me now if I would go for a
ride with him to help divert his thoughts from her and to pass the
time. I was more than willing, because from the moment he had
confided in me he could rest assured that I would be of unconditional

service to him. I used the half-hour while we waited for the carriage to take care of some business correspondence. I suggested he fill his pipe, or flip through some of the magazines that were lying about. He didn't need to do anything, however, to fill the time. He was so preoccupied with his own thoughts that he could not even remain seated, but paced back and forth. His gait, his movements, his gestures were all eloquent. He glowed with love. Just as a grape becomes bright and transparent as it ripens, the juice flowing through the fine veins, just as the skin bursts when it reaches the peak of ripeness, so did love break almost visibly forth from him. I could not help occasionally stealing a glance over at him, because such a youth is as seductive a sight as a young girl.

Just as lovers often seek refuge in the words of poets in order to allow the sweet anxiety of love a joyous expression, this was also the case with him. He repeated again and again as he paced back and forth a poem by Poul Møller:*

> There comes a dream from the spring of my youth
> > To my old easy chair
> I feel a passionate longing for you
> > My queen with the golden hair.*

His eyes filled with tears and he threw himself down in a chair. He repeated the verse again and again. This scene made a deep and moving impression on me. God in heaven, I thought, I have never before seen such melancholy. I had known he tended toward melancholy, but that to be in love could have such an effect on him! And yet are not most admittedly abnormal emotional conditions consistent in this way when they are generally present? People are always crying that a depressive should try to fall in love, because if he does, [14] he will forget about everything else. To the extent that he really is a depressive, how could he possibly avoid a melancholy preoccupation with what was now the most important thing in the world to him? He was deeply and passionately in love, this was clear, and yet he was already, in the earliest days, in a position to recollect his love. He was basically finished with the whole relationship. Simply by having begun, he advanced such a terrific distance that he had leapt right over life. It would make no great difference if the girl died tomorrow. He would still throw himself into his love. His eyes would still fill with tears and he would continue to repeat the words of the poet.

What a strange dialectic! He longs for the girl, and is forced to do himself violence in order to avoid spending his entire day with her, and yet from the first moment, he became an old man with respect to the whole relationship. There must be some kind of fundamental misunderstanding. Nothing had moved me for a long time so strongly as this scene. It was clear he would become unhappy, and no less clear that the girl would as well, even though it was not possible at this point to predict precisely how this was going to happen. This much, however, is clear: if anyone can speak about the love of recollection, he can. The great advantage of recollection is that it begins with loss. This is its security—it has nothing to lose.

The carriage arrived. We drove up Strandveien,* with the intention of later looking for an actual wooded area. Since, against my own will, I had adopted the position of an observer relative to him, I could not resist trying all kinds of tricks, as sailors say, to log the momentum of his depression. I evoked all possible erotic moods—no result. I searched in vain for any effect the change of surroundings might have. Neither the vast energy of the ocean, nor the lulling stillness of the forest, nor the beckoning solitude of evening could relieve him of the melancholy longing, through which he did not so much bring his beloved closer as remove himself from her even more. His mistake was fatal. His mistake was that he stood at the end rather than at the beginning, but such a mistake is always a person's ruin.

I believe, however, that his mood was an appropriately erotic mood, and that anyone who has not experienced it at the beginning of a love has never loved. It is simply that he needs another mood alongside this one. This intensified recollection is the eternal expression for the beginning of romantic love, is a sign of genuine romantic love. An ironic elasticity is also required, however, in order for it to [15] be of use. This he lacked, his soul was too delicate. It may be true that in the first instant one's life is over, but one must also have the strength to do away with this death, to transform it into life. At the dawn of love, the present and the future battle for eternal expression. This recollection is precisely the reflux of eternity into the present, when, in any case, it is healthy recollection.

We returned home. I left him, but my sympathy had been almost too strongly set in motion. I could not rid myself of the thought that there would soon be a terrible explosion.

I saw him now and then during the next couple of weeks. He had himself begun to grasp the problem; the young girl he desired had already become almost an annoyance. And yet she was his beloved, the only one he had ever loved, the only one he would ever love. On the other hand, he did not really love her, but only longed for her. All this was accompanied by a strange change in him. A poetic productivity awakened in him, to an extent that I would not have thought possible. Now I understood everything. The young girl was not his beloved, she was simply the cause that awakened the poetic in him and thus transformed him into a poet. This was why he could love only her, never forget her, never wish to love anyone else, and yet still merely long for her. She had permeated every aspect of his being. The thought of her was always fresh. She had been important for him. She had made him into a poet, and with this signed her own death-sentence.

As time passed, his relationship became an increasing torment. His depression came more and more to have the upper hand, and his physical strength was consumed by emotional battles. He could see that he had made her unhappy, and yet he was not conscious of having done anything wrong. But precisely this, through no fault of his own, to become guilty of having made her unhappy, offended him and set his passion in violent motion. Yet to confess to her how things stood would, he feared, injure her profoundly. It would be as if to say that she had somehow become less perfect, that he had outgrown her, that he no longer needed the stairs by which he had [16] ascended to his present height. What would happen as a result? She would know that he would never love anyone else, thus she would become his grieving widow who lived only in her memories of him and their relationship. He could make no confession; he valued her too highly for that. His depression increased and he decided to continue with the deception. All his poetic talents were now used to amuse and entertain her. What could have provided amusement for many was used exclusively on her. She was and remained the beloved, the adored, even though he was near to losing his mind as a result of the lie that served only to enthral her more and more profoundly. Her existence or non-existence, in a certain sense, actually meant nothing to him, though his depression found joy only through bringing enchantment to her life. It goes without saying that she was happy, because she suspected nothing and was being sustained by what was all too delicious. He did not want to be productive in a more genuine sense, for this would have required leaving her. Thus, as he said, he kept his productivity continually pruned in order to produce bouquets for her from the cuttings. She suspected nothing. I believe this. It would be disturbing, in any case, to think that a young girl could be so vain as to be flattered by a person's depression. Such things do happen, however, and I was once very close to discovering such a relationship. There is nothing so seductive to a girl as to be loved by a poetic-depressive type. And if she is vain enough to deceive herself into thinking that she loves him faithfully by clinging to him instead of giving him up, then her task in life will be easy. She will enjoy both the distinction and the good conscience of being faithful, and at the same time the most finely distilled romantic love. God save everyone from such faithfulness!

His dark passions had completely gained the upper hand when he came up to me one day. He vehemently cursed existence, his love, and his beloved. He never came to me again after that. He apparently could not forgive himself for having confessed to another person that the girl had become a torment to him. He had ruined everything, even the joy he had taken in preserving her pride, in transforming her into a goddess. He avoided me when our paths crossed. If we ran into each other he would not talk to me, but made obvious efforts to [17] appear happy and confident. I was prepared to pursue him a little more closely, and to this end I had begun to make enquiries among the more subordinate of his acquaintances. One learns most about depressives, I have discovered, through such people. Depressives often open up more to a domestic, a footman or a maidservant, an old and overlooked family fixture, than to someone to whom he is connected more closely by education and social circumstances. I knew a depressive who danced through life, and deceived everyone, including myself, until a barber put me on the right track. The barber was an older man who lived in straitened circumstances and who thus took care of his customers himself. Sympathy with the barber's plight caused the man to reveal his depression; thus this barber knew what no one else knew.

The young person spared me the effort of tracking him down, however, because he came to me himself, though this time determined never to set foot inside my door again. He suggested we arrange to meet at mutually agreed-upon times at certain out-of-the-way places.

I was willing to do this and purchased, for this purpose, two tokens to fish in Stadsgraven.* This is where we met in the early morning, in that hour when the day battles with the night, when even during the summer a cold chill runs through nature. We met down there in the clammy morning mist when the grass was still wet with dew and the birds took off in fright at his cries. In the hour when day has finally won, when everything that lives again rejoices in existence, in the hour when the beloved young girl, whom he had adorned with his pain, lifted her head from its pillow and opened her eyes because the god of sleep, who had sat by her bedside, rose again, in the hour when the god of dreams placed his fingers on her eyelids so that she slipped briefly back to sleep while he told her of things she had never suspected, but whispered them so softly that she forgot them all when she woke up, in this hour, we parted. And whatever the god of dreams might have said to her, she could not have dreamed what transpired between us. It is no wonder he was pale and no wonder that I, who was his confidant and the confidant of many others like him, am also pale.

More time passed. I suffered a great deal for the young person who wasted away day by day. And yet I in no way regretted sharing in his suffering, because through his love the idea had been set in motion. (And such a love, God be praised, one sees sometimes in life, though one would search vainly for it in literature.) Only where this [18] is the case does romantic love have any meaning, and he who is not enthusiastically convinced that the idea is the life-principle of love, and that when it is demanded he must give his life for it, and what is more, must sacrifice love itself, he is excluded from poetry. Even though his situation is ripe with poetic possibilities, he is excluded from poetry. On the other hand, where romantic love is present as an idea, every movement, every feeling, even a fleeting one, has meaning because the main point is always there, the poetic collision which can, according to what I know, be even more horrific than the one I am describing here. But to serve the idea, which in relation to romantic love is not to serve two masters, requires strenuous effort, because no beauty can calculate so accurately as the idea can, and no girl's disapproval is so heavy as the idea's displeasure that is, more than anything else, impossible to forget.

If I were thoroughly to pursue all the moods of this young person to the extent that I was aware of them, not to mention if I were, in poetic fashion, to bring in a mass of unrelated things, parlours and dress and beautiful scenery, relatives and friends, this little story could become a lengthy novel. I would rather not do that, though. I like lettuce, but I eat only the heart; the leaves, it seems to me, are for pigs. I prefer, like Lessing, the pleasures of conception to the pains of giving birth.* If anyone has anything against this, he can go ahead and complain. I do not care.

Time passed. When possible, I came to his nightly devotions, where through wild cries he would get his daily exercise since he used the daytime to entertain the girl. As Prometheus, nailed to a cliff where a vulture pecked at his liver, enthralled the gods with his prophesies, so did he enthral his beloved. He mustered all his strength every day, because every day was like the last. It could not go on like this though, he chafed at the leash that held him. But the more his passion boiled, the more blissful his songs, the more tender his speech, the tighter became the leash. It was impossible for him to make a real relationship from such a misunderstanding; it would be to abandon her to an eternal deception. To explain to her the confusion, that she was just the visible form, whereas his thoughts, his soul, sought something else that he had attributed to her, that would be to wrong her so deeply that his pride protested against it. This was a method he despised more than anything. In this he was [19] correct. It is despicable to deceive and seduce a girl. It is even more despicable, however, to leave a girl in such a way that one avoids becoming a scoundrel, but instead makes a brilliant retreat in that one puts her off with the explanation that she was not the ideal, but comforts her with the fact that she was one's muse. This can be done, if one has some experience in dealing with girls, and she will accept this explanation if she is desperate. One makes a good escape this way, remains an upstanding, even admirable person, and yet she is in this way wronged more deeply than the girl who *knows* she was deceived. Thus, in every romantic relationship that cannot be fully realized, despite the fact that it has begun, delicacy is the insulting thing, and he who has an eye for the erotic, and is not a coward, easily sees that to be indelicate is the only means left to him to preserve the girl's honour.

In order to put an end to his suffering, I encouraged him to dare to go to extremes. The essential thing was simply to find a point of agreement. I made the following suggestion: lay waste to everything. Transform yourself into a contemptible person whose only pleasure

is in tricking and deceiving. If you can do this, then you will have
established equality. There could not, in such a case, be any talk
of an aesthetic difference that vindicated you in relation to her,
something people all too often are inclined to concede, a so-called
exceptional individuality. She would then be victorious; she would
be absolutely in the right, and you absolutely in the wrong. Do not
do it too quickly though, because this will only inflame her love. Try,
at first, if possible, just to be a little annoying to her. Do not tease
her, that will only excite her. No, be changeable, nonsensical. Do one
thing one day, and another thing the next, but all without passion,
blunderingly. Do not let this degenerate, however, into inattentive-
ness. On the contrary, your external attentiveness must be as great as
ever, just transformed into a kind of official duty lacking any genuine
passion. Instead of romantic ecstasy, constantly produce a mawkish
quasi-love, that is neither indifference nor genuine desire. Allow
your whole manner to be as unpleasant as it is to see a man drool. Do
not start though, unless you have the strength to complete the thing,
or the game is lost, because there is nothing so smart as a girl, that
is, when the question is whether she is loved or not, and there is no
operation so difficult as an extraction if one has to employ the instrument himself, an instrument that generally only time knows how to
handle. Come to me after you have got everything started, and I will
take care of the rest. Allow the rumour to be spread that you are [20]
involved with someone else in a very unpoetic relationship, because
otherwise you will only egg her on. That such a thing could not occur
to you yourself, I understand completely. It is understood between
us that she is the only one you love, even though it is impossible for
you to translate this poetic relationship into an actual love. There
must be some truth to the rumour. I will take care of that. I will find
a girl here in town with whom I can arrange something.

It was not merely concern for this young person that moved me
to come up with this plan. I cannot deny though that I had gradually
come to think ill of his beloved. That she failed to notice anything,
that she had not the least intimation of his sufferings, that she did
nothing, did not try to save him with what he needed and what she
could give him — freedom. This would save him if she gave it to him,
because in this way she would, through her magnanimity, be in the
superior position, she would not be wronged! I can forgive a girl anything, but I cannot forgive that in her love she mistakes love's task.

When a girl's love is not self-sacrificing, then she is not a woman but a man, and I will always take pleasure in allowing her to become a laughing-stock. And what a subject for a comic writer, to let such a lover, whose love first sucked the blood out of her beloved to the point where he in despair and desperation breaks with her — to let such a lover appear an Elvira,* who performs brilliantly in this role, whose situation is bemoaned by relatives and friends, an Elvira who is the lead singer in the chorus of the deceived, an Elvira who can speak impressively about the faithlessness of men, a faithlessness that apparently is going to be the death of her, an Elvira who does all this with confidence and assurance, to whom it does not for one second occur that her faithfulness was more closely calculated to be the death of her beloved. Feminine fidelity is great, particularly when it is declined. It is always unfathomable and incomprehensible. The situation would have been priceless if her lover, despite his need, had preserved enough humour not to waste an angry word on her, [21] but had confined himself to a more profound revenge, to strengthen her in the delusion that she was shamefully deceived by him. If she believed this, then the revenge, if the young person were able to carry out my plan, would affect her terribly, yet with poetic justice. He is convinced that he is doing the best thing he can, but this, if she is selfish, will be the worst punishment. He treats her with the greatest possible erotic solicitude. Yet his method will be supremely painful, if she is selfish.

He was willing and applauded my plan. I found what I sought, in a milliner's shop, a young and very lovely girl, whose future I promised to take care of if she participated in my plan. He would be seen with her in public places, visit her at such times that there could be no doubt that they had an understanding. To this end, I secured an apartment for her in a house with access to two streets, so he need only walk through the house late in the evening to confirm the suspicions of the servant-girls, and others, and to get the rumours started. Once everything was in place, I would make sure his beloved did not remain ignorant of his new relationship. The seamstress was attractive, but in such a way that the beloved, quite apart from being jealous, would be astonished that such a girl was preferred to her. If I had focused on the beloved, the seamstress would have been a little different, but because I could know nothing in this respect with any certainty, and because I did not want to be too devious in relation to the young person, my choice was thoroughly consistent with his method.

The seamstress was engaged for one year. The relationship had to be maintained for this long in order fully to deceive the beloved. During this time he was, in addition, if possible to work on his transformation into a poet. If he succeeded in this, then a *redintegratio in statum pristinum*[1] could be effected. In the course of the year—and this is very important—the young girl would have the opportunity to extricate herself from the relationship in that he would have failed to make its direction clear. If this should happen, that she, when the moment of repetition came, had become tired, well, he would in any case have behaved magnanimously.

Thus everything was prepared. I already had a tight grip on the reins. I was unusually anxious concerning the outcome. But the young man disappeared. I never saw him again. He had not had [22] the strength to carry out the plan. His soul lacked the elasticity of irony. He had not had the strength to swear irony's promise of silence, to keep the promise, and only he who keeps silent amounts to anything. Only he who can really love, only he is a human being, only he who can give his love any sort of expression whatever, only he is an artist. In a certain sense, it was perhaps right that he did not even attempt it, because he could hardly have endured the horrors of the adventure. I was concerned from the beginning by the fact that he needed a confidant. He who knows how to keep silent, he discovers an alphabet that has just as many letters as the ordinary one, so he is able to express everything in his secret language. No sigh is so deep that he does not have laughter that corresponds to it in this secret language, and no entreaty so obtrusive that he is not clever enough to redeem it. There would come a point for him where he would be near to losing his mind. This is just a phase though, even though it is a terrible one. It is like the fever one gets between 11.30 and 12.00 at night. By 1.00 though, one works more intrepidly than ever. If one can endure this insanity, one will win in the end.

But I digress. I had actually intended this story to show that the love of recollection in fact makes a person unhappy. My young friend did not understand repetition. He did not believe in it, and thus failed to will it with enough strength. His fate was sad in that

---

[1] Return to the original state of things.

he really loved the girl, but in order actually to love her, he first had to be freed from the poetic confusion into which he had fallen. He could have confessed this to the girl. This is the seemly thing to do when one wants to end a relationship with a girl. He did not want to do this, though. I agreed with him entirely in his view that this would be wrong. He would in this way have deprived her of the opportunity to exist autonomously, and freed himself perhaps from becoming an object of her contempt as well as from a gathering anxiety concerning whether he would ever be able to recover what he had lost.

If he had only believed in repetition, what might this young person not have become? What heartfelt intensity could he not have achieved in his life?

I have, however, gone further into this story than I had intended. My point was simply to present the first phase, where it became clear [23] that this young person was, in a very real sense, the grieving knight of recollection's one happy love. The reader will perhaps allow me to reflect once again on the moment when, intoxicated with recollection, he came to my room, when his heart constantly '*ging ihm über*'[1] in that verse of Poul Møller's, when he confided to me that he had to restrain himself to keep from spending the entire day with his beloved. He repeated this same verse the evening we parted. I will never be able to forget that verse. I could more easily erase the memory of his disappearance,* than the memory of this moment, the facts of which caused me much less anxiety than this situation. I am constituted in such a way that in the first shudder of foreboding my soul has at once run through all the consequences that often require a long time actually to become apparent. One never forgets the concentration of foreboding. I believe that an observer must be constituted in this way, yet when he is so constituted, he will suffer a great deal. The first phase must overwhelm him almost to the point of fainting. In this moment of weakness, the idea impregnates him, and from that point begins his relation to actuality. If a person does not have this feminine quality that allows the idea to come into the proper relation to him, which is always to impregnate, then he will not be fit to be an observer, because he who does not discover the whole, really discovers nothing.

[1] Overflowed.

After we parted that evening, and he once again thanked me for having helped him pass the time that went all too slowly in relation to his impatience, I thought then to myself that presumably he is open-hearted enough to tell the young girl everything. Would she then love him even more? What if he did this? If he had asked me, I would have advised against this. I would have told him: 'Be firm in the beginning, erotically, this is the smartest thing to do, unless your soul is so serious that you can direct your thought to something much higher.' If he had told the girl the truth, he would not have acted wisely.

Anyone who has had an opportunity to observe young girls, to lure them into conversation, will often have heard this sort of statement: 'N.N. is a good person, but he is boring; on the other hand F.F. is so exciting and interesting.' Every time I hear these words in a little miss's mouth, I think: you should be ashamed of yourself. It is sad to hear a young girl say such a thing. If a young man lost himself in the realm of the interesting, who, other than a young girl, could save [24] him. Is she not also guilty? Either the one concerned is unable to do it, and then it is indelicate to demand it, or he can do it and so... A young girl should always be careful never to coax forth the interesting. The girl who does this always loses from the perspective of the idea, because the interesting can never be repeated. The girl who does not do this is always victorious.

Six years ago I took a trip thirty miles into the country. I stopped at an inn where I also ate lunch. I had consumed a pleasant and tasty meal, was in a good mood, had a cup of coffee in my hand whose aroma I was in the process of inhaling, when suddenly a lovely young girl, delicate and charming, passed by the window and into the courtyard that was part of the inn. I concluded that she was headed for the garden. I was young—thus I gulped down my coffee, lit a cigar, and was in the process of pursuing the signal of fate and the girl's tracks, when there was a knock on my door and in walks—the girl. She gives me a friendly curtsy and then asks whether it was my carriage that was in the courtyard, whether I was going to Copenhagen, and whether I would allow her to ride along. The modest and yet genuinely feminine way she did this was enough to cause me to immediately lose sight of the exciting and interesting. And yet it is much more interesting to ride thirty miles alone with a young girl, in one's own carriage with a driver and a footman, to have her entirely under one's power, than it is to meet her in a garden. And yet, I am convinced that even a less considerate person than myself would not have felt tempted. The trust with which she placed herself under my power is a better defence than all the shrewdness and cunning a young girl could muster. We rode together. She could not have been more secure if she had travelled with a brother or a father. I was silent and reserved. Only when it seemed that she was going to speak was I obliging. My driver had orders to hurry. We spent five minutes at each stop. I got out. With my hat in my hand I asked whether she wished for some refreshment. My footman stood behind me, also hat in hand. As we approached the city I had my driver take a side-road, where I alighted and walked the remaining two miles to Copenhagen, in order to avoid meeting anyone and thus coming into a situation that might disturb her. I have never tried to learn who she [25] was, where she lived, what could have occasioned her sudden trip. She has always been a pleasant memory for me though, which I have not allowed myself to sully with even an innocent curiosity.—A girl who desires the interesting becomes a snare in which she herself is caught. A girl who does not desire the interesting, she has faith in repetition. All honour to one who was originally so. All honour to the one who became so with time.

I must constantly repeat, however, that repetition was the occasion for my saying all this. Repetition is the new category that must be discovered. If one knows something about modern philosophy, and is conversant with Greek philosophy, one will easily see that precisely this category explains the relation between the Eleatics and Heraclitus,* and that repetition is really that which has mistakenly been referred to as mediation. It is unbelievable how much Hegelian philosophy brags about mediation, so much foolish nonsense, which under its auspices enjoyed honour and glory. It would be better to think through mediation and to do justice to the Greeks. The Greeks' development of the doctrine of being and nothing, the development of 'the moment', 'non-being', etc., beats everything in Hegel. 'Mediation'* is a foreign word. 'Repetition' is a good Danish word, and I congratulate the Danish language for its contribution to philosophical terminology. It has not been explained in our own time how mediation comes about, whether it is a result of a movement of the two phases and in what sense it is already contained in them, or whether it appears as something new and, if so, how.

In this respect, it is important to take the Greek ruminations on the concept of κίνησις,[1] which corresponds to the modern category of 'transition', into account. The dialectic of repetition is easy, because that which is repeated has been, otherwise it could not be repeated; but precisely this, that it has been, makes repetition something new. When the Greeks said that all knowing was recollecting, they were also thus saying that all of existence, everything that is, has been. When one says that life is repetition, one also says that that which has existed now comes to be again. When one lacks the categories of recollection and repetition, all of life is dissolved into an empty, meaningless noise. Recollection is the ethnic view* of life, repetition the modern. Repetition is the *interest* of metaphysics, and also the interest upon which metaphysics becomes stranded. Repetition is the solution in every ethical contemplation, repetition is the *conditio sine* [26] *qua non*[2] for every dogmatic problem.

Judge what one will concerning what I say here about repetition—that is, that I say it and in this way, following Hamann's example, *mit mancherlei Zungen mich ausdrücke, und die Sprache der Sophisten, der Wortspiele, der Creter und Araber, Weißen und Mohren und Creolen rede, Critik, Mythologie, rebus und Grundsätze durcheinander schwatze, und bald κατ'ἄνθρωπον bald κατ'ἐξοχην argumentire.** On the assumption that what I say here is not simply a lie, it would perhaps be best if I sent my aphorisms to a systematic appraiser. Perhaps something could come of this, a mention in the system—what a thought! Then I would not have lived in vain!

As far as the meaning repetition has for a thing, one can say a great deal without actually committing a repetition. When Professor Ussing,* in his time, gave a speech for the 28th of May Society,* and one of his remarks was not well received, what did the professor, who was then always resolute and vehement, do? He pounded on the table and said: 'I repeat.' That is, he waited until what he had said became accepted through repetition. A few years ago, I heard a priest give precisely the same speech on two ceremonious occasions. Had he been of the same opinion as the professor, the second time he climbed into the pulpit he would have pounded on it and said: I repeat what I said last Sunday. But he did not, and gave

---

[1] Motion.   [2] The indispensable condition.

no indication that he was repeating himself. He was not of the same opinion as Professor Ussing, and who knows, perhaps the distinguished Professor Ussing is no longer of the opinion that it was good for his speech to be repeated. When, during a royal celebration, the queen had told a story and all the courtiers, including a deaf minister, had laughed at it, this minister then stood up and asked to be allowed to tell a story of his own and told the same story. Question: what view did he have of the meaning of repetition? When a schoolteacher says: this is the second time, I repeat, that Jespersen must sit quietly, and this same Jespersen receives a mark for repeated disruptiveness, then the meaning of repetition is precisely the opposite.

I am not, however, going to dwell on such examples any longer. I'm going to speak instead about a voyage of discovery I undertook in [27] order to test the possibility and meaning of repetition. Unbeknownst to anyone (in order, namely, that too much discussion would not cause me to become unable to do the experiment, and in another sense bored with repetition) I sailed by steamship to Stralslund and then took the *Schnellpost*[1] to Berlin. There is a difference of opinion among the learned as to which seat in a stagecoach is the most comfortable. My *Ansicht*[2] is the following: they are all equally terrible. The previous time, I had one of the outer seats toward the front of the vehicle (this is considered by many to be a great coup) and was for thirty-six hours, together with those near me, so violently tossed about that when I came to Hamburg not only had I nearly lost my mind, but also my legs. The six of us who sat in this vehicle were worked together for these thirty-six hours so that we became one body, in such a way that I got an impression of what happened to the Molbos* who, after having sat together for a long time, could no longer recognize which legs were their own. In order to become a limb of what would at least be a smaller body, this time I chose a seat in the coupé.* This was a change. Otherwise, everything repeated itself. The postillion* blew the horn, I closed my eyes, surrendered to despair, and thought, as I am wont to do on such occasions: God knows whether you will be able to endure this, whether you will actually come to Berlin, and if so, whether you will ever be human again, able to free yourself in the individualism of isolation, or whether you will retain this memory that you are a limb of a huge body.

---

¹ Express coach.   ² View.

Then I arrived in Berlin. I hurried immediately to my old lodgings in order to ascertain the extent to which repetition was possible. I dare say that last time I was so fortunate as to get one of the best apartments in Berlin, I emphasize this because I have seen many. Gendarmenmarkt is the most beautiful square in Berlin, *das Schauspielhaus*,[1] the two churches, are luminous, seen from the window in the moonlight. That memory was a large part of why I set off on this trip. One ascends to the first floor of a gas-illuminated building, opens a little door, and is in the entryway. To the left there is a glass door that leads into a small room. If one continues straight ahead, one will come to the anteroom. Just off this room are two smaller, completely symmetrical rooms, identically furnished, so that they appear to be mirror-images of each other. The interior room is tastefully illuminated. A candelabra stands on a desk beside a tasteful and simply designed easy-chair, upholstered in red velvet. The first room is not illuminated. The pale moonlight is thus blended here with the stronger lighting of the inner room. One can sit here in [28] a chair by the window, gaze out at the square, and watch the shadows of the passers-by as they hurry across the walls. Everything is transformed into a scenic backdrop. One's soul becomes enveloped in a dreamlike dusk. One feels a desire to throw on a cloak and sneak stealthily along the wall like a spy, taking in every sound. One does not do it, of course, but only imagines a younger self doing it. One finishes one's cigar, and thus retires to the inner room and begins to work. It is past midnight. One extinguishes the candles and lights instead a little night candle. The moonlight now reigns supreme. A single shadow seems even darker, and the sound of a single footstep takes for ever to die away. The cloudless vault of heaven appears dreamy and sad, as if the end of the world had already come and heaven continued undisturbed in its self-preoccupation. One goes out again into the front room, the hall, into the little room and—if one is among the fortunate who can sleep—sleeps.

But no! Repetition was not possible here. My landlord, the chemist, *er hatte sich verändert*,[2] in the pregnant sense in which the Germans understand these words, and as far as I know, 'to change' is used in a similar way in some quarters of Copenhagen—i.e. he had married. I wanted to congratulate him, but because my command of

---

[1] The theatre.　　[2] He had changed.

the German language is limited to the extent that I do not know the precise expressions one would use in specific circumstances, and in particular in these circumstances, I restricted myself to a sort of pantomime gesture. I placed my hand over my heart and looked at him with an expression of tender appreciation. He shook my hand. After this exchange, he proceeded to produce a proof of the aesthetic validity of marriage.* And he succeeded, precisely as well as he had succeeded the last time in proving the perfection of bachelorhood. When I speak German, I am the most accommodating man in the world.

My previous landlord wanted very much to be of service to me, and I wanted to lodge with him, so I accepted a one-room apartment with a small foyer. Alas! Alack! I thought when I came home the first evening and lit the candles. Is this repetition? I became immediately out of sorts, or if one wishes, in precisely the sort of mood the day demanded, because fate had strangely arranged that I should come to Berlin on the *allgemeine Buß- und Bettag*.[1] Berlin was prostrate. One did not throw [29] ashes in the eyes of others with the words: *Memento o homo! Quod cinis esset in cinerem revertaris*;[2] but the whole city was nevertheless covered in dust. I thought at first that it was a government measure, but later I became convinced that it was the wind that was responsible for this inconvenience, and, without regard for what a person would like, followed its own mood or its unfortunate habit, because in Berlin at least every other day is Ash Wednesday. This is not really relevant, though, to my subject. This discovery did not concern 'repetition', because the last time I was in Berlin I did not notice this phenomenon, presumably because it had been winter.

Once one is comfortably installed in an apartment, when one in this sense has a fixed point from which to venture forth, a secure hiding-place, to which one can return to devour his prey — something I value very highly because, like certain predators, I cannot eat while anyone watches — then one sets out to learn what interesting sights the city has to offer. If one is a traveller *ex professo*,[3] an express courier, who travels just to be able to sniff everything others have also sniffed, or to write the names of important tourist attractions in one's travel diary, or alternatively to write one's own name in the volume of world travellers, one engages a *Lohndiener*[4] and in this way

---

[1] First day Lent (Ash Wednesday.) Literally, 'a day of universal fasting and penance'.
[2] Remember, O Man! That from ashes you came and to ash you will return.
[3] By trade.
[4] Literally, 'wage earner'. Here, however, it means a guide.

gets *das ganze Berlin*[1] for four *Groschen*. This method makes one an impartial observer whose statements any police report would count as trustworthy. If, on the other hand, there is nothing in particular one has to accomplish on one's trip, one can just wait for something to happen. One will sometimes see things in this way that others miss, look past the important sights, catch an accidental impression that has meaning only for oneself. Such a careless vagabond does not usually have much to communicate to others, and if he does try to communicate something, he easily runs the risk of undermining the positive opinion good people might have concerning his moral character and manners. If a person had been travelling abroad for a while, but had never travelled by train, would he not be expelled from all polite society! What if a person had been to London and had never been in the Tunnel!* What if a person arrived in Rome, fell in love with some small part of the city that was for him an inexhaustible source of pleasure, and then left Rome again without having seen a single tourist attraction!

Berlin has three theatres. The operas and ballets performed in Berlin's Opera are said to be *großartig*.[2] The pieces performed in the Theatre are not simply for amusement,* they must be instructive, must educate. I don't know. I do know, on the other hand, that there is a theatre in Berlin called the Königstädter Theatre. Tourists [30] rarely visit this theatre, though they visit it more often than they visit the more out-of-the-way places of amusement where a Dane would get the chance to jog his memory of Lars Mathiesen and Kehlet.* When I came to Stralsund and read in the paper that *der Talisman*＊ was going to be performed in this theatre, I was immediately in high spirits. The memory of this piece was awakened in my soul, and the first time I saw it, it was as if this first impression merely called forth a memory from within my soul that reached far back in time.

There is no young person with any imagination who has not at some time felt himself captured by the magic of the theatre and wished to become part of this mock actuality, in order, as a *doppelgänger*, to see and hear himself, to disperse himself into a multiplicity of all his possibilities, and yet in such a way that each possibility is a self. This desire naturally expresses itself at a very young age. Only the

---

[1] The whole of Berlin.   [2] Magnificent.

imagination is awakened to the dream of personality; everything
else continues to sleep securely. In such a self-contemplation of
the imagination, the individual has no actual shape, but is a mere
shadow, or more correctly, the actual shape is invisibly present and
is thus not content to cast one shadow. The individual has a multiplicity of shadows, all of which resemble him and each of which is,
at least fleetingly, equally justified as being his self. Personality has
not yet been discovered, its energy announces itself only in the passion of possibility, because it is in the life of spirit as it is with many
plants—the central shoot comes last. This shadowy existence also
demands satisfaction, and it is never beneficial to a person if it does
not get time to express itself, while on the other hand it is sad, or
even comical, when the individual mistakenly confuses this shadow
with himself. And such a person's pretensions to be an actual person
are as doubtful as the demand for immortality, of those who are not
in a position to appear personally on the Day of Judgement, but
appear instead in the form of good intentions, resolutions, half-hour
plans, and such. The main thing is that everything happens at the
right time. Everything has its time in youth, and what has had its
time then has its time again later, and it is just as healthy for an older
person to have something laughable in his past as it is for him to have
something heart-rending.

[31]   When, in a mountainous region, one hears the wind, day in and
day out, steadfastly, unchangingly, play the same theme, one is
perhaps tempted to abstract, for a moment, from the imperfection
of the analogy, and take pleasure in this symbol of the consistency
and security of human freedom. One does not think, perhaps, that
there was a time when the wind that has now for many years resided
in these mountains, came as a stranger to this place, cast itself about
confusedly, meaninglessly, through the cliffs and caverns, produced
first a howl with which it almost startled itself, then a roar from
which it fled, then a moan whose origin was even to itself a mystery,
then a sigh from anxiety's abyss, a sigh so deep that it became frightened and doubted for a moment whether it dare take up residence in
this place, then an exuberant, lyrical waltz; until, after it had come to
know its instrument, it worked all these into the melody that it now,
day in and day out, unvaryingly plays. Thus the individual becomes
lost in his own possibility, discovering first one and then another
possibility. But the potential of the individual does not simply want

to be heard, it is not simply passing through like the weather. It is
gestaltende,[1] thus it also wants to be seen. Each of its possibilities is
thus a sounding shadow. The cryptic individual has as little faith
in great noisy passions as he has in evil's cunning whisper, as little
faith in the blessed shouts of joy as in sorrow's endless sighing. Such
an individual wants only to see and hear with pathos, but—and
this is important—to see and hear himself. He does not actually
want to hear himself, though. That is not the point. Now the cock
crows, twilight's phantoms flee, night's voices are silenced. If they
remained, then we would be in an entirely different region, where
everything takes place under the anxious watch of accountability;
then we would be in the region of the demonic. In order to avoid
getting an impression of his actual self, the cryptic individual needs
his environment to be as light and transitory as shadows, as the
effervescence of words without an echo.

   Such is a scenic environment, which is therefore particularly well
suited to the *Schattenspiel*[2] of the cryptic individual. Among the
shadows, where he discovers himself, whose voices are his voice,
there is perhaps a highwayman. He must recognize himself in this
mirror-image, the highwayman's manly form, his fleeting yet pene-
trating look, passion's mark on his furrowed brow. Everything is
there. He lies in wait at the mountain pass, he listens for the sound
of a coach approaching, he whistles, the band springs into action. His   [32]
voice must bellow above the noise. He must be cruel, allow everything to be cut down, indifferently turning away from it. He must be
chivalrous to the frightened girl, etc., etc. A highwayman is at home
in sinister woods. If one wished to place this imaginary hero in such a
setting, to provide him with the necessary trappings and request only
that he wait calmly until one had retreated a couple of miles away,
in order, in this way, to be able to surrender completely to his passionate rage—then I think he would be speechless. It would perhaps
be with him as it was with a man who, a few years ago, honoured
me with his literary confidence. He came to me and apologized for
the fact that he was so overwhelmed by an abundance of ideas that
it was impossible for him to write anything down, because he could
not write fast enough. He asked me if I would mind functioning as

---

[1] Creative.   [2] Shadow play.

his secretary, and write down his ideas as he dictated them to me. I immediately sensed mischief, and comforted him with the fact that my writing could keep pace with a galloping horse, because I wrote only one letter of each word and yet I assured him that I could read everything I had written. My desire to be of service knew no bounds. I had a large table brought in, numbered several sheets of paper in order that I would not have to waste time turning them, and laid out a dozen steel pens with shafts, dipped the first pen in ink — and the man began to talk as follows: yes! You see, Esteemed Sirs, what I would really like to say, is... When he was finished with his speech, I read it back to him, and since that time he has never again asked me to serve as his secretary.

This highwayman would presumably find the standard by which he is measured too great, and yet in another sense, too small. No, paint him a backdrop with a tree, hang a lamp in front that makes the light even stranger, and these woods are suddenly larger than any actual woods, larger even than North America's primeval forest, and yet his voice can penetrate them without his even becoming hoarse. This is the sophistical desire of the imagination, to have the whole world like this in a nutshell, a nutshell that is larger than the whole world and yet not so large that the individual cannot fill it.

Such an inclination toward dramatic performance and expectoration is in no way an indication of a theatrical vocation. A theatrical vocation shows itself immediately in a disposition to individuality, and even the richest awakening talent does not have this sort of range. This desire is simply the immaturity of the imagination. This is entirely different from the desire that has its foundation in vanity [33] and an inclination to show off. Then the whole thing has no deeper source than vanity, a source that unfortunately can be fairly deep.

Even if this phase in an individual's life disappears, it comes again at a more mature age, when the soul has seriously begun to take shape. While art was perhaps not important enough to the individual, he can still have the desire to return to this first state and take it up again. He wishes then to be comical, to relate comically to his theatrical performance. Since neither tragedy, nor comedy, nor satire will satisfy him, precisely because of their perfection, he returns to farce. The same phenomenon is found in other spheres. One sometimes sees that the more mature individual, who satiates himself on actuality's strong food, is not really affected by a particularly good painting. On the other hand, he can be moved by the sight of a Nüremberg print,* a picture like those that not so long ago were sold in many shops. One sees there a landscape that is meant to represent a typical rural scene. This abstraction does not admit of artistic representation. The objective is therefore achieved through a contradiction, namely with an accidental concretion. And yet I always want to ask people whether they do not, from such a landscape, get the impression of a rural scene in general and whether they still have this concept from their childhood. When one is a child, one has such enormous categories that they would now almost make one dizzy. Then one could cut from a piece of paper a man and a woman, who were man and woman in general in an even stricter sense than Adam and Eve were. A landscape painter, whether he endeavours to achieve his effect through a faithful reproduction or through an ideal presentation, leaves the individual perhaps cold. Such a picture, however, produces an indescribable effect, in that one does not know whether one should laugh or cry. The whole effect depends upon the mood of the observer. There is no one who has not been through a period when no richness of language, no passionate interjection, was sufficient, when no expression, no gesticulation was satisfactory, because nothing satisfied except the wildest spontaneous leaps and somersaults. Perhaps this person learned to dance, perhaps he often watched ballets and admired the dancers' art, perhaps there came a time when ballet no longer had any effect on him. And yet there were moments when he could retreat to his room, indulge himself, [34] and feel an indescribably humorous relief in standing on one leg in as aesthetically pleasing position, or tell the whole world to go to the devil with an entrechat.*

They show farces in the Königstädter Theatre. The people who gather there are thus naturally very diverse. He who would study the pathology of laughter in a variety of estates and temperaments ought not to lose the opportunity offered by the performance of a farce. The shouts and shrill laughter from the gallery and the second balcony are something completely different from the applause of a sophisticated and critical audience. It is a constant accompaniment without which farce could not be performed. Farce is associated, for the most part, with the baser aspects of life, and thus those in the gallery and the second balcony recognize themselves immediately. Their noise and shouts of 'bravo' are not judgements of the aesthetic approval of individual actors, but purely lyrical outbursts of their own well-being. They are not even conscious of themselves as an audience, but would like to be down with the actors on the street or wherever the scene happens to take place. Since, however, the theatrical distance makes this impossible, they conduct themselves like children who are allowed to watch a commotion in the street only through the window. The orchestra and the first balcony* also shake with laughter, even if it is of an essentially different sort from the Cimbrian-Teutonic* screeching emanating from the cheaper seats. There is an infinitely nuanced variety of laughter even here, and in a completely different sense from what one would have with the performance of a first-class comedy. Whether one considers it a perfection or an imperfection, this is how it is. Every ordinary aesthetic category fails when it comes to farce, which is in no way able to bring about a uniform mood on the part of the more sophisticated public, because with farce the effect depends largely upon the observer's own energetic contribution. The individuality of the observer asserts itself here in an entirely different sense, and is thus in its enjoyment emancipated from all aesthetic obligations, such as to be moved emotionally, to laugh, to admire, etc., in the traditional manner. To watch a farce is, for the sophisticated, like playing the lottery, only without the unpleasantness of winning money. Such uncertainty does not serve the ordinary theatregoing public. They like, therefore, to denigrate farce or look down on it contemptuously, which is the worse for them. A real theatregoing public generally has a certain narrow-minded seriousness. They want, or in any case imagine they want, to be educated and ennobled by the theatre. [35] They want to have had, or at least to imagine they have had, a rare aesthetic pleasure. They want, as soon as they have read the poster, to be able to know in advance how the evening will go. Such prescience is impossible with farce, because the same farce can leave two very different impressions, and what is strange is that it can be least effective when it is best performed. One cannot, therefore, trust the reviews of friends and neighbours and the newspapers concerning whether it was entertaining. That determination can be made only by the individual. No critic has yet been able to prescribe an etiquette for a sophisticated theatregoing public that watches a farce. No *bon ton*[1] can be established in this way. The otherwise so reassuring

---

[1] Good tone.

mutual respect between the theatre and the public is suspended. A farce can put one in the most unpredictable mood. One can thus never know with certainty whether, while in the theatre, one behaved as a respectable member of society who has laughed and cried in the right places. One cannot, as a conscientious spectator, admire the finely developed characters that are necessary in a drama, because the characters in a farce are all abstract generalizations. The situation, the action, the lines—everything is an abstract generalization. One can thus just as easily become sad as doubled over with laughter.

No effect of a farce is brought about through irony, but through naivety. The spectator must therefore become involved as an individual with the spectacle. The naivety of farce is so illusory that it is impossible for the sophisticated to relate to it naively. But it is precisely the relating of the spectator to farce from which much of the amusement comes, and he must be willing to dare to risk this, though he will seek vainly to the right and to the left and in the newspapers for a guarantee that he has actually been amused. For a sophisticated person, on the other hand, who is still unembarrassed enough to dare to be amused all by himself, who has enough self-confidence to know, without seeking advice from anyone else, whether he has been amused, farce will perhaps have a very special meaning, in that now with the spaciousness of abstraction and now with the presentation of a tangible actuality, it will affect his mood differently. He will, of course, refrain from bringing a fixed and definite mood with him so that everything affects him in relation to that mood. He will have perfected his mood, in that he will be able to keep himself in a condition where no particular mood is present, but where all moods are possible.

The farces performed in the Königstadter Theatre are, to my [36] mind, absolutely first class. My opinion is, of course, completely my own. I would not impose it on anyone else and decline any pressure to change it. In order for farce to be performed with complete success, the cast must have a particular composition. There should be two, or at most three, seriously talented, or more accurately, creative geniuses. They must be children of high spirits, intoxicated with laughter, humour's dancers, who even if at other times, even the moment before, they are just like everyone else, immediately upon hearing the stage-manager's bell are transformed, and like the noble Arabian horse, begin to snort and groan, while their nostrils expand, witnessing to the exertions of the spirit in them that wants to come out and tumble about wildly. They are not so much reflective artists who have studied laughter, as they are lyricists who plunge themselves into the abyss of laughter and then let its volcanic might cast them onto the stage. They have not, therefore, so much calculated what they are going to do as they have allowed the moment and the natural power of laughter to take care of everything. They have the courage to do what the individual ventures to do only when he is alone, what the insane do in the presence of everyone, what the genius knows how to do, with the authority of genius, certain of laughter. They know that their exuberance has no bounds, that there is in them an inexhaustible source of the comical which at each moment almost surprises themselves. They know that they are able to sustain the laughter for the whole evening, without any more effort than I exert in putting this down on paper.

When a theatre known for farces has two such geniuses, that is enough; three is the absolute maximum; more weakens the effect, just as a person dies of hypertension. The other actors do not have to be talents; it is better if they're not. They don't even have to be attractive. It's best if they are a completely contingent seeming collection, on the order of the group that, according to a drawing by Chodowiecki,* founded Rome. They can even have physical defects; in fact such defects can be a good thing. The fact that one of the actors might be bow-legged, or knock-kneed, overly tall or unnaturally short—all such defects can be of use in farce. The effects they [37] produce can be incalculable. The accidental is the closest thing to the ideal. It has been said that one can divide humanity into officers, serving-girls, and chimneysweeps. This remark is, I believe, not merely witty, but also profound. One would have to be a great speculative talent to come up with a better division. When categories do not ideally exhaust their objects, then the contingent is in all respects preferable because it gets the imagination going. A more or less correct classification, while not entirely satisfactory to the understanding, is nothing to the imagination and is therefore rejected even if it is useful in everyday contexts, as a result partly of the fact that people just are not very smart, and partly because they do not have much imagination. In the theatre, a character must be presented either as the absolutely perfect incarnation of some ideal, or as completely contingent. Serious theatres should deliver the first type. Too often, however, it is considered enough if an actor is a good-looking fellow, well built, with a face appropriate to the theatre and a good voice. This rarely satisfies me because his performance *eo ipso*[1] awakens the critic in me and as soon as this is aroused it becomes difficult to determine what is required to be a human being, and equally difficult to fulfil the requirement. One would have to agree with me on this point when one remembers that Socrates, despite being very knowledgeable about human nature and having a great deal of self knowledge, did not know with certainty whether he was 'a more complex creature and more puffed up with pride than Typhon, or a simpler, gentler being whom heaven ha[d] blessed with a quite un-Typhonic nature'.* In farce, on the other hand, the subordinate characters function very well in this sort of abstract category—person in general—and achieve this through being some contingent concretion. Thus one comes no further than to actuality. One should not come any further. The spectator is comically reconciled to the sight of this contingency laying claim to do ideality, which it does by appearing in the artificial world which is the theatrical stage. If there is to be an exception in one of the subordinate characters, then it must be the female love interest. She must, of course, in no way be an artist, but one must make sure, however, in selecting her that she is attractive, that her whole appearance, her movements on the stage, are warm and salutary, that she is pleasant to look at, pleasant, so to speak, to have around.

The composition of the actors at the Königstädter Theatre is more or less what I would wish. If I were to make an objection, it would [38] be in relation to the subordinate actors, because I have no problem whatever with Beckmann and Grobecker.* Beckmann is clearly a comic genius who loses himself lyrically in the comical, not through character development, but through ebullience. He is not great in terms of what is commensurable with art, but admirable in terms of what is incommensurable—the individual and unique. He requires no support from the other actors, and none from the scenery or music. Precisely because he is in the right mood, he brings with him everything that is required. He paints himself into the scene independently of any scenographer, even while he gives himself over to an ecstasy of abandon. What Baggesen says about Sara Nickles*,

---

[1] In itself.

that she comes charging into a scene bringing a whole rural landscape with her on her heels, is true of B. as well, except that he
walks into a scene. In the serious theatre one rarely sees an actor
who can actually walk or stand well. I have seen only one. But what
B. is able to do, I have never seen before. He does not just walk, he
comes walking. To come walking is something completely different,
and with this ingenious action he sets the whole scene. He does not
just represent an itinerant apprentice lad, he can walk into a scene
as this character in such a way that one experiences everything. One
glimpses the smiling village from the dust of the country road, hears
the sounds of its peaceful activity, sees the footpath that runs down
along the pond and how it swings off by the blacksmith's shop, when
one sees B. come walking with a little bundle on his back, his staff
in his hand, carefree and indefatigable. He can come walking into
a scene followed by invisible street urchins. Even Dr Ryge in *King
Solomon and Jörgen the Hatter* cannot produce such an effect.* Yes,
Mr. B. is a real economy for a theatre, because if one has him, there
is no need either for the urchins or, for that matter, any props. This
itinerant apprentice is, however, not a developed character; it is too
thrown together in what are in truth its masterful contours. It is an
incognito in which the lunatic demon of the comical lives and from
which it leaps forth, transporting everything into licentiousness. In
this respect, B.'s dancing is incomparable. He has sung his couplet
and now begins to dance. What B. dares here is back-breaking because
he does not presumably venture to affect the audience in the strictest
sense through his graceful movements. He is well beyond this. The
lunatic laughter that is in him cannot be contained in either physical
[39] form or spoken lines. Only a Münchhausen-like* grabbing oneself
by the neck and repeatedly transcending oneself in a crazy, riotous
sort of leapfrog captures this spirit. An individual can, as I said,
recognize what relief lies in this, but to be able to do this on stage,
that takes a genius. That requires the authority of genius, otherwise
it will be utterly loathsome.

Every burlesque comic ought to have a voice that is instantly recognizable from the wings, so that he can thus prepare the way for himself.
B. has an excellent voice, which is not, of course, identical here with
good vocal chords. Grobecker's voice is harsher, but one word from
him on the stage has the same effect as three blows on a trumpet in
Dyrhavesbakken.* It makes one receptive to the humorous. In this

respect I would say that Gr. has an advantage over B. There is in B. a fundamental wildness, an unruly intelligence through which he achieves a kind of lunacy. Gr., on the other hand, climbs at times through the soulful and sentimental to lunacy. I remember having seen him once in a farce represent an estate manager, who, because of his devotion to the noble family he served and because of his belief that the purpose of festive occasions was to beautify the lives of this family, thinks only of having the rural pleasures in readiness for the family's ceremonious arrival. Everything is ready. Gr. chose to represent the god Mercury. He did not alter his overseer's costume at all. He simply put wings on his feet and a helmet on his head. He affects a picturesque pose, standing on one leg, and prepares to give his speech. Gr. is not so great a lyrical talent as B., but he is on the same lyrical good terms with laughter. He has a certain inclination towards correctness, and in this respect often performs masterfully, especially in the dryly comical. He is not a leavening agent for the entire farce in the sense that B. is. He is a genius though, and a genius for farce.

One enters the Königstädter Theatre. One takes one's seat in the first balcony, because the crowd will be relatively small, and when one watches a farce one needs to be comfortable and not in the least disturbed by the importance of art that leads people to allow themselves to be packed into a theatre in order to see a piece as if their eternal salvation depended on it. The air in the theatre is also quite fresh, free of contamination from the sweat of artistic connoisseurs, or the exhalations of art lovers. One can be fairly certain of securing [40] a box all to oneself in the first balcony. If this does not happen, then may I suggest to the reader, in order that he can gain some useful knowledge from what I write here, box no. 5 or 6 to the left. There is a nook in the back where there is a single seat that is incomparably comfortable. One sits alone in one's box. The theatre is empty. The orchestra plays an overture. The music rings throughout the hall, somewhat *unheimlich*,[1] given that the place is so empty. One has not come to the theatre as a tourist, not as an aesthete or critic, but if possible as nothing whatever, and one is as satisfied with the fact that one is as comfortably seated as if in one's own living-room. The orchestra is finished. The curtain has already begun to rise, just slightly.

[1] Eerily.

Then the other orchestra begins, the one that does not follow the conductor's baton but follows an inner instinct, this other orchestra, the natural sounds from the gallery, which has already sensed B. in the wings. I generally sat far back in the box and thus could not see either the second balcony or the gallery, which cast a shadow over my head like that of a huge hat. What had an even more fantastical effect was that while this noise penetrated everything, everywhere I looked the place appeared to be largely empty. The huge space of the theatre thus became for me transformed into a belly, like that of the whale in which Jonah sat. The noise from the gallery was like the rumblings of the whale's viscera. From the moment the gallery begins to stir no other music is needed, because B. animates it and it B.

My unforgettable nursemaid, you fugitive nymph who lived in the stream that ran past my father's farm and who always played along with me when I was a child even though it was simply for your own pleasure! You, my faithful comforter, you who with the passing of the years preserved your innocent purity, who never aged, even while I became old, you quiet nymph in whom I repeatedly sought refuge, so tired of people, so tired of myself, that I needed an eternity to rest, so sad that I needed an eternity to forget, you never denied me what human beings wanted to deny me by making eternity just as busy and even more terrible than time. I would lie next to you then, and lose myself in the immense space of the sky above me and in your peaceful murmuring! You, my happier self, you fleeting life that lives in the stream that runs next to my father's farm, where I lie stretched out as if I were a walking-stick someone had lain on the ground, but I am saved and liberated in the melancholy murmuring! — Thus I lay in [41] my box, tossed away like the clothes of a bather, stretched out beside the stream of shouting and laughter and general abandon that continuously rushed past me. I could see nothing apart from the space of the theatre, hear nothing but its sounds. Only now and then would I get up to watch Beckmann, laugh until I was so tired and satisfied that I would sink back down again by the side of the rushing stream.

This was wonderful, and yet I was still missing something. Then I discovered in the vast emptiness around me a form that delighted me more than Friday delighted Robinson Crusoe. In the box across from me sat a young girl in the third row, half-hidden by an older gentleman and lady who sat in the first row. This young girl could not have been in the theatre in order to be seen, in that in this theatre one is free of these loathsome feminine performances. She sat in the third row, her clothing was simple and modest, almost like that which she would wear at home. She was not wrapped in sable and marten, but in a large shawl, and from underneath this shawl her modest head extended slightly, as the top blossom on a stalk of lily of the valley extends gently from beneath the protection of its leaf. After I had watched Beckmann, had allowed the laughter to shake me through to the core, after I had sunk back in satisfaction and allowed myself to be carried away by the stream of shouting and merriment, after I had risen and returned again to myself, my eyes sought her, and the sight of her gentle mildness refreshed my whole being. Or when a wilder emotion surfaced in the farce, I would look at her and lose myself in the sight of her as she sat there with her peaceful smile and childlike wonder. She came there every evening, just as I did. I would sometimes fall into thought, occasioned by the sight of her, but these thoughts were merely moods that related back again to her. At one moment I would think she must be a girl who had already had enough of the world, and who thus wrapped her shawl tightly about herself as a kind of withdrawal from the world, and then something in her demeanour would reassure me that she was a happy child who pulled the shawl about herself in pleasure. She had no idea she was being observed, much less that I kept watch over her. It would not have been good for her had she known, and it would have been even worse for me, because there is an innocence, an unselfconsciousness, that even the most pure thought can disturb. One does not discover these things oneself, but if a man's positive genius confides to him where this original hiddenness conceals itself, then he does not offend this and distress his genius. If she had sensed my dumb, half- [42] love-struck joy, then everything would have been damaged beyond repair, even all her love could not have made it right again.

I know a place where a young girl lives, just a few miles from Copenhagen. I know the large, shaded garden with its many trees and bushes. I know where, not far from it, there lies a sloping little thicket from which one can peer undetected down into the garden. I have not told anyone about it, not even my coachman. I deceive him by getting out of the carriage before we reach the spot, and heading off to the right rather than the left. When I cannot sleep, and the sight of my bed frightens me more than an instrument of torture, more than a straitjacket frightens the deranged, then I go out for a drive that lasts the whole night. I lie in this little thicket in the wee hours of the morning, when life begins to stir again, when the sun first begins to open its eyes, when the birds begin to rustle their wings, when the fox sneaks out of its den, when the farmer stands in his door and looks out over his fields, when the milkmaid heads down to the meadow with her pail, when the farmhand fills the air with the bell-like tones of his scythe as he whets it, happily absorbed in this prelude to what will be the musical accompaniment to the day and its activities—then the young girl emerges from the house. Who could sleep! Who could sleep so easily that sleep does not become a heavier burden than the burdens of the day! Who could rise from his bed, as if no one had rested there, so the bed was cool and pleasant and refreshing to look at, as if the sleeper had not rested there, but only bent over it in order to make it! Who could die in such a way that even his deathbed, as he was borne away, was more inviting to look at than if an attentive mother had carefully fluffed up the down coverlet and pillows so that the child might sleep more soundly. Then the young girl emerges to enjoy the garden (but where is there more enjoyment, in the girl or in the trees!); she kneels to pluck a few flowers from their bushes, then skips about happily, then pauses thoughtfully. What wonderful persuasion does not lie in all this! Here finally my soul finds rest. Happy girl! If a man ever wins your love, I hope you make him as happy by being everything to him, as you make me by doing nothing for me.

Der Talisman was to be performed in Königstädter Theatre. The memory of this awakened in my soul. Everything stood before me as vividly as it had that first time. I hurried out to the theatre. I could [43] not get a box to myself though, not even no. 5 or 6 to the left. I had to go to the right. I encountered a group there who did not know whether they should be amused or bored. This sort of company is unequivocally annoying. There was hardly a single empty box. The young girl did not appear to be there, or if she was there, she must have been there with some group. Beckmann failed to make me laugh. I held out for half an hour and then finally left, thinking that repetition was impossible. This made a deep impression on me. I am not all that young. I have had some experience of life. Even before I came to Berlin the first time, I had weaned myself of the practice of trying to calculate uncertain outcomes. I had believed, however, that the pleasure this theatre had provided me was of an enduring sort. One had to have learned to be humbled and yet aided by existence before one could appreciate this kind of humour, and this seemed to me to suggest that such appreciation would be permanent. Could existence be even more disappointing than a bankrupt! He gives 50 per cent, or at least 30. He gives something, anyway. The comical is the least one can ask; is not even that capable of repetition?

I went home with these thoughts. My desk was prepared. The velvet armchair was still there. The sight of it made me so bitter though, that I almost destroyed it. Everyone in the house had gone to bed, so no one could remove it? What good is a velvet armchair when nothing else corresponds to it. It is like a man going naked while wearing a three-cornered hat. I got into bed without having had one sensible thought. It was so light in the room that, half-waking and half-dreaming, I could still see the velvet armchair. When I finally got up again in the morning I did what I had resolved to do in the night. I tossed the chair into a corner where I could no longer see it.

My home had become dismal to me precisely because it was the wrong sort of repetition. My thoughts were barren, my anxious imagination constantly conjured up tantalizing memories of how the thoughts had presented themselves the last time, and the weeds of these recollections strangled every other thought. I went out to the café I had visited every day on the last trip, to enjoy the beverage that, according to the poet's recipe, when it is 'pure and hot and strong and not misused' can always stand alongside that to which the [44] poet compares it — friendship.* I am a coffee-lover at least. Perhaps the coffee would be just as good as the last time, one would have thought so anyway, yet I did not like it. The sun burned through the café windows. The atmosphere of the place was oppressive, almost like the air in a casserole, one nearly stewed in it. A draught, like a small trade wind, pierced everything, prohibiting me from thinking about any repetition, even if there would otherwise have been an opportunity to do so.

In the evening I went to the restaurant where I had been in the habit of going on the last trip, and where, presumably through force of habit, I had enjoyed myself. Since I had gone there every evening, I had intimate knowledge of the place. I knew, for example, when the punctual guests left, how they parted from the company they left behind, whether they put their hats on in the inner or the outer room, when they opened the door or only when they were outside. No one escaped my notice; like Proserpina, I plucked a hair from every head,* even from the bald.—Everything was exactly the same, the same jokes, the same courtesies, the same patrons, the place was exactly the same—in short, uniform in its sameness. Solomon says a quarrelsome woman is like a constant dripping.* What might he say about this still life? Repetition was possible here, God help me.

I was at the Königstädter Theatre the next evening. The only thing that repeated itself was that no repetition was possible. Unter den Linden* was intolerably dusty, every attempt to mingle with people, and thus to bathe in the waters of humanity, was highly discouraging. Whichever way I turned, it was hopeless. The little dancer who had bewitched me the last time with a graceful manoeuvre that resembled the beginning of a leap, had made the leap. The blind man in front of the Brandenburg Gate, my harp player—for I was the only one who showed any concern for him—had a sort of greyish coat instead of the light green one for which I had a nostalgic longing, the one that had made him look like a weeping willow. He was lost to me and won by common humanity. The beadle's* amazing nose had paled; Professor A.A. had got a new pair of trousers that hung in an almost military fashion.

[45] After several days' repetition of this, I became bitter, so tired of repetition that I decided to return home. I made no great discovery, yet it was strange, because I had discovered that there was no such thing as repetition. I became aware of this by having it repeated in every possible way.

My home was my last hope. Justinus Kerner tells somewhere* of a man who became so tired of his home that he had his horse saddled, so that he could ride out into the wide world. After he had ridden a short way, his horse threw him. This turn of events became decisive for him because, as he turned to remount his horse, his eyes fell once again on the home he wanted to leave. He beheld it, and it looked so beautiful that he immediately turned back. I knew that at home I could count on finding everything prepared for repetition. I have always been very suspicious of revolutions, even to the extent that, for this reason, I hate all forms of cleaning or straightening-up, in particular the scrubbing of floors. I had thus left the strictest instructions to ensure that my conservative principles would be maintained even in my absence. But what happened? My faithful servant was of another mind. He supposed that if he initiated a frenzied cleaning immediately after my departure, the whole thing would be completed by the time I returned home again, and he was certainly the man to accomplish this. I return. I ring the doorbell; my servant appears. It was a moment rich with import. My servant became as pale as a corpse. Through the half-opened door to my rooms I glimpsed the horror: everything was in a state of chaos. I was stunned. He was so confused he did not know what to do. His conscience smote him and — he slammed the door again in my face. That was too much. My distress had reached a climax, my principles sank, I feared the worst, to be treated as a ghost in the manner of Grønmeyer the businessman.* I realized that there was no such thing as repetition, and my earlier view of life triumphed.

I felt ashamed, that I, who had been so stern with this young man, was now brought to the point where I felt as if I were he, as if all my lofty speeches, which I would not repeat now for any price, had simply been a dream from which I had awakened in order to allow life continuously and faithlessly to *take* everything back *again* that it had given without allowing a *repetition*.* Or is it not the case that the older one becomes, the more life reveals itself to be deceptive; the smarter one becomes, the more ways one learns to help oneself; the [46] worse off one is, the more one suffers? A small child is completely helpless, and yet it thrives. I remember once having seen a nurse-maid on the street pushing a baby-carriage in which there were two children. The one, just barely a year old, had fallen asleep and lay in the carriage dead to the world. The other was a little girl around two years old, chubby, in short sleeves, just like a little woman. She had pushed herself forward in the carriage and easily took up two-thirds of the space. The smaller child lay next to her as if it were a package the woman had brought with her. With an admirable egoism, the older child appeared not to care for anyone or anything except herself, if she could just make herself comfortable. Then a coach came down the road. The baby-carriage was clearly in danger. People ran to help, but with one healthy shove the nurse managed to push the carriage into a doorway. Everyone was horrified, including myself. Yet throughout this commotion the little madame was completely calm. She continued peacefully to pick her nose, her expression never changing. Presumably she thought, what do I care? It is the nurse's problem. One will seek in vain for such courage in an older person.

The older one gets, the better one understands life and the more one comes to care for and appreciate comfort. In short, the more competent one becomes, the less one is contented. One will never be completely, absolutely, and in every way content, and it is hardly worth the trouble to be more or less content, so one might as well be thoroughly discontented. Anyone who has really thought through the issue will agree with me that no one is ever granted even as little as half an hour out of his entire life where he is absolutely content in every conceivable way. It goes without saying that more is required for this sort of contentment than that one has food and clothing. I was close to achieving it once. I got up one morning in unusually good humour. This positive mood actually expanded as the morning progressed, in a manner I had never before experienced. By one o'clock my mood had climaxed, and I sensed the dizzying heights of complete contentment, a level that appears on no scale designed to measure moods, not even on the poetic thermometer. My body no longer seemed weighed down by gravity. It was as if I had no body, in that every function hummed along perfectly, every nerve rejoiced, the harmony punctuated by each beat of my pulse which served in [47] turn only to remind me of the delightfulness of the moment. I almost floated as I walked, not like the bird that cuts through the air as it leaves the earth, but like the wind over the fields, like the nostalgic rocking of waves, like the dreamy progress of clouds across the sky. My being was transparent as the clear depths of the ocean, as the night's self-satisfied stillness, as the soft soliloquy of midday. Every mood resonated melodically in my soul. Every thought, from the most foolish to the most profound, offered itself, and offered itself with the same blissful festiveness. Every impression was anticipated before it came, and thus awoke from within me. It was as if all of existence were in love with me. Everything quivered in deep rapport with my being. Everything in me was portentous; all mysteries explained in my microcosmic bliss that transfigured everything, even the unpleasant, the most annoying remark, the most loathsome sight, the most fatal collision.

As I said, it was exactly at one o'clock that my mood reached its peak, where I sensed the heights of perfect contentment. But then suddenly I got something in my eye. I do not know whether it was an eyelash, an insect, or a piece of dust. I know this though, that my mood immediately plummeted almost into the abyss of despair. This is something that everyone who has ever experienced these heights of contentment, and still speculated to what extent complete contentment was possible, will easily understand. Since that time I have given up any hope of ever being completely contented in every way, given up that hope that I had once nourished, of being, if not always completely content, then at least occasionally completely content, even if these occasions never became more numerous than, as Shakespeare put it, 'a tapster's arithmetic was capable of summing up'.*

I had already learned all of this before I became acquainted with the young person in question. As soon as I asked myself, or as soon as the question came up, whether complete contentment was possible, even if only for a half an hour, I always passed.* It was around then that, time and again, I grasped and became enthusiastic about the idea of repetition, through which I became once more a victim of my own theoretical zeal, because I am convinced that if I had not taken that trip with the purpose of deciding this issue, I would have got immense pleasure from it. But I cannot be content with the ordinary. I have to understand the underlying principles. I cannot go about dressed as other people; I have to go in stiff boots! Does not every- [48] one, spiritual and secular orators, poets and writers of prose, skippers and undertakers, heroes and cowards, agree that life is a stream?* Where does one get such a foolish idea, and what is even more fool-ish, elevate it to the level of a principle? My young friend thought: let go, and with that he would be better off than if he had initiated a repetition. Then he would have got his beloved back again, just like the lover in the popular ditty who wanted a repetition, as a nun with shorn hair and pale lips. He wanted a repetition, therefore he got one, and the repetition killed him.

> The little nun came walking
> In a snow white veil;
> Her hair was shorn and taken,
> Her lips were thin and pale.

> The youth sank down dejected,
> He sat on a stone apart:
> He shook and wept pale tears,
> Asunder broke his heart.*[1]

Long live the post-horn!* It is my instrument, for many reasons, principally because one can never be certain of coaxing the same tone out of it twice. A post-horn is capable of producing an infinite number of tones, and the one who puts it to his lips and invests his wisdom in it will never be guilty of a repetition. And he who, instead of answering his friend, hands him a post-horn for his amusement, says nothing, yet explains everything. Praised be the post-horn! It is my symbol. Just as the old ascetics sat a skull on their desks, so shall the post-horn on my desk always remind me of the meaning of life. Long live the post-horn! But the journey is not worth the trouble, because one need not move from the spot in order to become convinced that repetition is impossible. No, one can sit peacefully in [49] one's living-room, when everything is vanity and passes away;* then one travels more briskly than if one travelled by train, despite the fact that one is sitting still. Everything should remind me of this. My servant should wear a postal uniform and I should myself not go to dinner except in a post-chaise.* Farewell, farewell, rich hope of youth! Why do you hurry away? What you are hunting does not exist, has no more existence than you do. Farewell, manly strength, why do you stamp so violently on the ground? What you are treading on is a phantom of your own imagination. Farewell, conquering resolve, you will reach your goal because you cannot take the deed with you without turning back, and this you cannot do. Farewell, you beauty of the forest. When I wanted to see you, you had faded! Go then, you rushing river! You are the only one who really knows what you want, because what you want is to flow, to lose yourself in the ocean that is never filled! Play on, life's drama, which no one calls a comedy, no one a tragedy, because no one knows how it ends! Play on, you existential drama, where life, like loans, is never repaid! How is it that no one has returned from the dead? Because life does not know how to captivate in the way death does, because life is not so persuasive as death. Yes, death is brilliantly persuasive, if only one will not argue with it, but just let it speak. Then it persuades

---

[1] [Kierkegaard's note.] Herder's *Volkslieder*, ed. Falk (Leipzig, 1825), i. 57.

instantly, in such a way that no one has ever been able to object, or to long for the eloquence of life. O death! Great is your persuasiveness. There is no one who can speak so well as the man whose eloquence gave him the name πεισιθάνατος,* because he spoke with such powerful persuasion of you!

REPETITION

Some time passed. My servant, like a conscientious housewife, made up for his earlier wrong. A monotonous and uniform order was re-established in my living-quarters. All the inanimate objects were in their rightful places, and all the animate ones—my clock, my servant, and myself—went about their usual business, with me pacing about the apartment in my usual measured strides. Despite the fact that I had convinced myself that repetition was impossible, inflexibility combined with a dulling of the powers of observation results in a certain uniformity that is far more stupefying than the most whimsical diversion, and which, in addition, becomes even more stupefying over time, like some kind of magical incantation. The excavation of Herculaneum and Pompeii revealed everything in its place, just as the owners had left it. If I had lived then, the archae-ologists would have perhaps been surprised to find a person who paced with measured strides back and forth across the floor. I used every means in order to maintain this existing order. At times, I even went about the room like the emperor Domitian,* armed with a fly-swatter, pursuing every revolutionary fly who dared buzz about the room. Despite this, however, I showed mercy on three flies. Thus I was living, forgetting the world and believing myself forgotten by it, when I received one day a letter from my young friend. This letter was then followed by more letters, at more or less monthly inter-vals, without, however, my being able to draw any conclusions with respect to where he was living. He did not want to reveal anything himself. He could well have been deliberately trying to maintain a [51] certain mystery in this respect, by allowing the intervals between his letters to fluctuate from five weeks to just a day over three weeks. He did not want to inconvenience me by initiating a correspondence. Even though I was willing to respond to his letters, he didn't want responses—he just wanted to get things off his chest.

I could see from his letters what I already knew: that, like every depressive, he was extremely sensitive, and that despite this irrit-ability, as well as because of it, he was fundamentally torn. He wants me to be his confidant, and yet he doesn't want this; it makes him anxious. He feels a certain security in my so-called superiority, and yet also a certain discomfort. He confides in me, and yet wants no answer. He does not even want to see me. He demands that I keep silent, absolutely silent 'by all that is holy', and yet it makes him furious that I have the power to keep silent. No one, not a single soul, may know that I am his confidant. He does not even want to know it himself. He does not want me to know it. In order to explain this confusion to his satisfaction and gratification, he very politely hints that he really thinks I am mentally ill. How can I respond to such a bold interpretation? Any response would only further support the correctness of the charge—in my mind anyway—while my failure to respond would, in his eyes, serve only as new evidence of my detachment and derangement in that I do not allow myself to be personally affected, let alone offended. This is the thanks one gets when one has disciplined oneself for years to have only an objective intellectual interest in human beings, but to have such interest, if possible, for anyone who is animated by an idea! I tried, for a time, to help the idea that animated him, and now I am reaping the rewards—that I shall both be and not be Being and Nothing, whatever he wishes and without any appreciation for being able to do it, and in this way to help him again with his internal conflict. To the extent that he thought himself of how much indirect recognition there was in this sort of *Zumutung*,[1] he would presumably again become furious. It is more difficult than the most difficult task to be his confidant. He forgets that with one word—if, for example, I refused his correspondence—I could offend him deeply. It was not simply those who betrayed the Eleusinian mysteries* who were punished, but also those who offended the institution by refusing to be initiated into them. This latter crime, according to the account of a Greek author, was committed by a man named Demonax, who [52] escaped intact through the agency of an ingenious defence.* My position as a confidant is even more critical, because he is more chaste with his mysteries. He even becomes angry when I do what he most urgently requests—when I keep silent.

If, however, he thinks I have completely forgotten him, then again he does me an injustice. His sudden disappearance made me actually fear that, in his despair, he had done away with himself. Such an action seldom remains hidden for long, so when I read and heard nothing, I decided that he must still be alive, wherever he might be.

---

[1] Unreasonable demand.

The girl he left in the lurch knew absolutely nothing. He just failed to appear one day, without a word of explanation. Her pain was not immediate. First came a certain fearful foreboding, then the pain began to sink in, with the effect that she slipped softly into a kind of waking dream, unclear about what had happened and what it could mean. The girl became a new object for my observation. My friend was not one of those types that tortures his beloved to an extreme before tossing her aside; on the contrary, she was, at the time of his disappearance, in an enviable position, radiant, full of vitality, enriched by the poetic gifts he had bestowed on her, well nourished on the costly cordial of poetic illusions. It is rare to meet a jilted girl in such a state. When I saw her a few days later, she was still as lively as a freshly caught fish, whereas such a girl is normally as emaciated as a fish that has been kept in a tub. In my conscience I was convinced that he must be alive, and I was thankful that he had not seized in his despair upon the desperate gesture of faking his own death. It is unbelievable how much confusion can be occasioned by the erotic when one party decides he would like to die of sorrow, or would like to be dead as a means of escaping the whole thing. A girl will, according to her own solemn declaration, die of sorrow over the fact that her lover deceived her. But look! Perhaps he was not really a deceiver. Perhaps there was a positive explanation for the whole thing. What he might have done, however, in the fullness of time he is no longer free to do, simply because she had once allowed herself to frighten him with this assurance, because, as he said, she had played this rhetorical trick on him, or in any case said, what a girl must never say, even if she thinks he really is a deceiver, because if he is a deceiver, then she should be too proud to do such a thing, and if she still believes in him, then she should see that she does him the most terrible wrong. To want to be dead as a means of escaping the whole thing is about as pathetic as one can get, and dishonours the girl in the most offensive way. She believes he is dead, she grieves, she weeps, she mourns honestly and sincerely. She must come to be almost disgusted with herself for having grieved so sincerely when she later discovers that he is still alive and had never had any thoughts whatever of doing away with himself. Or if she first comes to have suspicions in the next life, not over whether he is actually dead—that would be indisputable—but over whether he had been dead back then when she had grieved for him. Such a situation is

[53]

stuff for an eschatologist who has understood his Aristophanes (I mean the Greek, not the men, who were called that like *doctores cerei* in the Middle Ages) and his Lucian.* One could maintain this confusion for a while, in that he was certainly dead and he remained dead. The grieving girl would then awaken, to begin again where they left off, until she discovered there was a little intermediate period.

The memory of the whole thing was reawakened in me when I received his letter. It was in no way a dispassionate recollection. When I came to the clever explanation in his letter that I was deranged, it occurred to me immediately that he now had a secret, deeper even than the deepest secret, and that this secret was jealously guarded by more than a hundred eyes. When we were together it did not escape me that, before he would say anything, he would very carefully insinuate that I was 'strange'. Yes, an observer must be prepared for this. He must know to offer the confessor a little guarantee. A girl who makes a confession always demands a positive guarantee, a man a negative one; the reason for this is feminine humility and devotion and masculine pride and wilfulness. What a comfort it is, then, that the one from whom one seeks advice and explanation is deranged! One need not therefore be ashamed. To talk to such a person is like talking to a tree, 'something one does purely for the sake of curiosity', in case anyone should ask about it. An observer must know how to make himself seem easygoing or else no one will open up to him. Above all, he must guard against ethical stringency or against presenting himself as a morally upright person. [54] This man, one says, has been corrupted. He has been part of, has had, really depraved experiences — ergo, I can easily confide in him, I who am a much better person than he is! That is how it is; I demand nothing of people other than the contents of their consciousness. I weigh these contents, and if they are weighty enough, then no price is too high for me.

I could tell, just from skimming the letter, that this love affair had left a much deeper impression on him than I had suspected. He must have hidden some of his moods from me. I can understand that. I was only 'eccentric' then, now I am deranged, that is *was Andres.*[1] If this is really how it is, then a religious movement is the only thing left to him. Love thus leads a person further and further. I have often attested to what I will attest to again here: 'Existence is infinitely

---

[1] Something else entirely.

profound, and the controlling power constructs intrigues that are entirely different from any constructed by all the poets *in uno*.'[1] This young person was constituted in such a way, and by nature so gifted, that I would have wagered he would never be caught in the net of romantic love. There are, of course, exceptions in this respect that cannot be inflected according to the normal case rules. He had an exceptional intellect, especially in terms of the size of his imagination. As soon as his creativity was awakened, he had enough for his whole life, especially if he understood himself correctly and restricted himself to that cosy domestic diversion of following the activities of the intellect and the pastimes of the imagination; which is the most perfect compensation for romantic love, does not involve love's difficulties and fatalities, and which can be described as equal to the most beautiful aspects of romantic bliss. Such a nature does not long for a woman's love, which I always think to myself must be a result of the fact that he had been a woman in an earlier life, and that he has retained the memory of this now after he has become a man. To fall in love with a girl only disturbs him and frustrates his objective, because he can almost play her part as well. This is unpleasant both for her and for himself. On the other hand, he was a very melancholy soul. Just as the former would prevent him from becoming close to a girl, so would the latter protect him if it should please some clever beauty to try to win his love. A deep melancholy of the sympathetic sort has always been a complete humiliation for all feminine wiles. If [55] a girl succeeded in drawing him to herself, the instant she began to celebrate her victory, he would think: are you not doing her an injustice, committing a sin against her by giving in to these feelings, will you not simply be in her way? Thus it is good-night to all feminine intrigue. The situation is now strangely altered. He has gone over to her side. He is more than willing to recognize all her excellent qualities, knows how to present them perhaps even better than she does herself, admires them perhaps even more than she requires. But she will never be able to bring him any further than this.

I never expected that he would have such difficulty getting over a love affair. Existence is ingenious however. What has ensnared him is not the girl's charms, but regret over having wronged her by disturbing her life. He had thoughtlessly got too close to her.

---

[1] Together.

He assures himself that love cannot be realized, that he can be happy without her, to the extent that he can be happy, especially given this new insight. But now he cannot forget that he has wronged her, as if it were wrong to break something off that cannot be completed. If he had been detached, if he had been asked: 'Here is the girl. Do you want to become close to her, to fall in love with her?' he would certainly have answered: 'Not for the whole world. I have learned what comes of that.' Such things one never forgets. This is how the situation ought to be expressed if he does not want to deceive himself. He still believes that, humanly speaking, his love cannot be realized. He has arrived at the border of the miraculous, so if it is to happen it must be by virtue of the absurd. He is not thinking at all of the difficulties, or am I so clever that I am actually inventing things here! Does he love the girl, or is she just another thing that moves him? It is unquestionably neither possession in the strict sense, nor what develops from possession, that concerns him. It is simply his return, in a purely formal sense. He would not be more disturbed if she died the next day. He would not really feel a loss, because he would essentially be at peace. The split that his encounter with her had precipitated in him would be reconciled by the fact that he had gone back to her. The girl has, again, no actuality, but is simply a reflection of, and occasion for, movements within him. The girl has enormous significance for him. He will never be able to forget her. But that through which she has significance is not herself, but her relation to him. She is like the limit of his being. But such a relation- [56] ship is not erotic. Religiously speaking, one could say that it is as if God had used this girl to capture him. And yet the girl is not herself an actuality, but is like the flies with which fishermen bait their hooks. I am completely convinced that he does not know the girl at all, despite the fact that he was attached to her and that since that time she has never been out of his thoughts. She is the girl, period. Whether, in a more concrete sense, she is this or that, attractive, lovable, faithful, self-sacrificing, someone for whom one would risk anything, move heaven and earth, does not enter his thoughts at all. If he were to give an account of the happiness, the joy, he really expects from an actual erotic relationship, he would presumably have nothing to say. What concerns him is achieved the instant he can redeem his honour and his pride! As if it were not also an issue of honour and pride to defy such childish anxieties! Perhaps he even

expects some sort of damage to his personality. This would be nothing though, if he could only get revenge on existence for mocking
him by causing him to become guilty when he had been innocent,
by making his relation to actuality on this point meaningless, so that
he must endure being seen as a deceiver by every genuine lover! Is
this not almost unbearable? But then, perhaps I do not completely
understand him. Perhaps he is hiding something. Perhaps he truly
loves. Then the whole thing would probably end with his killing me,
since he had confided to me his most sacred thoughts. One can see
that it is dangerous to be an observer. Meanwhile I wish that, purely
out of an interest in human psychology, I could briefly remove the
girl, get him to believe that she had married. I bet I would get a
different sort of explanation, because his sympathy is so melancholy
that I believe he has convinced himself out of respect for the girl that
he loves her.

The problem that has confounded him is nothing more nor less
than repetition. He is right not to look for clarification of this problem either in Greek or modern philosophy. The Greeks make the
opposite movement. A Greek would choose to recollect without
being troubled by his conscience. Modern philosophy makes no
movement. In general, it merely makes a commotion. To the extent
[57] that it makes a movement, it is always within the sphere of immanence. Repetition, on the other hand, is transcendence. It is good that
he does not seek clarification from me, because I have abandoned
my theory, the one I have been propounding. Repetition is too
transcendent for me. I can circumnavigate myself, but I cannot get
beyond myself. I cannot find this Archimedean point.* My friend,
fortunately, seeks no clarification, neither from some world-famous
philosopher nor from some professor *publicus ordinarius*.[1] He seeks
refuge in a private thinker who once had the world at his feet, but
later withdrew from life. In other words, he seeks refuge in *Job*, who
does not posture from a pulpit, attesting to the truth of his claims
with comforting gesticulations, but who sits among the ashes and
scrapes himself with potsherds* while making the occasional sign or
remark. He believes he has found here what he sought. In this little
circle that includes Job and his wife and three friends, the truth, he

---

[1] Roughly: an assistant professor at a university.

believes, sounds more glorious and joyful and true than in a Greek symposium.*

Even if he still sought my help, it would be for nothing. I cannot make a religious movement. It is against my nature. I do not for this reason, however, deny the reality of such a movement. Nor do I deny that one can learn a great deal from a young person. If he succeeds, he will be free of any irritation in relation to me. I cannot deny, however, that the more I think about the thing, the more I begin to think ill of the girl, that she in one way or another has allowed herself to trap him in his melancholy. If this is the case, then I would not want to be in her shoes. She will pay. Existence always wreaks the most terrible revenge on such behaviour.

15 August [58]

My Silent Confidant!

You will perhaps find it strange suddenly to receive a letter from one who has long been dead for you and as good as forgotten, or forgotten and as good as dead. I do not dare expect any further surprise on your part. I imagine that you will instantly recall my case, saying to yourself: right, he was the one with the unhappy love affair. Where was it we left off? Oh yes, so of course these are going to be the symptoms. There is in truth something terrible in your composure! My blood boils when I think about it, and yet I cannot tear myself loose. You have imprisoned me through some strange power. There is something indescribably soothing and beneficial in talking to you, because it is as if one were talking to oneself or to an idea. When one has expressed oneself and found solace in this release, and then suddenly sees your unaltered expression and thinks that this is a human being who is before him, an enormously intelligent person one has spoken to, then one becomes very frightened. Good God, the mourner is always slightly jealous in relation to his grief. He will not confide in just anyone. He demands silence. One can be certain enough of this with you. And yet, after one has reassured oneself of this, one becomes afraid again because your silence, which is more silent even than the grave, presumably conceals many similar confessions. You know everyone's situation, never get confused, can instantly recall another secret and begin again where you left off. Then one regrets having confided in you. Good God, the mourner is always a little jealous of his grief. He wants the one to whom he confides it to feel its full weight and meaning. You do not disappoint because you grasp the finest nuance better than one does oneself. The next moment, this superiority that is part of knowing every-thing, that nothing is new or unfamiliar, drives me to despair. If I ruled over all human beings, God help you! I would lock you up with [59] me in a cage, so that you would belong only to me. And then I would presumably experience the most painful anxiety in seeing you every day. You have a demonic power that can tempt a person to want to risk everything, to want to have powers that he does not ordinarily have, which he would not otherwise desire, but desires only so long as you look at him, desires only to be thought to be something he is not, desires simply in order to purchase the indescribable rewards of that appreciative smile. I would love to spend the day with you, listen to you through the night, but when I would have to act, then I would not do it in your presence for any price. You could disturb everything with a single word. I do not have the courage to admit my weakness in front of you. If I ever did, then I would become the most cowardly person of all, because it would seem to me that I had lost everything. Thus you captivate me with an indescribable power that both frightens me and causes me to admire you. And yet sometimes it seems to me that you are deranged. Or it is not a kind of mental ill-ness, to have subjected every passion, every movement of the heart, every mood, to the cold discipline of reflection! Is it not a kind of mental illness to be like this, an idea rather than a person, not like other people—pliant, forgiving, lost, and damned? Is it not a kind of derangement never to sleep, always to be conscious, never drowsy, never dreaming?—Right now, I do not want to see you, and yet I cannot get along without you. Therefore I write and ask that you do not inconvenience yourself by answering. Just to be safe, there is no return address on the letter. This is how I want it. This makes it safe to write to you, makes me feel secure and grateful for you.

Your plan was excellent, yes, unparalleled. I still sometimes reach out like a child toward the heroic form you once held up for my admiration with the explanation that it was my future, the heroic form that would have made me a hero if I had had the strength to don it. I was enraptured by it back then, drawn by the power of illusion into a state of complete imaginative intoxication. To determine one's entire life in such a way, for the sake of a single girl! To transform

oneself into a scoundrel, a deceiver, for the sole purpose of showing
how highly one prized her, because one does not sacrifice one's
honour, brand oneself a scoundrel, forfeit one's life, for something
insignificant! To carry out the act of revenge in a manner more perfect than that of which the empty chatter of human beings is capable!
To be a hero in such a way, not in the eyes of the world, but in one's
own eyes, to be unable to appeal to human beings, living within the [60]
walls of one's own personality, to be one's own witness, one's own
judge, one's own accuser, one's only accuser! To put one's future
at the mercy of the onslaught of thoughts that would certainly be a
consequence of such a step, with which in a way, humanly speaking,
one abandons reason! To do all this for the sake of a girl! And if it
could be transformed, as you suggested, into the most chivalrous
and erotic compliment, one that surpassed all others, even the most
fantastical exploit, precisely because one had used only oneself. This
proposition made a deep impression on me. It had naturally not been
said in the heat of passion — you and passion! — but coolly and rea-
sonably, with an official knowledge obtained from a thorough perusal
of the history of chivalry, undertaken precisely in order to gain such
knowledge. Just as the discovery of a new category affects a thinker,
so did this discovery in the realm of the erotic affect me.

Unfortunately, I was not an artist with the strength or stamina for
such a performance. Fortunately, I saw you infrequently and only
in out-of-the-way places. If you had been by my side, you could
have sat in the room, even in a corner, reading, preoccupied with
something entirely unrelated, and yet, as I know only too well, and
yet observing everything — I believe I would have at least begun the
thing. If that had happened, it would have been terrible. Or is it not
terrible, coldly and calmly, day after day, to bewitch the beloved
into believing a lie! Say she had seized what means were available
to her — feminine appeals; say she had beseeched me with tears in
her eyes, appealed to my honour, my conscience, my happiness both
in this life and the next, my temporal and eternal peace! The mere
thought of it makes chills run up and down my spine.

I have not forgotten those suggestions you made that I was all too
entranced to dare to oppose. 'If the girl is within her rights', you said,
'when she uses such means, then one should allow them to have an
effect; what is more, one should assist her in their employment. In
relation to a girl one is chivalrous enough, not only to be oneself, but

also for her sake to rise to her defence. If she is wrong to use such
means, then one should simply let them slide off one's back.' This
[61] is true, absolutely true, but I am not so reasonable. 'What foolish
contradiction one often meets in human courage and cowardice. One
fears seeing something terrible, but one has the courage to do it.
You leave the girl; this is terrible. You have the courage to do this,
but to see her pale, to count her tears, witness her distress, for that
you have no courage. And yet this is nothing compared to the other.
If you know what you want, why, and to what extent, then you
ought to see, you ought to respect, every argument and not try to
sneak away from them in the hope that your imagination is duller
than actuality. In this respect you deceive yourself because your
vibrant imagination will behave quite differently when the time
comes for you to imagine her distress, than if you had seen it,
had helped her to make everything as terrible and excruciating for
you as possible.'

This is true, every word is true. Yet it is so cold and logical that
it seems to come from the dead. It fails to convince me, to move me.
I admit that I am weak, I was weak, will never be so strong or intrepid.
Consider everything, imagine yourself in my place, but do not forget
that you really love her as much as I loved her. I am convinced you
would be victorious, you would prevail, you would overcome any
fears you might have, you would fool her. What would happen? If
you were not so lucky that, in the same instant that your struggles
were over, your hair turned grey and your soul an hour later left
your body, you would, according to your plan, have had to continue
the deception. You would have succeeded. I am convinced of that.
Do you not fear losing your mind? Do you not fear losing yourself
in the terrible passion that is called contempt for humanity? To be
right in such a way, to be faithful and yet to make oneself out to be
a scoundrel, and with this deception to mock all the wretchedness of
which people often boast, but to mock as well all that is good in the
world. That anyone could endure such a thing! Does it not occur to
you that you would have to get up often in the middle of the night
and drink a glass of cold water, or sit by the side of your bed and go
through it all again in your mind!

Say I had begun the plan, it would have been impossible for me
to carry it through. I chose another means, left Copenhagen in the
still of night for Stockholm. According to your plan, this would have

been wrong. I should have left openly. Just think if she had come out there and stood at the customs-house; it gives me chills. Imagine if I had first caught sight of her the second the engine started. I believe I would have lost my mind. I do not doubt that you would have had the strength to remain calm. If it had been necessary, if you had [62] expected her to appear at the customs-house, then you would have taken the seamstress with you. If it had been necessary, you would not only have bribed a girl, but actually seduced her, simply in order to serve the beloved. You would have seduced a girl, actually seduced, ruined, and branded her, if the situation had required it. But say you once woke suddenly in the night, and could not recognize yourself, confused yourself with the character you used for this pious deception. Because I have to admit, you certainly did not mean that one should thoughtlessly undertake such a thing. You even intimated that this method would not be necessary if the girl were not also guilty either through having been so thoughtless as to fail to notice tokens of sympathy, or so egotistical as to ignore them. But precisely this is the point—would there not come an instant when she would understand what she ought to have done, would despair over the consequences of her failure to do it, which was the result not so much of any insensitivity on her part as of the whole personality of the other? Would it then not have gone with her as it went with me? She would not have dreamed, would not have had the slightest intimation, of the powers she had unleashed, on what passions she played. Thus she became guilty in everything, despite being innocent. Would this not be too strict for her? If I had to do something here, I would rather quarrel, become angry, than issue this sort of silent, objective condemnation.

No! No! No! I could not, I cannot, I will not, not for anything would I do it. No! No! No! I could despair over these letters, which stand here next to each other as cold and indolent as idlers, the one 'No' saying no more than the others. You should hear how my passion modulates them. If only I stood next to you. If only I could tear myself away from you with my last 'No', like Don Juan from the Commandatore* whose hand is no colder than is the reason with which you irresistibly enrapture me. Though if I stood before you, I would probably not say more than a single 'No', because before I could say anything else, you would have interrupted me with the cold answer: Yes! Yes!

What I did was more mediocre and bungling. Go ahead, laugh at me. When a swimmer, who is used to diving off the mast of a ship and doing some incredible gymnastic feat before he hits the water, [63] challenges someone else to follow his example, and this other person, instead of doing this, goes down the steps, sticks first one leg in and then the other, before finally entering the water—then I do not need to know what the first one did. I disappeared one day, without having said a word. I got on a steamship to Stockholm, fled, hid from everyone. God in heaven, help her to find some kind of explanation herself! Have you seen her—the girl I never mention by name, whose name I am not man enough to write, because my hand would tremble with terror? Have you seen her? Is she pale, or perhaps even dead? Does she grieve, has she cobbled together an explanation that is comforting to her? Does she still have a spring in her walk, or is her head bent, her form troubled? Great God, my imagination can produce everything. Are her lips pale, those lips I admired, even though I allowed myself only to kiss her hand? Is she weary and pensive, she who was happy like a child? Write, I beg you. No, do not write, I do not want any letters from you, do not want to hear about her. I believe nothing, no one, not even her. Even if she appeared before me now in the flesh, even if she were more confident than ever, it would not make me happy. I would not believe her. I would think it was a deception, designed either to mock or to comfort me. Have you seen her? No! I hope you have not permitted yourself to see her, or to interfere in my love affair. If I ever found out that you had! When a girl becomes unhappy, hungry monsters suddenly appear, monsters that want to satisfy their psychological hunger and thirst by writing novels. If I only dared to keep these flies from the fruit that was sweeter to me than everything else, more delicate and tender to look upon than a peach when, in its happiest hour, it clothes itself in the finest silk and velvet.

What do I do now? I begin again from the beginning, and thus also from the end. I flee from every external reminder of the whole thing, while my soul, day and night, waking and dreaming, continues to be obsessed with it. I never speak her name, and I thank fate for the fact that I have accidentally gained a false name. A name, my name—that really belongs to her. If only I could be rid of it. My own name is enough to remind me of everything. All of existence seems to me to contain nothing but allusions to this past. The day before

I left, I read in *Adresseavisen*,* '16 yards of heavy, black silk for sale [64]
because of change of plans'. What could have been the original purpose, perhaps a wedding dress? If only I could sell my name through
the papers because of a change of plans. If some powerful spirit took
my name from me and offered it back to me decorated with immortal honours, I would throw it away, cast it as far away as I could. I
would beg for the most insignificant, the most meaningless name. I
would ask to be called No. 14, like one of the blue boys.* How would
a name help me that was not mine, what help would a glorious name
be, even if it were mine:

> Because of what value is a name with glory blessed
> Compared to a sigh of love from a young girl's breast?*

What do I do now? I sleep during the day and lie awake at night.
I'm active and industrious. A model of domesticity and diligence.
I moisten my hands, pump the pedal with my leg, stop the wheel, set
the spindle in motion—I spin. But when, at night, I have to put the
spinning-wheel away, it is not there, and only my cat knows what has
become of my yarn. I am restless and active, indefatigable, but what
comes of it? The peat-stamper performs miracles compared to me. In
short, if you want to understand, if you want to get an impression of
how fruitless is all my activity, then interpret the words of this poem
as applying to my thoughts. That's all I can say:

> The clouds are drifting to and fro
> They are so tired, so heavy though,
> That down they plunge, as if a wave—
> The lap of earth becomes their grave.*

I do not need to say any more to you, or more correctly, I would
need you in order to be able to say more, in order to express clearly
and comprehensibly what my groping thoughts can understand only
as insane.

If I actually related everything, my letter would become infinitely
long, at least as long as a bad year and like the days of which it is
said: I have no pleasure in them.* I have the advantage, though, in
that I can break off at any point I wish, just as I can snip the thread I
spin, God willing. He who believes in existence, he has ensured that
he will accomplish everything as certainly as a man hides his feelings
who holds a hat without a crown before his face as he prays.

[65] Sir! I have the honour, etc.
        —yes whether or not I want to, I remain
                                    Your
                        Devoted, nameless friend.

[66]

                                                    19 September
  My Silent Confidant!

Job! Job! O! Job! Did you really say no more than these beautiful
words: the Lord gave, and the Lord has taken away; blessed be
the name of the Lord?* Were these the only words you uttered?
Did you continue in all your distress only to repeat them? Why
were you silent for seven days and seven nights, what was going on
in your soul? When all of existence collapsed on you and lay about
your feet like potsherds, did you immediately have this superhuman
self-possession, did you immediately have this interpretation of love,
this boldness of trust and faith? Is your door closed to one who is
grief-stricken, can he expect no other relief from you than the misery
offered by worldly wisdom when it gives its little speech on life's
perfection? Do you have nothing else to say, do you not dare say any
more than the official consolers sparingly dole out to a person, what
the official consolers stiffly and ceremoniously prescribe, that in the
hour of anguish it is appropriate to say, the Lord gave, and the Lord
has taken away, blessed be the name of the Lord, nothing more nor
less, just as one says 'bless you' to a person who sneezes! No, you who
in the days of your youth* were the sword of the oppressed and the
staff of the aged and down-trodden, you did not disappoint people
when everything went to pieces—then you became the voice of the
suffering, and the cry of the repentant, the shriek of the fearful, and a
comfort to all those silenced by pain, a faithful witness to the distress
and anguish that can reside in a heart, an unfailing spokesman, who
dared to complain 'in the soul's bitterness' and to battle with God.
Why does one hide this? Woe unto him who consumes widows and
orphans, and defrauds them of their inheritance, but woe also unto
those who cunningly defraud the grief-stricken of grief's temporary
comfort, to vent itself and to 'quarrel with God'. Or is the fear of
God so great in our age that the grieving person no longer needs
what was customary in days of old? Does one no longer dare to complain to God? Has the fear of God, or merely fear and cowardice in

general, become greater? Nowadays people believe that the genuine expression of grief, passion's despondent language, should be left to [67] poets, who, like attorneys on behalf of a client, present the case of the sufferer before the tribunal of human sympathy. No one dares to do more than this. Speak, therefore, memorable Job! Repeat everything you said, you mighty spokesman who appears before the highest tribunal as unafraid as a roaring lion! Your speech is pithy, your heart is pious, even when you complain, when you defend your despair to your friends, your friends who, like thieves, try to overwhelm you with their speeches, even when you, provoked by your friends, trample on their wisdom, scorn their defence of the Lord as if it were a decrepit servant's or a politically savvy government official's wretched cleverness. I need you, a man who knows how to complain loudly, so that it echoes in heaven, where God consults with Satan concerning His plans for a person. The Lord has no fear of complaints. He can defend himself. But how can he defend himself when no one dares to complain as seems fitting to him. Speak, lift up your voice, speak loudly, God can always speak more loudly—after all, he has thunder. This is also an answer, an explanation, dependable, faithful, original, an answer from God himself, which, even if it crushed a person, is more glorious than gossip and rumours concerning the justice of providence, invented by human wisdom, spread by hags and half-men.

My unforgettable benefactor, tormented Job! Dare I join your company, may I listen to you? Do not thrust me away, I do not stand fraudulently at your hearth, my tears are not false, even if I am able only to cry with you. Just as one who is happy seeks happiness, partakes of it, even if that which makes him happy is the happiness that is within him, so does one who grieves seek sorrow. I never owned the world, did not have seven sons and three daughters, but even one who had very little can lose everything. He can also feel as if he has lost sons and daughters, he who has lost the beloved. He can also feel as if he has been struck down with sores, he who has lost his honour and pride, and with them meaning and the will to live.

Your
Nameless friend.

My Silent Confidant!

I cannot endure my life any longer. I loathe existence; it is insipid, without salt* or meaning. Even if I were hungrier than Pierrot,* I hope I would not stoop to eating the explanation people offer. One sticks his finger in the ground in order to judge where one is. I stick my finger in existence—it feels like nothing. Where am I? What is the 'world'? What does this word mean? Who has duped me into the whole thing, and now leaves me standing there? Who am I? How did I come into the world; why was I not asked, why was I not informed of the rules and regulations, but thrust into the ranks as if I had been forced by a *Seelenverkopper*?* How did I come to be involved in this great enterprise called actuality? Why should I be involved in it? Am I not free to decide? Am I to be forced to be part of it? Where is the manager, I would like to make a complaint! Is there no manager? To whom then shall I make my complaint? Existence is after all a debate. I would like to request that my opinion be taken into account. If one has to take existence as it is, would it not be best if one were told how it is? What does it mean: a deceiver? Does not Cicero say that one discovers deceivers by asking: *cui bono*?[1] I will allow anyone to ask me, and I will ask anyone myself, whether I have benefited at all from making myself and a young girl unhappy. Guilt—what is that? Is it witchcraft? Do we not know specifically how it is that a person becomes guilty? Will no one answer? Is it not crucial for all the gentlemen involved?

My mind has become paralysed; or would it be more correct to say that I have lost my mind? At one moment I am so tired, so dulled, it is as if I had died of indifference. The next moment I am raving mad, travelling from one end of the world to the other in search of some-one on whom I could vent my rage. The whole of my being shrieks [69] in self-contradiction. How did it happen that I became guilty? Or am I not guilty? Why am I called guilty in every tongue? What a miser-able invention is human language, which says one thing and means something else!

Has something not happened to me, was the whole thing not an event? Could I know in advance that my whole essence would undergo a change, that I would become a different person? Did something which lay hidden in my soul simply burst forth? Yet if

---

[1] Who benefits from this?

it lay hidden, how could I have foreseen its appearance? And if I could not have foreseen it, then I am innocent. If I had had a nervous breakdown, would I still have been guilty? What is the human jabbering one calls language but miserable gibberish understood only by a clique! Are dumb beasts not wiser for never speaking of such things? — Am I unfaithful? If she continued to love me, and never wanted to love another, then she would be faithful. If I continued to want to love only her, am I therefore unfaithful? We both do the same thing, how is it that I have become a deceiver because I show my fidelity with the deception? Why should she be in the right, and I in the wrong? If we are both faithful, why does human language characterize her as faithful and me as a deceiver?

Even if the whole world were against me, even if all the scholastics disputed with me, even if it meant my life, I am right. No one is going to take this from me, even if there is no language in which I can say it. I have behaved correctly. My love will not admit of expression in a marriage. If I tried, it would crush her. Perhaps this possibility seemed enticing to her. I cannot help that. It was also this way for me. The instant actuality enters in, everything is lost, then it is too late. Then actuality, in which her meaning must reside, is merely a shadow for me that runs beside my genuine intellectual actuality, a shadow that at one moment will cause me to laugh and at the next will intrude disturbingly upon my existence. It would end with my grasping her, fumblingly, as if I were grasping a shadow, or as if I stretched my hand out toward a shadow. Would her life not thus be wasted? She would become for me as if she were dead. Yes, she could actually tempt my soul to wish her dead. If I crush her, make her into something fleeting and insubstantial at precisely the moment I wanted to make her actual, instead of, on the other hand, preserving her in a true, yet in another sense apprehensive, actuality—what then? Language says that I am guilty because I should have foreseen this.

What kind of a power is it that wants to take my honour and my [70] pride from me, and does it in such a meaningless way? Am I lost? Will I be guilty and a deceiver in whatever I do, even if I do nothing?—Or am I perhaps crazy? Then it would be best to lock me up, because human cowardice is particularly afraid of the utterances of the insane and the dying. What does that mean: crazy? What must I do in order to enjoy the respect of the bourgeoisie, to be considered intelligent? Why does no one answer? I promise a reasonable reward to anyone

who comes up with a new word! I have presented the alternatives. Is
there anyone so clever that he knows more than two? But if he does
not know more, then is it nonsense to suggest I am crazy, faithless,
and a deceiver, while the girl is faithful, reasonable, and respected?
Or will it be held against me that I made the first part as beautiful as
possible? Thank you very much! When I saw her joy at being loved,
then I placed myself, and everything she pointed to, under the magical power of romantic love. Is it blameworthy that I was able to do
this, or blameworthy that I did it? Who is guilty in this if not also
she herself and some third, whose origin no one knows, that which
moved me, changed me with its blow? What I have done is praised in
others.—Or is it my compensation that I became a poet? I refuse all
compensation. I demand my rights—i.e. my honour. I did not ask to
become a poet, and would not pay this price to become one.—Or if
I am guilty, then I should be able to repent of this and make it right
again. Explain to me how. Should I perhaps in addition regret the
fact that the world allows itself to play with me like a child with an
insect?—Or is it perhaps best to forget the whole thing? To forget, I
would cease to be if I forgot it. What kind of a life is it, when I have,
with my beloved, lost honour and pride, and lost it in such a way
that no one knows how it happened or why I can never make it right
again? Must I allow myself to be snuffed out in this way? Why was I
ever born then? I didn't request it.

He who is restricted to bread and water is better off than I am. My
reflections are, humanly speaking, the strictest diet imaginable, and
yet I feel a certain satisfaction in gesticulating my microcosmicness
in as macrocosmic a manner as possible.

I do not like to speak with people, but in order not to break off all
communication with them, as well as to give them something more
[71] than gossip for their money, I have collected a pile of verse, pithy
sayings, proverbs, excerpts from the immortal Greek and Roman
authors who have been admired throughout all time. To this I have
added many excellent quotations from Balle's Catechism,* published
under the auspices of the Orphan's Home. If anyone asks me anything, I have my answer ready. I can quote from the classics just as
easily as Per Degn,* and, in addition, I quote from Balle's Catechism.
'Even if we attained all the honours we could wish for, we should
not allow ourselves to become arrogant or proud.' I deceive no one.
How many people are there who always speak the truth, or who

always have a meaningful observation. 'The expression "the world" is generally taken to include both heaven and earth and everything found therein.'

What good would it do if I said something? There is no one who understands me. My pain and my suffering are nameless, just as I am myself, I who despite having no name, perhaps will always be something for you, and in any case remain.

Devotedly yours

15 November [72]

My Silent Confidant!

What would I do without Job! It is impossible for me to describe how complex and subtle is the meaning he has for me. I read him not as one would read some other book, with the eyes. I lay the book over my heart and read it with the heart's eye. I understand with a kind of *clairvoyance* each individual point in a unique way. Just as a child sleeps with his school-book under his pillow in order to be sure that he will remember his lessons when he wakes in the morning, so do I take the book with me to bed at night. Every word from Job is food and clothing and succour for my miserable soul. At one moment a word from him will awaken me from my lethargy, so that I face a new restlessness; the next moment it quiets my fruitless inner raging, stops the horror in the dumb qualms of passion. Have you read Job? Read it. Read it again and again. I do not have the heart to write a single one of his exclamations in a letter to you, even though it makes me happy to copy again and again what he said, first with Gothic characters and then with Latin ones, first in one format, then in another. Each copy is then laid like a poultice from the hand of God on my sick heart. And on whom was God's hand not laid but on Job? But quote him—that I cannot do, that would be to put my oar in, to want to make his words mine in the presence of another. When I am alone, then I do it, appropriate everything, but as soon as someone else is present, then I understand what young people do when old people talk.

In the whole of the Old Testament, there is no figure that one can approach with the confidence, boldness and hope of consolation with which one can approach Job, precisely because everything about him is so human, because he lies on the border of poetry. Nowhere has the passion of pain found such expression. What is Philoctetes* with his complaints, which remain terrestrial and do not thus dismay the [73] gods? What is Philoctetes' situation compared with Job's, where the idea is in constant motion?

Forgive me that I tell you everything. You are my confidant though, and you cannot answer. If anyone ever learned of all this, it would cause me an unbelievable amount of anguish. At night I can allow all the candles to be lit in my room, illuminating the entire house. Then I stand and read aloud, almost yelling, one or another passage from Job. Or I open my window and shout his words out into the world. If Job is a poetic figure, if there has never been a man who has spoken in such a way, then I will make his words my own and take on the responsibility for doing that. I cannot do more than that, because who is so eloquent as Job, who is in a position to improve upon anything he has said?

Even though I have read the book again and again, each time every word is new to me. Each time I come to a word, it is again made original or becomes original in my soul. I imbibe the intoxication of passion like a drunkard, gradually, until through this slow sipping I become almost insensible with inebriation. Yet I also rush toward it with indescribable impatience. Half a word, then my soul hastens into his thoughts, into his exclamations, more swiftly than a jettisoned weight sinks to the bottom of the ocean, faster than lightning seeks the rod, my soul slips in and remains there.

At other times I am quieter. I do not read, I sit sunken like an old ruin overlooking everything. Then it seems to me as if I am a little child who messes about in a room, or who sits in a corner with his toys. Then the strangest mood comes over me. I cannot understand what it is that makes adults so passionate, I cannot imagine what they quarrel about, and yet I cannot help but listen. Then I think that evil people are the source of Job's troubles, that it is his friends who now sit and bark at him. Then I sob loudly, fear for the world, and life, and people, pressing in upon my soul.

I wake and begin again with all my strength and all my heart to read him aloud. I stop suddenly. I hear nothing more, see nothing, I sense Job only in vague outline, sitting there among the ashes with his friends. No one says a word, but this silence hides a terror within it as a secret that no one dares to mention.

Then the silence is broken and Job's tormented soul breaks forth with powerful cries. These I understand. I make these words my [74] own. In the same instant I feel the contradiction and smile at myself, as one smiles at a child who has put on his father's clothes. Or is it not something to smile at, when someone other than Job wants to say: 'Can one assert the rights of a man as against those of God, like a man can assert his rights against those of his neighbour?'* But then fear comes over me, as if I still did not understand what I would come one day to understand, as if the horror about which I read already sat in wait for me, as if I brought it upon myself by reading about it, just as one comes to have the disease about which one reads.

14 December [75]

My Silent Confidant!

Everything has its time, the raging fever is past, I am now like a convalescent.

The secret in the story of Job, the vital force, the core, the idea is: that Job, despite everything, is in the right. This claim makes him an exception to all human considerations; his endurance and strength prove his authority, his warrant. Every human explanation is simply a misunderstanding to him, and all his distress is to him, in relation to God, a mere sophism that he knows he cannot solve himself, but which he has confidence that God can solve. Every *argumentum ad hominem* is used against him, yet he is undaunted in his conviction. He claims that he and God are on good terms, that he knows he is innocent and pure in his innermost heart where, in addition, he knows this with God, and yet all of existence seems to refute him. This is what is great in Job, that the passion of freedom in him is not quelled or calmed through a false expression. This passion is often quelled in a person under similar circumstances, in that a faint-heartedness or trivial anxiety has allowed him to believe he suffered for the sake of his sins, when he did not do this at all. His soul lacked the endurance to think through a thought when the world thought the opposite. It can be beautiful, and true and humble, when a person thinks that he suffers misfortune because of his sins, but it can also be that he has a vague conception of God as a tyrant, which he expresses in a meaningless way in that he immediately places Him under ethical determinations.——But neither did Job become demonic in the way a person can who, for example, wants to see God as in the right, even while believing that he is in himself in the right. It is as if he wants to show that he loves God, even while God tests him. Or he thinks that God cannot change the world just for him, but he will nevertheless be magnanimous enough to continue to love God. This is a completely demonic passion that deserves its own psychological treatment, independently of whether it humorously breaks off the [76] quarrel in order to avoid further fuss, or whether it culminates in a selfish assertion of the strength of his feelings.

Job continues to maintain that he is in the right. He does this in such a way that he demonstrates noble human boldness, which knows what a person is, that he, though delicate and quickly withered like the life of a flower, from the perspective of freedom is something great, has a consciousness that not even God, though He gave it, can wrest from him. In addition, Job maintains his claim in such a way that one sees in him the love and confidence that assures him that God can explain everything, if one can simply get Him to talk.

Job's friends give him enough to do. His dispute with them is a purgatory where the thought that he is in the right is tested. If he lacked the strength or ingenuity to try his conscience and frighten his soul, lacked the imagination to become afraid for himself, for the guilt and transgressions that might hide in the innermost reaches of his self, then his friends help him with their clear allusions, their offensive accusations, which, like envious divining-rods, are supposed to be able to call forth what lies most deeply hidden. His unhappiness is their main argument. This is how things are for them. One would think that Job would either lose his mind or collapse from misery and surrender unconditionally. Eliphas, Bildad, Zophar, and most of all Elihu,* who, unaffected, stands up *integer*[1] when the others are tired, and presents variations on the theme that his misfortune is a punishment, that he should repent, pray for forgiveness, and everything would be made right again.

Job, on the other hand, sticks to his position. His claim is like a permit with which he departs from the world and human beings. It is a demand people reject, but which Job maintains. He uses every means to persuade his friends. He tries to move them to sympathy ('have pity on me').* He terrifies them with his voice ('you whitewash

---

[1] Still vigorous.

with lies').* Everything is to no avail. His cries of pain become louder and louder in proportion to his friends' protests; reflection is precisely deepened in his suffering. Though this fails to move his friends, that is not important. They would gladly agree that he suffers, that he has reason to cry out, 'does the wild ass bray when he has grass?'* but they demand that he should see that he is being punished.

How can one explain Job's claim? The explanation is this: the whole thing is a *test*. This explanation creates a new difficulty, how- [77] ever, which I have endeavoured to make clear to myself in the following way. Scholarship treats and explains existence and, in existence, the relation of human beings to God. But what discipline is of such a sort that it has a place for a relationship that is characterized as a test, which when conceived in the abstract, really is not, but is such only for the individual? There is no such discipline, and there could not be one. It would have to address how the individual would come to know that it was a test. Anyone who has any sort of conception of an existence in thought and of a being of consciousness easily sees that this is neither so easily done as said, nor so easily transcended as said, nor so easily maintained as said. The event must first be wrenched from its cosmic context and be given a religious baptism and a religious name. It must then be placed in the context of ethics, and from this comes the expression: 'a test'. Before this, the individual would not appear to exist in terms of thought. Any sort of explanation is possible and passion's vortex is unleashed. Only those who have no conception, or a worthless conception, of what it is to live by virtue of spirit are quickly finished with this problem. They console themselves with half-an-hour's reading, just as many novices in the field of philosophy offer a hastily drawn conclusion.

What is great about Job is therefore not that he said: 'The Lord gave and the Lord took away, praised be the name of the Lord', which he said at first, but did not later repeat. Job's significance is that the disputes at the boundaries of faith are fought out in him, that this tremendous insurrection of passion's desire and combative force is presented here.

Job does not, therefore, reassure like the hero of faith, but he soothes temporarily. Job is in a way the whole rich contribution from the side of human beings in the huge dispute between God and man, the extended and dreadful process that stems from the fact that Satan placed discord between God and Job, and which ends with recognizing that the whole thing was a test.

This category — test — is neither aesthetic, nor ethical, nor dogmatic; it is completely transcendent. It is primarily knowledge about the category of a test, that something is a test, which would have a place in dogmatics. As soon as such knowledge comes into play, however, then the elasticity of the test is weakened and the category becomes something other than it was. This category is absolutely transcendent and places a person in a purely personal relation of [78] opposition to God, in such a relation that he cannot allow himself to be satisfied with a second-hand explanation.

That there are a certain number of people who have this category at hand and will pull it out on every occasion, as soon as the porridge begins to stick, shows only that they do not understand it. A person who has acquired a sophisticated understanding of the world will take an enormously long detour before he reaches it. This is the case with Job, who shows the breadth of his world-view through the firmness with which he knows how to avoid all shrewd escapes and cunning ethical exits. Job is not a hero of faith; he gives birth, in enormous pain, to the category of a 'test' precisely because he is so developed that he does not possess it in childlike immediacy.

I am aware that the purpose of such a category could be to remove and suspend all of actuality by characterizing it as a test in relation to eternity. This doubt has not, however, got the better of me, because then the test would be a *provisional* category, which would mean it was determined *eo ipso* in relation to time, and may therefore be transcended in time.

This much I see now, and since I have allowed myself to initiate you into everything, I am also writing this to you, though for myself. You know that I demand nothing of you, except that you would allow me to remain

Devotedly yours

[79]   13 January
My Silent Confidant!

The storm has blown itself out — the thunder is past — Job has been chastened before the ranks of humanity — the Lord and Job have come to an understanding, they are reconciled, 'the secret of God' is again upon Job's tabernacle as in the days of his youth.* People understand Job. *Now* they come and eat bread with him and sympathize with him and comfort him. His brothers and sisters each give him 'a piece of money and an earring of gold'.* Job is again blessed: 'and the Lord gave Job *twice* as much as he had before'.* That is what I call a *repetition*.

A thunderstorm can really do one good though! How glorious it must be to be chastened by God! It so often happens that one becomes obdurate when one is corrected, but when God judges, one loses oneself and forgets the pain in the love that wishes to educate.

Who could have thought of such an ending? And yet, no other ending is conceivable, even if this one also is inconceivable. When everything has ground to a halt, when thought ceases and speech is silenced, when explanation retreats in despair — then a thunderstorm is necessary. Who can understand this? And yet who could think of anything else?

Was Job then in the wrong? Yes, eternally, because there is no higher court before which he could come. Was he in the right? Yes, eternally, in that he was in the wrong *before God*.

So repetition is possible. But when? No human language can say. When did it happen for Job? When, from a human perspective, the impossibility was *conceived* as probable, even certain. Job gradually loses everything, and thus hope also gradually disappears in that actuality, rather than mitigating the accusations, makes increasingly harsh claims against him. Viewed immediately, everything appears to be lost. His friends, especially Bildad, know of only one escape: he must submit to the punishment, daring to hope for a repetition to the point of excess. But Job does not want to do this. Thus the knot, the [80] tangle, is tightened. Only a thunderstorm can loosen it.

This tale is indescribably comforting to me. Was it not fortunate that I did not follow your clever, admirable plan? Perhaps from a human perspective it was cowardly of me, but perhaps it will be easier this way for providence to help me.

There is only one thing I regret, that I did not ask the girl to give me my freedom. I am convinced she would have done it. Who can grasp a girl's magnanimity? And yet, I cannot really regret it because I know that I did not ask this because I respected her too much.

What would I have done without Job! I will not say any more for fear of burdening you with my eternal refrain.

Devotedly yours.

[81]   17 February
My Silent Confidant!

Here I sit, pleading innocence (as one would say in the language of thieves) or by the king's pleasure? I do not know. The only thing I know is that I sit, that I do not move from my place. Here I am, at the peak or at the foot? I do not know. All I know is that I have been here in *suspenso gradu*[1] for a whole month without moving a foot, or indeed, making the slightest movement.

I wait for a thunderstorm—and for a repetition. And yet, if only a thunderstorm would come, I would be indescribably happy, even if my sentence were that repetition was impossible.

What would be the effect of this thunderstorm? It would make me fit to be a husband. It would destroy my whole personality, I would be finished. It would make it so that I would hardly know myself. I do not waver, even though I stand on one leg. My honour would be saved, my pride redeemed and however it might change me, I hope the recollection will remain with me as an inexhaustible comfort, remain after it has happened. What I fear is, in a sense, worse than suicide because it is going to disturb me in an entirely different way. If the thunderstorm does not come, then I remain deceitful. I do not die, but only make myself out to be dead so that my friends and family can bury me. After I have been laid in my coffin, then I will quietly embrace my expectation. No one will know of this, because otherwise they would be afraid to bury a man in whom there was still life.

I do everything in my power to transform myself into a husband. I sit and pare myself down, remove all the incommensurable in order to become commensurable. Each morning I lay aside my soul's impatient and infinite striving, but to no avail, for in the next instant it is there again. Each morning I shave myself to make myself presentable, but to no avail, the next morning my beard is back. I
[82] *re*call myself as banks recall their notes in order to put new ones into

---

[1] Immobilized.

circulation, but it does not work. I convert all my intellectual property, my mortgage into conjugal currency — alas, alas, my wealth is worth very little in this coin!

I realize my account here is brief. My situation does not allow me many words.

Devotedly yours.

Despite the fact that I long ago renounced the world and abandoned all theorizing, I cannot deny that my interest in this young person drew me, to some extent, out of my pendular movements. It was easy to see that he laboured under a complete misunderstanding. What he suffers from is a misplaced melancholy magnanimity whose only place is in a poet's brain. He waits for the thunderstorm that will transform him into a husband, a nervous breakdown perhaps. He has got it all wrong. He is one of those people who says: 'About face' to the whole battalion, instead of turning around himself, which can be expressed here as: 'The girl must go.' If I were not so old I would enjoy the pleasure of taking the girl myself, if only to help the man.

He is pleased that he did not follow my 'clever' plan. That is just like him. Even now, he cannot see that that would have been the only right thing to do. One cannot really engage him. It is fortunate, therefore, that he does not want me to answer his letters. Corresponding with a person who has such a trump card as a thunderstorm in his hand would be laughable. If only he had my intelligence. That is all I am going to say on the matter. If he, when what he had calculated would happen did happen, would give it a religious expression, that is his business. I have no objection to that. But it is always good to have done everything that human sagacity can prescribe. It should have been me. I could have been more help to the girl. Now it is going to be much harder for her to forget him. It is unfortunate that she did not come to the point of screaming. There should be screaming, it is beneficial, just as is bleeding with a contusion. One must allow a girl to scream, to get it out of her system. She will forget faster that way.

He failed to follow my advice and now, presumably, she sits and grieves. I understand that this is extremely serious for him. If there were a girl who would be faithful to me in this way, then I would fear her more than anything in the world, more than lovers of freedom fear a tyrant. She would be a source of constant anxiety. She would

[83]

[84]

be like a sore tooth of which I was aware at every instant. She would cause me anxiety because she would be an ideal, and I am too proud to endure that another human being could be stronger and more enduring in that sense than I. If she remained at the pinnacle of the ideal, then I would find that my life, instead of going forward, would exist *in pausa*.[1] Perhaps if someone could not endure this painful admiration she extorted from him and became jealous, he would employ all possible means to topple her: marriage.*

Even if she said, as is often said and read and forgotten and repeated, 'I have loved you, I will confess now' (*'now'*, despite the fact that she has presumably already said it hundreds of times); 'I have loved you more than God' (this is not often said… especially not in our God-fearing age, where the fear of God is actually an even rarer phenomenon)—it would not disturb him. The ideal is not to die of grief, but to preserve oneself healthy and, if possible, happy, and yet also to preserve one's feelings. To accept another is no virtue. It is a weakness, a very simple and plebeian virtuosity which only the bourgeoisie would sound an alarm about. Anyone with an artistic view of life easily sees that this is a mistake that cannot be corrected, even if one married seven times.

He regrets that he did not ask her for his freedom. He could save himself that trouble. It would not have helped much. He would, in all probability, simply have given her ammunition to use against him, because genuinely to request his freedom is quite different from crediting her with being his muse. One sees again here that he is a poet. A poet is born to be a fool for girls. Even if the girl had made a fool of him right in front of his face, he would have believed it was high-mindedness. He is much better off thanking his lucky stars he did not do that. She would then presumably really have become serious. She would then not simply have manipulated the little multiplication table of the erotic, which is of course legitimate and her right, but also the larger table of marriage. She would have had God vouch for her, called on all that was holy, seized every one of his precious memories. In this respect, many girls will, when the opportunity presents itself, make unabashed use of a falsehood that [85] not even a seducer would allow himself to use. Whoever, in the context of the erotic, calls on God's help and wants to be loved for God's

---

[1] In a stationary state.

sake ceases to be himself and strives to be stronger than heaven and more meaningful than eternal salvation.—Assume the girl had done this, he would perhaps never have forgotten it, never have recovered from it, since he presumably would have been so chivalrous as not to listen to a single reasonable word from me, but would have taken every outburst from her at face value and preserved it as an eternal truth. Assume that afterwards it would have become apparent that the whole thing had been an exaggeration, a little lyrical impromptu, an emotional divertissement... Now what! But then perhaps his high-mindedness would also have helped him here.

My friend is a poet, and the fanatical belief in the feminine ideal is essential to poets. I am, respectfully, a writer of prose. I have my own opinions concerning the opposite sex, or more correctly, I have no opinions because I very seldom have seen a girl whose life could be grasped in an intellectual category. Girls normally lack the coherence that is necessary in order for one to either admire or despise a person. A woman is self-deceived even before she deceives anyone else, and therefore one lacks any standard by which to measure her.

My young friend will see. I have no confidence in his thunderstorm. I believe he would not have acted badly had he followed my advice. The idea was in motion in the young man's love. This was the reason I became involved with him. The plan I suggested used the idea as a yardstick. That is the most reliable yardstick in the world. If one employs it consistently throughout life, then anyone who would deceive one becomes himself a fool. The idea had taken aim. In my mind, that was the fault of both himself and his beloved. If she were capable of living in this way, a way that required no extraordinary abilities, but simply inwardness, then in the same instant that he left her she would have said to herself: 'I will have nothing more to do with him. It does not matter if he was a deceiver or not, if he should come back or not. I will preserve the ideality of my own love. That, I will certainly know how to honour.' If she had done that, my friend's position would have been painful enough, because then he would have remained in sympathetic pain and distress. But who would not want to be in such a position, when in the midst of his grief he had the joy of admiring his beloved? His life would have halted like hers, but it would have halted as a river halts, bewitched by the power of music.—If she were unable to use the idea as regulative for her life, [86] then his pain would not have interfered with her use of another mode of advance.

[87]

My Silent Confidant!

She is married, to whom I do not know, because when I read it in the newspaper I felt as if I had been struck and I dropped the paper. Since then I have not been able to bring myself to take a closer look at the announcement. I am back to my old self. This is a repetition. I understand everything, and existence seems more beautiful than ever. So there was a thunderstorm, even if it was caused by her high-mindedness. Whoever it is she has chosen—I will not say 'preferred', because in terms of the qualities required of a husband, anyone would be preferable to me—she has been magnanimous toward me. Even if he were the handsomest man in the world, the very ideal of masculine perfection, able to enchant any girl, even if she could bring the whole feminine sex to the point of despair by agreeing to marry him, she has behaved magnanimously, if in no other respect, at least to the extent that she has completely forgotten me. What is as beautiful as feminine generosity? Terrestrial beauty may wither, the sparkle in her eye may one day be extinguished, she may become bent and stooped with the years, her locks may lose their power to ensnare when they are hidden by a matronly cap, her regal glance, that ruled the world, may one day shrink to one of maternal concern for her small brood—a girl who has been magnanimous in this way will never age. Let existence reward her as it has, let it give her what she loved more; it has also given me what I loved more—myself; and it gave me this through the agency of her magnanimity.

I am back to my old self. This 'self', which another would not pick up off the street,* is mine again. The schism in my being has been removed. I am whole again. The anxieties of sympathy, which my pride nourished and supported, no longer force splits and separations.

Is repetition not possible? Have I not received everything back, only doubled? Have I not myself again, and in such a way that I have
[88] a double appreciation of what this means? And what is a repetition of worldly goods, which have no meaning in relation to spiritual

matters, compared to such a repetition? Only Job's children were not returned to him twofold, because a human life does not allow itself to be doubled in this way. Here only a spiritual repetition is possible, even though it cannot be so complete temporally as in eternity where there is true repetition.

I am myself again. The machinery has been set in motion. The traps in which I had been caught have been hewn asunder. The magic spell that had been placed on me so that I could not come to my senses has been broken. No one raises his hand against me now, my freedom has been secured, I am born again to myself, because as long as Ilithyia* folds her hands the one who is in labour cannot give birth.

It has passed, my yawl is afloat. In the next minute I will be back to the place of my soul's craving, there where ideas effervesce with elemental force, where thoughts are as deafening as migrating nations, there where at other times it is calm, as still as the silent South Sea depths, a stillness where one hears oneself speak, even if the movement takes place only within, there where one ventures one's life every minute, every minute loses it, and then wins it back again.

I belong to the idea. When it beckons me, I follow. When it summons me, then I wait day and night. No one calls to dinner, no one waits supper on me. When the idea calls, I leave everything, or more correctly, I have nothing to leave. I disappoint no one, distress no one, by being true to it. My spirit is not distressed by having to distress another. When I return home, there is no one to read anything in my face, no one to grill me, no one to worm an account out of me, which I would not be able to give anyone anyway, of whether I am happy or sunk in misery, of whether I have been victorious in life or been vanquished by it.

I am again handed intoxication's beaker. I can already catch its fragrance, sense its bubbling music. But first, a toast to her who saved my soul that had sat in the loneliness of despair: praised be feminine magnanimity! Long live thought's flight, long live mortal danger in the service of the idea, long live the misery of battle, long live the festive shouts of victory, long live dancing in the eddy of the infinite, long live the wave that drives me down into the abyss, long live the wave that slings me up again over the stars.

[89]

> To:
>
> Mr. X, Esq.
>
> the real reader of this book

[91]   Copenhagen, August 1843

My Dear Reader!

Forgive me for speaking confidentially to you, but we are *unter uns.*[1]
Despite the fact that you are an imaginary person, you are in no way
a multiplicity, but only one, so there is only you and I.

If one assumes that everyone who reads a book for some contingent reason having nothing to do with the book's content is not a
genuine reader, then there would not be many genuine readers left,
even for authors with a large readership, because to whom would it
occur in our day to waste an instant on the ludicrous thought that to
be a good reader is actually an art, let alone to spend time to become
such a reader? This unfortunate situation naturally influences an
author, who according to my opinion does well to write after the
fashion of Clemens Alexandrinus,* in such a way that heretics cannot
understand it.

A curious female reader, who reads the end of every book on her
night table in order to see if the lovers are finally united, will be disappointed because, although two lovers are united, my friend, who is
also a man, is not one of them. Since this is apparently not the result

---

[1] There are only the two of us.

of some minuscule contingency, then the case becomes significant for girls who are both ready and eager to marry and who, by having to cross off a single eligible man, make this prospect less probable.— A concerned father may fear that his son will go the same way as my friend, and thus be of the opinion that the book does not make a good impression, in that it does not provide a ready-made uniform that would fit any musketeer.— An ephemeral genius will perhaps find that the exception creates far too many problems for himself and takes the situation much too seriously.— An amiable family friend will search in vain for an explanation of the trivialities of the parlour or a glorification of tea-party gossip.— A realist would perhaps think the whole thing a lot of to do about nothing.— A woman experienced in matchmaking would judge the book to be flawed, in that the most [92] interesting issue was the determination of what qualities would be required of a girl in order for her to be able 'to make such a man happy', because she reassures herself that it stands to reason that such a girl must exist, or at least must have existed.— A parish priest will proclaim that there is too much philosophy in the book; the more reflective bishop will seek in vain that of which the contemporary congregation is in such great need, the genuinely speculative.— My dear reader, we can certainly talk about this *unter uns*, because you can understand that I do not mean to suggest that all these opinions will actually be held by anyone, since the book will not have many readers.

The book will possibly provide a welcome occasion for an ordinary reviewer to demonstrate in detail that it is neither a comedy, tragedy, novel, epic, epigram, nor novella. He will also find it unforgivable that one searches in vain for a 1. 2. 3. development.* He will find the actual development difficult to understand, because it is inverse. It is not addressed to him, in any case, because reviewers generally explain existence as follows: both the universal and the particular are annihilated. Most importantly, however, it is too much to expect of an ordinary reviewer that he should have any interest in the dialect-ical battle through which the exception emerges from the universal,* the extended and incredibly complicated procedure through which the exception fights for and asserts its legitimacy, because the ille-gitimate exception is recognizable in that it wants to bypass the universal. This conflict is very dialectical and infinitely complex. It assumes an absolute proficiency in the dialectic of the universal, demands speed in the imitation of the movements, it is, in a word, as difficult as killing a man while letting him live. On the one side is the exception, on the other side the universal, and the struggle is itself a strange conflict between the impatience and anger of the universal in relation to the spectacle the exception causes, and its besotted infatuation with the exception; because the universal delights in the exception to the same extent that heaven delights in the reformed sinner—more than in ninety-nine righteous souls. On the other side is the resistance and defiance of the exception, its weakness and infirmity. The whole thing is a rupture, in which the universal breaks with the exception, breaks with it violently, and strengthens [93] it with this rupture. If the exception cannot endure the anguish, the universal will not help it, just as heaven will not help a sinner who cannot endure the pains of repentance. The vigorous and determined exception which, despite its struggle with the universal, is an offshoot of it, preserves itself. The relationship is this: the exception grasps the universal to the extent that it thoroughly grasps itself. It works for the universal in that it works through itself. It explains the universal in that it explains itself. The exception thus explains the universal and itself, and when one really wants to study the universal, one need only examine a legitimate exception, because it will present everything much more clearly than the universal would itself. The legitimate exception is reconciled with the universal; the universal is at its basis polemically opposed to the exception. It will not reveal its infatuation with the exception until the exception forces it to do so. If the exception does not have the strength to do this, then it is not legitimate, and it is therefore very shrewd of the universal not to reveal anything too quickly. If heaven loves a sinner more than ninety-nine righteous souls, the sinner does not know this in the beginning; on the contrary, he senses only heaven's wrath, until he finally, in a sense, forces heaven to speak.

Over time, one tires of the interminable chatter about the universal and the universal, which is repeated until it becomes boring and vapid. There are exceptions. If one cannot explain them, then neither can one explain the universal. One generally fails to notice this, because one does not normally grasp the universal passionately, but only superficially. The exception, on the other hand, grasps the universal with intense passion.

When one does this, a new order of precedence emerges, and the poor exception, if it is ever any good, appears again, as the poor stepdaughter in the fairy tale, restored to a position of honour.

A poet is such an exception. He serves as a transition to the genuinely aristocratic exceptions, the religious exceptions. A poet is generally an exception. One is generally grateful for such a person and his productions. I have thought myself that it could be very valuable to allow such a thing to come into being. The young person I have allowed to come into being is a poet. More than this I cannot do, because the most I can do is to conceive of a poet and present him through my thoughts. I cannot become a poet myself. My inter- [94] est lies in another direction. My concern in this project has been purely aesthetic and psychological. I have included myself, but when you, dear reader, look closely, you will easily see that I am only an assisting spirit and far from being what the young person fears; I am actually indifferent to him. This was a misunderstanding that I occasioned as a means of presenting him more clearly. Every movement I made was made simply in order to illuminate him. I have had him constantly *en mente*,[1] every word I wrote was either ventriloquism or said in relation to him. Even where humour and flippancy seem to be tossed about without reference to anything in particular, it was with reference to him. Even when everything ends sadly, there is a gesture to him, to something in him. For this reason, all the movements are purely lyrical, and what I say one can see only darkly in him,* or through what I say one will be better able to understand him. Thus have I done for him what I could, just as I now endeavour to serve you, dear reader, by again being another.

The life of a poet begins in a struggle with all of existence. The point is to find something reassuring, or legitimizing, because he must always lose the first struggle. He is not justified in wanting to win immediately. My poet finds a justification in that existence absolves him in that instant when he wishes, in a sense, to destroy himself. His soul then wins a religious resonance. This is what actually sustains him, despite the fact that it never breaks through. His dithyrambic joy in the last letter is an example of this, because this joy is unquestionably based on a religious attunement which remains, however, hidden in him. He has a religious attunement

---

[1] In mind.

like a secret he cannot explain, even while this secret helps him to explain actuality poetically. He explains the universal as repetition, and yet he understands repetition in another way himself, because while actuality becomes repetition, for him the exponential power of his consciousness is repetition. He has had, what belongs essentially to a poet, a love affair; but this is equivocal: happy, unhappy, comic, tragic. In relation to the girl, everything appears comical, because he was presumably affected sympathetically in such a way that his suffering lay largely in the suffering of the beloved. If he was mistaken in this, then the situation appears comical. If he considers himself, then [95] the situation appears tragic, just as it does when, in another sense, he considers the beloved ideally. He has preserved an ideal picture of the whole love affair, to which he can give whatever expression he wishes, but only in terms of a mood, because he has no facticity. He has a consciousness-fact, or more correctly, he has no consciousness-fact, but a dialectical elasticity that allows him to produce moods. While this productivity becomes his outward appearance, he is carried by something ineffably religious. Thus was the movement in the earlier letters, especially in certain of them, much closer to a genuine religious event, but the instant the temporary tension is relieved, he comes back to himself, but as a poet, and the religious is driven underground—i.e. becomes like an ineffable substratum.

If he had had a more devoutly religious background, he would not have become a poet. Then everything would have received a religious meaning. The situation in which he had become ensnared would definitely have been significant for him, but then the hesitation would have had a higher source; he would also then have had an entirely different authority, though it would have been purchased with even more painful suffering. He would then have acted with an entirely different iron-like consistency and firmness. He would have gained a fact of consciousness he could have stuck with, and which would never have been equivocal to him, but pure seriousness, because he would have established it himself by virtue of a relationship to God. In the same instant the whole question of finitude would become insignificant; genuine actuality would, in a deeper sense, make no difference to him. He would have religiously exhausted every possible horrific consequence of the situation. Whether things turned out to be other than he had thought would not disturb him at all. Even if the worst had happened, this could not have frightened him any more than it already had. He would, with religious fear and trembling, but also with faith and confidence, understand what he had done from the beginning, and what he was as a result obligated to do later, even if this obligation occasioned something strange.* It is characteristic of this young person that, as a poet, he can never fully understand what it is he has done, precisely because he will both see it and yet not see it in the external and visible, or will see it in the external and visible, and therefore will see it and not see it. [96] A religious individual, on the other hand, rests in himself and does not take seriously the childish pranks of actuality.

My dear reader! You will understand now that what is of interest here is the young person, while I pale into insignificance, just as a woman giving birth does in relation to the child she delivers. Thus it is with me, because I have in a way delivered him, and as the elder, I am allowed to speak. My personality is a presupposition of consciousness, which must be present in order to force him out, whereas my personality could never come to the place where he arrives, because the primitive simplicity in which he appears is the important thing. He has therefore, from the beginning, been in good hands, even though I frequently had to tease him out in order that he should be visible. I saw he was a poet when I first laid eyes on him, if for no other reason than that an event which had happened to a more superficial person, would in time have become nothing, for him expanded into an earth-shaking event.

Despite the fact that it is generally I who am speaking, you, my dear reader (you have a good understanding of intimate psychological states and emotions, and it is for this reason that I call you 'dear'), you will read about him everywhere. You will understand the variety of the transitions, even if now and then, when the mood suddenly showers down upon you and makes you feel peculiar, you will see afterwards how everything was modified, the one mood in relation to the other, together with the fact that the individual mood is essentially correct, which is the most important thing, since the lyrical is so important here. You might once let yourself be distracted by an apparently pointless joke or purposeless threat, but afterwards you will perhaps reconcile yourself with it.

Your devoted
Constantine Constantius

Philosophical Crumbs

or

A Crumb of Philosophy

By

JOHANNES CLIMACUS

Published

by

S. KIERKEGAARD

Can an eternal consciousness have a historical point of departure; could such a thing be of more than historical interest; can one build an eternal happiness on historical knowledge?

Better well hanged than ill wed.
(Shakespeare)*

WHAT is offered here is just a little piece, *proprio Marte, propriis auspiciis, proprio stipendio*,[1] without any pretension to participation in the scholarly striving wherewith one acquires the right to exposition, to transitions, such as concluding and preliminary, to participation as a colleague or simply an enthusiast, as a hero, a relative hero, or at least an absolute trumpeter. It is just a little piece and remains such, even though I, like Holberg's magister, *volente deo**[2] would follow it with a sequel in seventeen parts; it remains such, just as one who writes half-hour pieces produces only half-hour pieces, even if he produces volumes. The work is, however, in accordance with my abilities, I who do not, as that noble Roman *merito magis quam ignavia*,[3] refrain from serving the system, but am a comfortable idler, *ex animi sententia*,[4] and for good reason. I would not wish, however, to commit an ἀπραγμοσύνη,[5] which is always a crime against the state,* but chiefly in a tumultuous age, since in olden times it was prohibited on pain of death. But suppose that one, by one's interference, was guilty of a greater crime, to the extent that he caused only confusion; would it not have been better had he kept his concerns to himself? Not everyone is so fortunate that what preoccupies his thoughts corresponds to the interests of the general public, corresponds so perfectly that it is difficult to determine to what extent he is concerned for his own sake or for the sake of the general public. Did not Archimedes* sit calmly contemplating his circles while Syracuse was being taken, and did he not say to the Roman soldier who murdered him: '*nolite perturbare circulos meos*'?[6] He who is not so fortunate can look to another model. When Philip threatened to lay siege to Corinth and all the inhabit- [216] ants were busily occupied preparing to defend the city, with the one polishing his weapon, another collecting stones, and a third repairing the wall, Diogenes* saw this and hastily drew his robe about himself and rolled his tub zealously back and forth through the streets.

---

[1] By one's own effort, at one's own expense.
[2] God willing.
[3] On the basis of my excellence, not from any baseness of motive.
[4] By inclination.
[5] Illegal failure to participate in public affairs.
[6] Do not disturb my circles.

When asked why he did this, he answered: 'I do not wish to be the only idler amongst so many diligent people, so I busy myself rolling my tub.' Such behaviour is at least not sophistical, if Aristotle's explanation that the art of sophistry is that with which one makes money is correct. Such behaviour can at least not result in a misunderstanding, in that it was unthinkable that anyone would have taken Diogenes for the saviour and benefactor of the city. It is similarly impossible that anyone could attribute world-historical significance* to such a modest piece (what I at least consider the greatest misfortune that could befall my project), or to suppose that its author was the systematic Salomon Goldkalb,* eagerly awaited in our beloved royal city of Copenhagen. Such a misunderstanding could happen only if the guilty party were by nature extraordinarily stupid, and would presumably be the result of bellowing day in and day out the antistrophic response every time someone made him believe that a new era was beginning, a new epoch, etc., to such a degree that his economically apportioned *quantum satis*[1] of good sense was driven completely out of his head, so that he was made ecstatic in what one could call the roaring insanity of a higher madness, whose symptoms are bellowing, the convulsive bellowing, the content of which is these words: 'era', 'epoch', 'era and epoch', 'epoch and era', 'the system'; and the ecstatic person's condition is an irrational exaltation, in that he lives as if every day were not simply one of the *extra* days, that come only every four years, but one of those that comes only once in a millennium, while the concept like a juggler in this circus-like time at every moment must perform these continual tricks of tossing things over and over until finally the man himself falls over.* Saints preserve me and my piece from the fate that such a noisy 'comedian' could, with his meddling slapstick, tear me away from my carefree self-satisfaction as the father of a piece, or prevent a kind and good-natured reader from freely investigating whether there is anything in it he can use. God forbid that he should bring me into the tragic-comic situation of having to laugh at my own bad luck, as the good people of Fredericia had to laugh at their bad luck when [217] they read in a report in the newspaper of a fire there, that 'the alarm sounded and the fire-engines raced through the streets', even though there is only one fire-engine in Fredericia, and not much more than one street, and the paper thus compelled one to conclude that the

---

[1] Sufficient amount.

one truck, instead of heading for the fire, had executed ceremonious manoeuvres up and down the street. My little piece could least of all be thought to resemble the sound of an alarm, and its author is less inclined than anyone to sound an alarm.

What is my opinion?... Let no one ask me about it, and next to having an opinion, nothing can be less important to another than what my opinion is. To have an opinion is both too much and too little for me. It assumes a sense of well-being and security with one's existence, just as, in a worldly sense, having a wife and children does, which is not granted to him who must keep himself in readiness day and night without, however, having financial security. This is my situation in the world of the spirit, because I have cultivated and continue to cultivate in myself the ability to dance nimbly in the service of thought, as much as possible to the honour of God and for my own amusement, renouncing domestic happiness and civic esteem, the *communio bonorum*,[1] and unanimous happiness, which is to have an opinion. Am I compensated for this, do I, like the person who serves at the altar, partake myself of what is offered there?... That is my business. The one I serve is good for it, as financiers say, and in another sense than the financiers mean. If, however, anyone were to be so polite as to assume that I had an opinion, if he pressed this gallantry to the extreme of adopting this opinion because it was mine, I would be pained by this courtesy, in that I would feel unworthy of it, and for his opinion, in that he has no other opinion than mine; I can stake my own life, I can play, in all seriousness, with my own life—but not with the life of another. This I am able to do, the only thing I can do for thought, I who cannot offer erudition, 'hardly the one drachma course, not to mention the great 50 drachma course' (*Cratylus*).* I have only my own life, which I offer as soon as a difficulty appears. Then the dance is easy, because my partner is the thought of death and it is a lively dancer. People are too heavy for me, therefore I request *per deos obsecro*:[2] No one invite me, because I will not dance.

J. C.

---

[1] The common good, the good of the community.
[2] I swear by the gods.

PROPOSITIO

The question is posed by one who is ignorant, who does not
even know what has led him to ask such a question

CHAPTER I

THOUGHT PROJECT

A

To what extent can the truth be taught?* We will begin with this
question. It was a Socratic question, or became so with the Socratic
question of whether virtue could be taught since virtue was determined to be insight (cf. *Protagoras, Gorgias, Meno, Euthydemus*).*
To the extent that the truth is to be learned, it must be presumed
not to exist. That is, in that it is to be learned, it is sought. Here
we encounter the difficulty that Socrates draws attention to in the
Meno as a 'trick argument' (80e 2), that it is impossible for a person
to seek what he knows and equally impossible for him to seek
what he does not know; because what he knows he cannot seek, because
he knows it, and what he does not know he cannot seek, because he
does not know what he should seek. Socrates ponders this difficulty
and suggests as a solution that all learning and seeking are merely
recollection, so that the ignorant person needs only to be reminded,
in order by himself to recollect what he knows. The truth is thus
not imparted to him, but was in him. Socrates develops this further in a way that concentrates the pathos of Greek thought, in that
[219] it becomes a proof for the immortality of the soul, though—
and this is important—retrogressively, that is, a proof of the pre-
existence of the soul.[1] This shows with what wonderful consistency

---

[1] [Kierkegaard's note.] If the thought is thought absolutely, so one leaves out of
account the various forms this pre-existence can take, then this Greek thought is found
in both ancient and modern speculation: an eternal creation; an eternal departure from
the father; an eternal evolution of the divine; an eternal sacrifice of the self; a past resur-
rection; a transcended sentence. All these thoughts are the same as the Greek theory
of recollection; it is just that one does not always notice it because one has arrived
at them by going further. If the theory is broken down into the variety of forms of

Socrates was true to himself and realized artistically what he had understood. He was and remained a midwife; not because he 'lacked the positive',*[1] but because he understood that this was the highest relationship one person could have to another. And in this he is eternally correct. Because even if there is ever given a divine point of departure, between one person and another this remains the true relationship, provided one reflects on the absolute and does not fool around with the contingent, but from the bottom of his heart renounces any understanding of the half-truth that seems to be man's desire and the system's secret. Socrates, on the other hand, was a divinely sanctioned midwife; the feat he accomplished was a divine errand (cf. Plato's *Apology*); even if he seemed a bit odd to others (ἀτοπώτατος[2] *Theaetetus*, 149); and it was God's intention, which [220] Socrates also understood, that he was forbidden from giving birth (μαιεύεσθαί με ὁ θεὸς ἀναγκάζει, γεννᾶν δὲ ἀπεκώλυσεν.[3] *Theaetetus*, 150); because between one person and another the μαιεύσθαι[4] is the highest. To give birth belongs to God.

From a Socratic perspective, every temporal point of departure is *eo ipso* contingent, something vanishing, an occasion; the teacher is no more significant, and if he presents himself or his teachings in any other way, then he gives nothing, but removes, then he is not even a friend of the other, let alone his teacher. This is the profundity of the Socratic teaching, his noble humanity, he who refused superficial and vain association with the clever, but who also felt just as much kinship with a tanner, which is why he 'discussed moral questions in the workshops and the marketplace, being convinced that the study of nature is no concern of ours' (Diogenes Laertius II. 5, 21),*

pre-existence, then is this approximating thought [an] eternal 'pre' like the corresponding approximations eternal 'post'? One explains the contradiction of existence by proposing a pre, according to need (by virtue of an earlier condition the individual has come to his present or inexplicable condition), or by proposing a post, according to need (on another planet the individual is better placed, and from this perspective his new condition is not inexplicable).

[1] [Kierkegaard's note.] Thus it is characterized in our age where one has the positive sort of like a polytheist disparaging the negativity of monotheism because polytheism has many gods, monotheism only one. Philosophers have many thoughts, each of which is to a certain extent valid. Socrates only one, which is absolute.

[2] Eccentric.

[3] The god directs me to help others give birth but prevents me from giving birth.

[4] To deliver another (into the world), to give birth to another.

but was just as purely philosophical no matter with whom he spoke. Half-baked thoughts, cheap haggling, assertions and concessions, as if the individual to a certain extent owed something to another person, but then to a certain extent did not; loose speech that explains everything, except what this 'to a certain extent' is, cannot advance beyond Socrates. Neither can one in this way reach the concept of revelation, but will remain instead at the level of idle chatter. The Socratic view is that each individual is his own centre and the world is centred around him, because his self-knowledge is a knowledge of God. This is how Socrates understood himself and, according to him, how everyone must understand himself and, with this in mind, how he must also understand his relation to another individual, always with equal humility and equal pride. For this, Socrates had enough courage and self-possession to be sufficient unto himself, but also in relation to others to be only an occasion even for the stupidest person. O rare magnanimity, rare in our time, where the priest is above a clerk, where every other person is an authority, while all these differences and all this authority is mediated by a common craziness, a *commune naufragium*;[1] because while no human being has ever truly been an authority, or helped another by being one, or has been capable, in truth, of taking the client with him, this is better accomplished in another way; because it is always the case that when a fool goes, he takes others with him.

If this is the situation with respect to learning the truth, then the [221] fact that I have learned something from Socrates, or Prodicus,* or a parlour-maid, can concern me only historically, or, to the extent that I have a Platonic sort of enthusiasm, poetically. Even if this enthusiasm is beautiful, even if I wish both for myself and for everyone else this εὐκαταφορία εἰς πάθος[2] which only the stoics would warn against, even if I had enough Socratic magnanimity and Socratic selflessness to be able to imagine this void—this enthusiasm is still only an illusion, as Socrates would say, an ambiguity within which worldly differences ferment voluptuously. Neither can it interest me other than historically that Socrates' or Prodicus' teachings were this or that, because the truth in which I rest was within me and came to the surface by itself. Socrates could no more give it to me than

---

[1] Common shipwreck.*   [2] Disposition to passion.

could a coachman pull a horse's burden, even if he can help it a little through the use of his whip.[1] My relation to Socrates and Prodicus is of no concern to me in relation to my eternal blessedness, because this is given retrogressively in my possession of the truth I had from the beginning without knowing it. If I imagine meeting Socrates, or Prodicus, or the parlour-maid, in another life, once again none of them could be more than an occasion, as Socrates expresses it when he boldly asserts that even in the underworld he would continue to question others, because at the basis of all questioning lies the assumption that the one questioned must have the truth himself, or must be able to get it all by himself. The temporal point of departure is nothing, because the instant I discover that I have always known the truth, without knowing it, is immediately hidden in the eternity of this 'always', taken up into it in such a way that I could not find it, even if I looked for it, because there would be no here or there, but only a *ubique et nusquam*.[2]

B

If the situation is to be different, then the moment in time must have decisive significance so that I could not for a moment forget it, neither in time nor in eternity, because the eternal, which did not exist before, came to be in this moment. Let us consider now, from the perspective of this assumption, the situation with respect to the question of the extent to which the truth can be taught.

(a) *The Prior State*

We begin with the Socratic problem of how one can seek the truth, in that it appears equally impossible whether one has it or does not have it. The Socratic view genuinely abolished the disjunction, in that it appeared every human being had the truth. This was Socrates' explanation; we saw the consequences with respect to

---

[1] [Kierkegaard's note.] There is a place in *Clitophon** to which I will direct the reader as a piece of hearsay, in that this dialogue is not considered to be genuine. Clitophon complains that, in relation to virtue, Socrates is merely encouraging (προτετραμμένος) in such a way that from the moment he has sufficiently recommended virtue in general, he leaves everyone to himself. Clitophon believes that such behaviour must stem from the fact that Socrates either does not know any more than he says, or that he does not want to communicate what he knows (cf. 410).

[2] Everywhere and nowhere.

the moment. If the moment is now to have decisive significance, then the seeker must lack the truth right up until the moment he receives it; he cannot even possess it in the form of ignorance, because then the moment becomes merely an occasion. No, he cannot even be a seeker. This is how the problem must be characterized if we do not want to revert to a Socratic account. He must be defined as being outside the truth (not approaching it as a proselyte, but going away from it), or as being in error. He is thus in a state of error. How could one remind him, or what good would it do him to be reminded of something he never knew and thus cannot recollect?

(b) *The Teacher*

If the teacher is to be the occasion that reminds the learner, then he cannot contribute to the learner's remembering that he really knows the truth, because the learner is actually in a state of error. [223] That with respect to which the teacher can be an occasion is the learner's remembering that he is in error. But this recollection precisely excludes the learner from the truth even more than when he was ignorant of the fact that he was in error. In this way, the teacher actually thrusts the learner away, precisely by reminding him, as he turns inward and discovers, not that he already knows the truth, but that he is in error. With respect to this act of consciousness the Socratic applies. That is, the teacher, whoever he might be, even if he is a god, is only an occasion; because I can discover my own error only by myself. Only when I discover it, and not before, has it been discovered, even if the whole world knew it. (According to our supposition concerning the moment, this is the only analogy to the Socratic situation.)

If the learner is to obtain the truth, then the teacher must bring it to him, and not just the truth, but also the condition for understanding it; because if the learner had himself the condition for understanding the truth, then he would need only to recollect it; because the condition for understanding the truth is like being able to ask about it, the condition and the question contain the conditioned and the answer. (If this is not the case, then the moment can be understood only Socratically.)

But one who gives the learner not merely the truth, but also the condition for understanding it, he is not a teacher. All instruction is based on the assumption that, when all is said and done, the condition for understanding it is there. If it is missing, the teacher can do nothing; because in that case he could not transform the learner, but would have to re-create him before he could begin to teach him. But no human being can do this. If it is to happen, then it must be done by the god himself.

To the extent that the learner is, he has been created, and to this extent, God must have given him the condition for understanding the truth (because otherwise he would earlier have been a mere animal, and this teacher who, along with the condition, gave him the truth would actually have had to make him into a human being first); but to the extent that the moment is to have decisive significance (and if this is not assumed, then we remain in the Socratic situation), he must lack the condition, that is, be deprived of it. This could not have been brought about by the god (because that would be a contradiction), nor could it have happened by accident (because it is a contradiction to say that the lower could overcome what is higher); he must have then been responsible himself for having lost it. If he could have lost the condition in such a way that he was not responsible for having lost [224] it, and could remain in a state of deprivation through no fault of his own, then he would have possessed the condition only accidentally, which is a contradiction, in that the condition for understanding the truth is an essential condition. Error is not simply outside the truth, but is polemically opposed to it, which is expressed by saying that he has himself forfeited and continues to forfeit the condition.

The teacher is thus the god himself, who functions as an occasion, and occasions the learner's recollection that he is in error, and this is through his own fault. But this condition, to be in error and to be this through one's own fault, what should we call it? Let us call it sin.

The teacher is then the god, who gives the condition and the truth. What should we call such a teacher, because we are in agreement that we have already gone far beyond the definition of a teacher? To the extent that the learner is in error, but is there through his own fault (since, according to the foregoing, he could not have been there in any other way), one might think he was free; since to be responsible for one's own state is certainly freedom. And yet he is not free, but bound and exiled, because to be free of the truth is to be exiled from it, and to be exiled through one's own act is to be bound. But because he has bound himself, can he not loosen these bonds, or liberate himself? Because what binds me must also be able to liberate me if it wished, and since this is himself, he should be able to do it. He must certainly first will it. But assume now that he is reminded so deeply, of what the teacher gave him occasion to remember (and this must never be forgotten) that he does will it. In this case (if, by willing it, he could do it himself), then that he had been bound in a previous situation would, in the moment of liberation, be lost without a trace, and the moment would not become decisively significant. He would become ignorant of the fact that he had bound himself and then liberated himself.[1]

[225] Viewed in this way, the moment is not decisively significant, yet it

---

[1] [Kierkegaard's note.] There is no need to hurry. We can take our time. One can sometimes fail to reach one's goal by going slowly, but too much haste can also sometimes cause one to go right past it. We will converse a bit on this subject as the Greeks would. Suppose there were a child who had got a little money and could now with this [225] money buy, for example, either a good book or a toy, because they were the same price. If he buys the toy, can he then for the same money buy the book? By no means, because the money has been spent. He could perhaps go to the bookstore and ask the proprietor whether he would be willing to take the toy in exchange for the book. Assume now that the proprietor answered: 'My dear child, your toy is worthless; it is true that back when you still had the money you could just as well have bought the book as the toy; but this is the peculiar thing with toys, once you have bought them, they lose all value.' Would not the child think: that is very strange. There was also a time when a person could have purchased either freedom or bondage for the same price, and this price was the soul's free choice and the choice's surrender. He chose bondage; but if he would come to the god again and ask whether he could not exchange it, would not the answer be: 'There was undeniably a time when you could have bought whichever you chose, but the strange thing about bondage is that, once one has bought it, it has no value even if it was originally very expensive.' Would not such a person say: that is very strange. What if two opposing armies faced each other and a knight came along whom both armies endeavoured to enlist, but he joined the side that lost and was taken prisoner. Suppose he was then presented as a prisoner before the victor and was foolish enough to offer his services under the same conditions he was earlier offered. Would not the victor say to him: 'Oh dear, now you are my prisoner; there was definitely a time when you could have chosen otherwise, but now everything has changed.' Was that not strange! If that were not the relationship, then the moment would not have decisive significance, then the child would fundamentally have bought the book, but simply have been ignorant of the fact, mistakenly thinking he had bought the toy; then the prisoner would fundamentally have fought on the other side, but overlooked, because of fog, would fundamentally have been on the side whose prisoner he now imagined himself to be.— 'The dissolute person and the virtuous person do not have control over their moral character. They did initially, however, have the power to become the one or the other, just as he who has thrown a stone initially had the power to throw it, even though, once it is thrown, he cannot recall it' (Aristotle);* otherwise, throwing would be an illusion and the thrower would retain the stone in his hand despite all his attempts to throw it, because, like the sceptic's arrow, it would not fly.

was just such significance we wanted to assume as our hypothesis. Therefore, according to our hypothesis, he is unable to free himself. (And this is how it truly is; because he uses freedom's force in the service of bondage in that he is freely in it, and thus the united forces [226] of bondage grow, making him a slave of sin).— What should we now call such a teacher who gives him the condition again and, with it, the truth? Let us call him a saviour, because he liberates the learner from his bondage, saves him from himself; a deliverer, because he delivers from bondage one who had bound himself, and no one is so terribly bound, and no bondage so impossible to escape, as that in which the individual places himself! And yet we still have not said enough, because the learner is guilty of having chosen bondage, and this teacher who gives him the condition and the truth is then himself an atonement that removes the wrath that lay over the guilty one.

Such a teacher the learner will never be able to forget; because in that same moment he would sink back into himself again, like the one who had once had the condition, by forgetting there was a God, sank into bondage. If they met each other in another life, this teacher would again be able to give the condition to him who had not received it. But one who had once received it would be a stranger to him. The condition was something entrusted, for which the receiver would always be required to give an account. But such a teacher, what shall we call him? A teacher can certainly assess whether a pupil makes progress, but he cannot judge him, because he must be Socratic enough to see that he cannot give the pupil what is essential. This teacher is thus not really a teacher, but a judge. Even when the learner has thoroughly appropriated the condition and immersed himself in the truth, he can never forget the teacher, or let him vanish Socratically, which is, however, much more profound than all premature pettiness and illusory enthusiasm, yes, is the highest, if the other is not the truth.

And now the moment. Such a moment is unique. It is, of course, brief and temporal, as moments are, ephemeral, as moments are, passed, as moments are, in the next moment, and yet it is decisive, and yet it is filled with eternity. Such a moment must have a special name. Let us call it: the fullness of time.*

[227]   (c) *The Disciple*

When the disciple is in a state of error (otherwise we go back to the Socratic), yet is a human being, and now receives the condition and the truth, he does not become a person for the first time, because he was a person; he becomes a different person, not in the facetious sense of becoming another of the same quality, but a qualitatively different person, or as we will call it, a new person.

To the extent that he was in error, he was constantly moving away from the truth; but in having received the condition in the moment, his course was altered, which is to say that he was turned around. Let us call this change *conversion*; though this word has not yet been used, it is precisely therefore that we chose it, in order to avoid confusion; because it is as if it had been created to refer to the change of which we speak.

To the extent that the disciple was in error through his own fault, this conversion cannot happen without being taken up in his consciousness, or without his being conscious of the fact that it was through his own fault that he was in error; and with this consciousness he takes leave of what went before. But how does one take leave without sadness? His sadness, however, is over the fact that he had remained for so long in the earlier state. Let us call such sadness *repentance*; because what else is repentance, but that which certainly sees what lies behind a person, yet in such a way that precisely this act hastens his course to what lies before him!

To the extent that the disciple was in error and now receives the truth as well as the condition for understanding it, a change takes place in him that is like the transition from not being to being. But this transition from not being to being is precisely that of birth. He who exists already can hardly be born, and yet he is born. Let us call this transition *rebirth*, with which he comes into the world again just as with birth, an individual human being, who knows nothing of the world into which he is born, whether it is populated, whether there are other people in it; because while baptism is certainly possible *en masse*, one is never reborn *en masse*. Just as he who, through Socratic midwifery, gave birth to himself, forgot everything else in the world, and in a deeper sense was not beholden to anyone, he who is born [228] again owes nothing to any other human being, but everything to this divine teacher, and just as the former forgot the whole world in relation to himself, he forgets himself in relation to this teacher.

If *the moment* is to have decisive significance, and without this we would speak only Socratically, no matter what we said, even if we used many special and unique expressions, even if we without understanding ourselves thought that we had gone much further than this simple wise man, who uncompromisingly distinguished between God, other human beings and himself, more uncompromisingly than Minos, Aeachus, and Rhadamanthus;*—the break has been made, and the person cannot go back and will not enjoy remembering what reminiscence will cause him to remember; even less will he be able through his own power once again to pull God over to his side.

But is that which has been developed here conceivable? We will not be hasty in answering. It is not simply the person who through the protracted nature of his deliberations on a subject never got around to answering it, but also the person who displayed marvellous speed in answering, but not the desired slowness in considering the difficulties before he explained them, who fails to provide an answer. Before we reply, we must ask who it is who should answer the question. To be born, is that conceivable? Yes, why not; but to whom is it conceivable, one who has been born or one who has not been born? The latter is preposterous and could not have occurred to anyone, because he who has been born could never get such an idea. When he who has been born thinks of himself as having been born, he thinks of this transition from not being to being. This must also be the case with respect to rebirth. Or does it make the situation more difficult that the non-being that precedes rebirth contains more being than the non-being that precedes birth? But who can conceive of this? It must be he who is reborn, because it would be preposterous for one who had not been reborn to think it, and would it not be laughable that such a thing could occur to him?

If a person is originally in possession of the condition for under- [229] standing the truth, then he thinks there is a God, in that he exists himself. If he is in error, he may think this about himself, but recollection could not help him to think anything else. If he is to progress beyond this, *the moment* must decide (even if it were already active in allowing him to see that he was in error). If he does not understand this, he should be referred to Socrates; even if, in his opinion, he has progressed far beyond Socrates; he has done this wise man a great disservice, just as those did who were so provoked by him, when he deprived them of some stupidity or other (ἐπειδάν τινα λῆρον αὐτῶν ἀφαιρῶμαι), that they actually wanted to bite him (cf. *Theaetetus*, 151c–d). A person becomes conscious in *the moment*, that he was born, because his prior state, to which he must not cling, was precisely one of non-being. He becomes conscious in *the moment* of being born again, because his prior state was one of non-being. If in either case his prior state had been that he did exist, then the moment would not have received decisive significance for him in the way described above. While Greek pathos is concentrated on recollection, the pathos of our project is concentrated on the moment, and no wonder, or is it not a highly pathos-filled thing, to come to be from not having been?

*   *
*

This is my project! But perhaps someone will say:

'That is the most laughable of all projects, or more correctly, you are the most laughable of all schemers, because even though one hypothesizes something foolish, there will always remain the truth that it was he himself who hypothesized it. But you on the other hand are behaving like a tramp who charges money to show people an area that anyone can see. You are like the man who exhibits for a fee a ram in the afternoon that anyone could see for free in the morning grazing in an open field.'

'Perhaps this is the case, I hide myself in shame. But assume I were so foolish, allow me to make amends with a new project. Gunpowder was invented hundreds of years ago; it would therefore be foolish for [230] me to pretend I had invented it; but was it also foolish that I assumed that someone had invented it? I am going to be so polite now as to assume that you have come up with my project; you cannot require more courtesy than that. Or if you deny that you have come up with it, will you then also deny that anyone has come up with it, that is, any human being? In that case I am as close to having come up with it as is anyone else. So you are not really angry with me because I am laying claim to something that belongs to another. You are angry with me because I am claiming responsibility for something that is not due to any human being, and you are just as angry when I falsely ascribe the authorship to you. Is this not strange, that there is such a thing about which everyone who knows it knows also that he has not invented it, so this "go to the next house"* never ends, would never end, even if one went to everyone. This peculiarity is extremely fascinating to me, because it both tests and proves the correctness of the hypothesis. It would be preposterous to demand of a person that he should by himself discover that he did not exist. But this transition is precisely that of being born again from not being to being. It makes no difference if he understands this retrospectively. Just because one knows how to use gunpowder, can break it down into its constituent elements, does not mean that one has invented it. So you can be angry with me, or with any other person who would purport to have come up with this. You need not, however, be angry with the thought itself.'

CHAPTER II

THE GOD AS TEACHER AND SAVIOUR
(A LYRICAL ESSAY)

Let us consider for a moment Socrates, who was also a teacher. He was born into specific circumstances, was educated within the culture to which he belonged, and when he reached maturity and sensed an inner stirring and call, he began in his way to teach others. After living for some time as Socrates, he appeared, when the time seemed right to him, as Socrates the teacher. He was himself influenced by circumstances and influenced them in turn. In [231] that he completed his task, he satisfied to the same extent both the demand within himself and the demand others could make on him. Understood in this way, and this is precisely the Socratic understanding, the teacher lies in a reciprocal situation, in that life and its circumstances are the occasion for him to become a teacher, and he again the occasion for others to learn something. His situation is consistently just as autopathetic* as it is sympathetic. This is also how Socrates understood it, which is why he would accept neither accolades, nor honorary posts, nor money for his instruction. He judged as incorruptibly as one deceased. O rare contentment, rare in our time when monetary awards and laurel-wreaths cannot be too large or too spectacular a compensation for the magnificence of teaching, but when worldly riches and laurels are precisely the compensation for teaching because they are worth just as little. Our age is positive and understands the positive. Socrates, on the other hand, lacked the positive. But it may well have been this lack that explained his narrow-mindedness, the foundation of which was surely his zeal in relation to what is specifically human, as well as a self-discipline practised with the same envy of the divine with which he disciplined others, and through which he loved the divine. Between one human being and another, this is the highest; the disciple is the occasion for the teacher to understand himself, the teacher the occasion for the disciple to understand himself. The teacher leaves at his death no claim upon the disciple's soul, just as the disciple cannot claim that the teacher owes him anything. And if I were as sentimental as Plato, if my heart pounded as violently as Alcibiades',* more violently than that of the Corybantic mystic,* when I listened to Socrates, and if the passion of my admiration for him could be stilled only by embracing this glorious man, Socrates would surely smile at me and say: 'Oh dear, you are a deceitful lover, because you want to deify me, proclaim my wisdom, and then you would be the one who had best understood me, he from whose admiring embrace I would not be able to free myself. Are you not a seducer?' And if I did not want to understand him, then his cold irony would cause me to despair when he would try to explain to me that he owed me just as much as I owed him. O rare rectitude that defrauds no one, not even him who would invest his happiness in being deceived, rare in our age where [232] everyone goes beyond Socrates in his self-estimation, in benefiting his disciple, in being sensitive in public, and in delighting in admiration's warm embrace! O rare fidelity that seduces no one, not even him who employs all the arts of seduction to be seduced!

But the god does not need any disciple in order to understand himself, and no occasion could be the occasion for him in such a way that there would be as much in the occasion as in the decision. What can then move him to appear? He must move himself, and thus continue to be as Aristotle says of him: ἀκίνητος πάντα κινεῖ.[1] But if he moves himself, no need moves him, as if he could not himself endure the silence but must break it by speaking. But if he moves himself, not because of a need, what is it that could move him, what else but love? For love does not satisfy itself through something external, but through something internal. His resolution, which does not stand

---

[1] Unmoved, he moves everything.

in a reciprocal relation to the occasion, must be from eternity even if, realized in time, it becomes precisely *the moment*; because where the occasion and the occasioned correspond to each other, in the same way as the answer in the wilderness to the cry, the moment does not appear, but is swallowed up by the eternity of recollection. The moment appears precisely in the relation between the eternal resolution and the incommensurable occasion. If the situation is not like this, then we return to the Socratic and get neither the god, nor the eternal resolution, nor the moment.

The god's eternal resolution must stem from love. But just as his love is the reason, so must love also be the goal, because it would be incoherent for the god to have a motive and a goal that did not correspond to it. The love must thus be for the learner, and the goal must be to win him, because only in love are the different made equal, only in equality or unity is there understanding, but without complete understanding the teacher is not the god, unless the reason is to be found in the learner who did not want what was made possible for him.

This love is, however, fundamentally unhappy because the parties are so unequal, and what would appear to be easy — that the god must be able to make himself understood — is not so easy if the difference is not to be destroyed.

We do not want to be hasty here. If it seems to anyone that we waste time instead of coming to some sort of resolution, we can comfort ourselves with the realization that it does not necessarily follow from this that our efforts have been for nothing. There is much talk in the world of unhappy love. Everyone knows what these words mean: that the lovers cannot be united. The reasons — well, there can be many reasons. There is another type of unhappy love, however, about which we speak and to which there is no perfect analogy among earthly relationships, though we can, if we allow ourselves to speak loosely for a moment, imagine in an earthly context. The unhappiness of this love does not lie in the fact that the lovers cannot be united, but in that they cannot understand each other. And this grief is infinitely greater than that of which people normally speak, because it aims at the heart of love and injures for an eternity, unlike the other, which touches only the external and the temporal. For the high-minded, in fact, that the lovers cannot be united in time is almost a matter of sport. But this infinitely more profound grief

[233]

belongs essentially to the superior one, because only he understands the misunderstanding; belongs essentially only to the god, because no human relationship can provide a valid analogy, even though we will point to one here in order to arouse the disposition to understand the divine.

Suppose there was a king who loved a peasant girl. But the reader has perhaps already lost patience when he hears that the beginning is like that of a fairy-tale and not at all systematic. Yes, the learned Polos found it tedious that Socrates constantly spoke only of food and drink and physicians and other such inconsequential things that Polos thought unworthy of discussion (see *Gorgias**). But did not Socrates have one advantage, however, in the fact that he, himself, and everyone else from childhood on was in possession of the required foreknowledge, and would it not be desirable, though far beyond my abilities, for me to confine my considerations to food and drink rather than be forced to include kings, whose thoughts are not always like everyone else's, if they are actually regal? But perhaps I may be forgiven, I who am only a poet who, mindful of Themistocles' lovely words,* would roll out the carpet of the discourse, so that its workmanship would not be hidden by being rolled up.

Suppose there were a king who loved a peasant girl. The king's heart was not polluted with the wisdom, which is proclaimed loudly enough, was unacquainted with the difficulties the understanding discovers in order to trap the heart and which preoccupy poets and make their magic spells necessary. His decision to marry the girl was [234] easy to carry out; because every politician feared his wrath and dared not even to hint at anything that might arouse it, every foreign state trembled before his power and dared not fail to send ambassadors to the wedding with congratulations, and no cringing courtier grovelling in the dust dared to hurt him, lest his own head be crushed. So let the harp be tuned, let the poets' songs begin, let everything be festive while love celebrates its triumph; because love exults when it unites the equal, but it triumphs when it makes that which was unequal equal in love.

But then there awoke a concern in the king's soul — who would dream of such a thing except a king who thinks regally! He spoke to no one of his concern, because had he done this, every courtier would have said: 'Your Majesty, you are doing this girl a favour for which she will never, in her whole life, be able to thank you.'

But then the courtier would have awakened the king's wrath, so that he would have executed him for high treason against the beloved, and thus in another way he would have caused the king grief. Alone the king grappled with this sorrow in his heart: would the girl be happy, would she win the confidence never to remember what the king wished only to forget: that he was the king, and that she had been a peasant girl? Because if this did happen, if the memory awakened and, like a favoured rival, sometimes called her thoughts away from the king, if it tempted her into the seclusion of a secret grief, or if it occasionally passed through her soul as death over the grave; what then would be love's glory? Then she would have been happier if she had remained in obscurity, loved by an equal, content in a humble cottage, but confident in her love, cheerful early and late. What a rich surplus of sorrow there is here almost ripe, almost sinking under the weight of its fecundity, merely waiting for harvest, when the king's thoughts will thresh the kernels of concern from it. Because even if the girl were satisfied with becoming nothing, this could not satisfy the king, precisely because he loved her and because it was harder for him to be her benefactor than to lose her. If she could not understand him (because when we speak loosely about the human, we can assume an intellectual difference between them which would make understanding impossible), what deep sorrow slumbers in this unhappy love, who dares to awaken it? A human being need not endure such a thing, however, because we would refer him to Socrates, or to what in an even more beautiful sense is able to make the unequal equal.

If *the moment* is to have decisive significance (and without this we [235] revert to the Socratic, even if we think we are going beyond this), the learner is in error, is there through his own fault—and yet, he is the object of the god's love, the god who wants to be his teacher, whose concern is to effect equality. If this cannot be effected, then the love becomes unhappy and the instruction meaningless, because they would not be able to understand each other. One might think the god would not care about this, since he does not need the learner. One forgets though—or more correctly, one shows how far one is from understanding him—that the god loves the learner. And just as the regal sorrow of which we spoke can be found only in a regal soul, and the speech of the masses of humanity does not touch on it at all, so is all human language so marked by self-love that it has no intimation of such sorrow. The god thus reserved this sorrow, this unfathomable grief, for himself; he knows he can repel the learner, can do without him, that the learner is lost through his own fault, that he can let him sink— he knows how nearly impossible it is to keep up the learner's confidence without which understanding and equality are lost and the love unhappy. Anyone who does not have at least an intimation of this grief is a shabby soul of base coinage, bearing neither Caesar's nor God's image.

The task is thus set, and we will invite the poet, if he has not already been invited somewhere else, and if he is not like those who, along with the flute-players and other noise-makers, must be driven out of grief's house* in order that happiness can come in. The poet's task is to find a solution, a point of union where there is true understanding in love, where the god's concern has overcome its pain, because this is the unfathomable love which is not satisfied with what the object of love might in his foolishness rate as happiness.

A. The union may be brought about by an elevation. The god wants to draw the learner up to himself, to glorify him, to delight him with a millennial happiness (because a thousand years is as a day to him), allow him to forget the misunderstanding in the tumult of joy. Ah yes, the learner would be inclined to consider himself happy with [236] this. And was it not glorious, just like the lowly peasant girl, suddenly to have his fortune made by the fact that the god's eye had fallen on him, glorious to help him take it all vainly, deceived by his own heart! The noble king had, however, already seen the difficulty. He knew something about human nature and so understood that the girl was fundamentally deceived, which is the worst thing possible when one has oneself no intimation of it but is as if bewitched by the change of costume.

The union could be brought about by the god's showing himself to the learner, accepting his adoration, allowing the learner to forget himself in this. The king could have shown himself in this way, in all his splendour, to the peasant girl. He could have allowed the sun of his magnificence to rise above her humble cottage, to shine upon that spot where he showed himself to her, and allowed her to forget herself in adoring wonder. Alas, this might have satisfied the girl. It could not satisfy the king though, because he does not wish his own glorification, but the girl's. This was why his sorrow that she did not understand him was so heavy. Even heavier still, though, would be his sorrow at deceiving her. Simply giving his love an imperfect expression was in his eyes a deception, even if no one understood him, even if reproaches tried to injure his soul.

Love cannot be made happy in this way. The learner and the girl may appear to be happy, but the teacher and the king cannot be happy. They cannot be satisfied with an illusion. Thus the god delights in decorating the lily more gloriously than Solomon. But if we are to speak of an understanding, then the lily would be the victim of a painful illusion if it thought that it was beloved because of its decoration; and while it now stands undaunted in the field, playing with the wind, as carefree as a gust of wind, then it would sicken and lack the boldness even to lift its head. This was precisely the god's concern, because the lily's shoot is tender and easily broken. But if the moment is to have decisive significance, would his concern not be inexpressible?

There was a people with a profound understanding of the divine. They believed that to see God was fatal. —Who grasps the contradiction of this grief? That not to reveal oneself is precisely the death of love, and to reveal oneself is the death of the beloved! O, how the minds of human beings crave power and might, and how their thoughts eagerly seek these things, as if when they were achieved, everything would be made clear. They do not understand that there [237] is not simply joy in heaven, but also sorrow, the sorrow of having to deny the learner what he longs for with his whole soul and to have to deny him this precisely because he is the beloved.

B. The union must therefore be brought about in another way. We must remember Socrates again here, because what was his ignorance if not an expression of union with the learner through his love for the learner? But this union was also the truth, as we have seen. If, on the other hand, the moment is to have decisive significance, then this is not the truth; because the learner will owe the teacher everything. Just as, from the Socratic perspective, the teacher's love was only that of a deceiver if he allowed the disciple to continue to believe that he actually owed him something, rather than helping him to become self-sufficient, when the god wants to become a teacher, his love must not simply be assisting but procreative. He must, through his love, give birth to the learner, or as we have called him, the one reborn, with which expression we designate the transition from not being to being. The truth is thus that the learner owes him everything. But it is precisely this that makes understanding so difficult: that the learner becomes nothing and yet is not annihilated, that he owes the teacher everything and yet becomes confident, that he understands the truth and yet the truth liberates him, that he grasps the guilt of error and yet triumphs confidently in the truth. Between one human being and another, to assist is the highest. To give birth is reserved for the god whose love is *procreative*, not that procreative love of which Socrates was able to speak so beautifully at a certain banquet. That love does not designate the relation of the teacher to the disciple, but the relation of the autodidact to the beautiful, in that by looking beyond beauty in its scattered forms, he glimpses the beautiful itself and then gives birth to many beautiful and glorious speeches and thoughts, πολλοὺς καὶ καλοὺς λόγους καὶ μεγαλοπρεπεῖς τίκτει καὶ διανοήματα ἐν φιλοσοφίᾳ ἀφθόνῳ (*Symposium*, 210d).[1] Here it is a case of his giving birth to or bringing forth what he has already long carried about within himself (209c). He has the condition within himself and the appearance (the birth) is only a manifestation of what was already there. Thus the moment is once again, in this birth, instantly swallowed up by recollection. And he who is born knows that he also dies, and that he can less and less [238] be said to be born in that he is only more and more clearly reminded that he is. And he who again gives birth to expressions of the beautiful does not himself give birth to them, but allows the beautiful that is within him to give birth to them.

If the union is not to be brought about by an ascent, then it must be attempted through a descent. Let the learner be an x, this x must include the humblest, because was not Socrates himself indifferent to the company of the clever? How could the god then care about such things! In order for the union to be brought about, the god must become equal to such a one. He will thus show himself as equal to the most lowly. But the most lowly is precisely he who must serve others. Thus the god will reveal himself in the form of a *servant*. But this servant form is not something put on like the king's humble cloak, the loose flapping of which, precisely because it was put on, betrayed that he was the king. It is not like the light Socratic summer robe* which, despite being woven from nothing, is both concealing

---

[1] '[H]e will find in such contemplation the seed of the most fruitful discourse and the loftiest thought, and reap a golden harvest of philosophy.'*

and revealing; it is his true form. This is the unfathomable nature of love, not in fun, but in seriousness and truth to want to be equal to the beloved. And this is the omnipotence of the decisive love, to be able to do what neither the king nor Socrates was able to do and which was the reason that their assumed forms were really a kind of deception.

Look, there he is—the god. Where? There; can you not see him? He is the god and yet he has no place to lay his head,* and he dare not seek shelter with another person in order not to offend him. He is the god and yet he makes his way more cautiously than if an angel bore him, not in order to avoid stumbling, but in order to avoid trampling people in the dust if they should be offended by him. He is the god and yet his eye rests with concern on the human race, because the tender shoot of the individual can be crushed as quickly as that of a blade of grass. What a life, sheer love and sheer sorrow: to want to express the unity of love and yet not to be understood; to fear for everyone's damnation and yet to be truly able to save only a single soul; sheer sorrow, even while his days and hours are filled with the sorrows of the learner who trusts in him. Thus the god is on earth like unto the lowest through his omnipotent love. He knows the learner is in error—if he misunderstood, if he weakened and lost his boldness! O, to bear heaven and earth with an omnipotent [239] 'Let it be!' so that if it were absent for even the briefest time, everything would collapse. How easy that is compared to bearing the possibility of offending the race when one would become its saviour through love!

But the servant form was not a costume. The god must, therefore, suffer everything, endure everything, hunger in the desert, thirst in anguish, be forsaken in death, absolutely equal to the lowest—behold the man!* It is not the suffering of death that is his suffering, the whole of this life is a story of suffering, and it is love that suffers, love that gives everything, which is itself needy. Marvellous self-denial, even if the learner is the lowest, still he asks anxiously: Do you now really love me? Because he knows where the danger lies, and yet he knows that any easier way would be a deception even if the learner did not understand this.

Any other revelation would, for love, be a deception, because it would either first have had to undertake a transformation of the learner and hidden from him that this had been necessary (but love does not alter the beloved, rather it alters itself), or it would have had to allow him to remain blissfully ignorant of the fact that the whole understanding was an illusion. (This is the untruth of paganism.) Any other revelation would, according to the god's love, be a deception. And if I cried more tears than a repentant sinner, and if my tears were more precious than the many tears of the woman whose sins were forgiven,* and if I should find a humbler place than at his feet, and if I could sit there more humbly than a woman whose heart's only wish was to sit this way, and whether I loved him more honestly than a faithful servant, who loved him to the last drop of his blood; whether I was more pleasing to his eyes than the purest among women—if I entreated him to change his decision, to show himself in another form, to protect himself, then he would look at me and say: Man, what have you to do with me,* get thee behind me,* for you are Satan's even if you do not understand this yourself! Or if he just once stretched out his hand to order that something should come to pass, and I thought that I understood him better or loved him more, then I would see him weep also for me and hear him say: That you could thus be unfaithful to me, and in this way wound love. Do you then love only the omnipotent one who performs miracles, not the one who lowered himself to be equal to you?

[240] But the form of the servant was not a costume; therefore he must breathe his last breath in death and once again leave this earth. And if my sorrow were deeper than the mother's when the sword pierces her heart,* and if my situation were worse than that of a believer when he loses his faith, and if my wretchedness were more moving than that of one who crucifies his hope and is left with only the cross—if I would ask him to protect himself and remain, then I would see him grieved unto death, but also concerned for me, because this suffering was to benefit me; but his sorrow was that I could not understand him. O bitter cup, more bitter than wormwood is the violence of death for one who is mortal, how bitter is it then for one who is immortal! O sour drink, more sour than vinegar, to be refreshed through the misunderstanding of the beloved! O what comfort there is in the necessity of suffering when one is guilty. What comfort is there though to suffer innocently!

Thus the poet presents our hypothesis. For how could it occur to him, that the god would want to reveal himself in such a way as to produce the most horrible decision; how could it occur to him to want to play lightheartedly with the god's suffering, deceitfully dismissing love in order to make room for wrath?

And the learner, his suffering is not that of the teacher, but has he no share or part in this story of suffering? And yet it must be like this and it is love that occasions all this suffering, precisely because the god does not think of himself, but wants, because of love, to be equal to the lowest. When one plants an acorn in a clay pot, the pot bursts. When one pours new wine in old skins, they burst. What happens then when the god plants himself in a frail human form, if he does not become a new person and a new vessel! But this becoming, how arduous it is, how like a difficult birth! And the situation of the understanding, how precarious it is, poised at every moment at the edge of misunderstanding as the anxieties of guilt threaten the peace of love; how terrifying, because it is less terrifying to fall prostrate while the mountains tremble at the voice of the god, than to sit with him as with an equal, and yet it is precisely the god's desire to sit this way.

*   *
*

If someone were to say: 'What you are making up here is the shab- [241] biest plagiarism ever produced, in that it is no more nor less than what every child knows', then I would have to shamefacedly hear that I was a liar. But why the shabbiest? Every writer who steals, steals from another writer; thus we are all equally shabby; my theft is perhaps less harmful in that it is more easily discovered. But who is the author? If I were so polite as to consider you, you who judge me, as the author, you would again become angry. Is there then no author when there is a story? That would be strange, like hearing a flute despite the fact that there was no flute-player. Is this story like a proverb, the author of which is unknown because it is as if the whole human race had written it? Was it perhaps therefore that you called my plagiarism the shabbiest, because I did not steal from some individual person, but robbed the race and arrogantly, despite the fact that I am only an individual person, and a shabby thief at that, pretended to be the whole race? Is the situation such that if I went around to everyone and everyone knew the story, but knew in addition that he had not written it, that I could conclude that the whole race had written it? Would that not be strange? If the whole race had written it, this should be expressed by saying that each and every person was equally close to having written it. Does this not seem to you a difficult situation we find ourselves in, given that it appeared in the beginning that the whole thing could be easily dismissed with your angry accusation that my story was a shabby plagiarism and with my shame at having to hear it? So perhaps it is not merely a story after all, or in any case neither the product of an individual human being, nor of the whole race. Now I understand you. This was why you called my conduct the shabbiest plagiarism, not because I stole from some individual, and not because I stole from the whole race, but because I robbed the deity, or hid him away and, despite the fact that I was only an individual person — worse, a shabby thief — blasphemously pretended to be God. O friend, now I understand you completely and understand that your anger is justified. But now my soul is gripped by a new wonder, is filled with adoration, because it would also be strange if it had been a human [242] story. It can easily occur to a person to present himself in likeness to God, or God in likeness to himself, but not to come up with the idea that it had occurred to God to present Himself in likeness to a human being; because if God allowed Himself no distinguishing mark, how could it occur to a person that the blessed God needed him? This would be the vilest thought, or more correctly, so vile a thought that it could not have occurred to him even if, after the god had confided this to him, he adoringly said: 'This thought did not originate in my heart', and found that it was the most fantastically beautiful thought. And is not the whole thing miraculous, and is this word not again a happy word of warning on my lips because do we not stand here, as I said we would, and as you yourself also involuntarily said: at *the miracle*? And in that we now thus both stand here at the miracle, the solemn silence of which cannot be disturbed by human squabbling about what is mine or yours, whose awe-inspiring speech infinitely drowns out all human disagreements about mine and yours. So you will forgive me the strange delusion that I came up with this story. That was a mistake. The story is so different from every human story that it is not a story at all, but the *miracle*.

CHAPTER III

THE ABSOLUTE PARADOX

(A METAPHYSICAL CAPRICE)

Despite the fact that Socrates used all his powers in an effort to understand human nature and to know himself, despite the fact that he has been lauded through the centuries as the person who best understood human nature, he claimed the reason he was disinclined to contemplate the natures of creatures such as Pegasus and Gorgon was that he was not quite certain whether he (the expert on human nature) was a stranger monster than Typhon* or a gentler and simpler being, that by nature participated in something divine (cf. *Phaedrus*, 229e). This appears to be a paradox. One should not think ill though of paradoxes, because the paradox is the passion of thought, and a thinker without a paradox is like a lover without passion: a poor model. But the highest [243] power of every passion is always to will its own annihilation. Thus it is also the highest passion of the understanding to desire an obstacle, despite the fact that the obstacle in one way or another may be its downfall. This is the highest paradox of thought, to want to discover something it cannot think. This passion of thought is fundamentally present everywhere in thought, also in the thought of the individual, to the extent that in thinking he transcends himself. One fails to discover this because of habit. In a like manner scientists have revealed that walking is a progressive falling. But a fine and upstanding gentleman who walks every morning to the office and home again at noon presumably believes this is an exaggeration, because his progress is clearly mediation. How could it possibly occur to him that he was constantly falling, he who follows so resolutely his own nose?

Just to get started though, let us make a bold proposition. Let us assume we know what a human being is.[1] With this we have the

---

[1] [Kierkegaard's note.] It may seem laughable to want to give this proposition the dubious form of an 'assumption', since this is something everyone in our theocentric time knows. Would that it were so. Democritus* knew this as well, because he defined human beings as follows: 'Human beings are what we all know', and then continued, 'because we all know what a dog, a horse, a plant, etc., is, but none of these things is a human being.' We do not want to be so malicious as, nor can we be so witty as, Sextus Empiricus, who famously concludes from this that a human being is a dog, since a human being is what we all know and since we all know what a dog is, ergo — We do not want to be so malicious. But if only the issue were seriously examined in our time, so one did not have to become a little anxious at the thought of poor Socrates and his dilemma!

criterion of truth sought throughout all of ancient philosophy, *sought*, or *despaired of*, or *postulated*, or *utilized*. And is this not strange that this is the situation with the Greeks? Is this not a kind of attack on the meaning of the Greeks, an epigram they have written on themselves and which serves them better than the sometimes rambling treatises written on them? Thus the proposition is well worth assum-

[244] ing, and also for another reason, since we already in the two preceding chapters have explained it, while someone, if he would explain Socrates otherwise than we have done, should be careful not to fall into the trap set by the later and more mature Greek scepticism. If the Socratic theory of recollection and the view that every individual person is the prototypical human being is not accepted, then Sextus Empiricus* stands ready to make the transition that lies in 'to learn' not simply difficult, but impossible. And Protagoras begins where he left off, that man is the measure of all things,* understood in such a way that he is the measure of others, which is not at all the Socratic view that the individual is the measure of himself, neither more nor less.

So we know then what a human being is, and this wisdom, the worth of which I least of all would denigrate, can become continually richer and more meaningful and thus also the truth. But there the understanding halts—just as did Socrates,* because now the paradoxical passion of the understanding that wills an obstacle and wills, without really understanding itself, its own annihilation, is awakened. Thus it is also with the paradox of romantic love. The individual lives unperturbed, sufficient unto himself, but then the paradox of self-love is awakened through the love of another, the one desired. (Self-love lies at the foundation of, or goes to the foundation of, all love, which is why, if we would like to think of a religion of love, it would be just as epigrammatic as true that it would have to assume a condition and accept it as given: that a person loves himself in order to be able to demand that he love the neighbour as himself.)* The lover is changed by this paradox of love, so that he hardly recognizes himself (this is witnessed to by poets, who are love's spokesmen, as well as by lovers themselves, in that they allow poets to take only the floor from them, not their passion). So this imperceptibly sensed paradox of the understanding affects a person and his self-knowledge, so he who believed he knew himself is no longer certain whether he is a stranger creature than Typhon, or whether there is not in his being a milder and more divine part (σκοπῶ οὐ ταῦτα, ἀλλὰ ἐμαυτόν, εἴτε τι θηρίον ὤν τυγχάνω πολυπλοκώτερον καὶ μᾶλλον ἐπιτεθυμμένον, εἴτε ἡμερώτερόν τε καὶ ἁπλούστερόν ζον, θείας τινὸς καὶ ἀτύφου μοίρας φύσει μετέχον,[1] *Phaedrus*, 230a).

But what is this unknown thing against which the understanding, in its paradoxical passion, collides, and which, in addition, disturbs even a person's self-knowledge? It is the unknown. But this cannot [245] be another person, to the extent that he knows what a person is, nor can it be any other thing he knows. So let us call this unknown *God*. This is just a name we give it. It can hardly occur to the understanding to want to prove that this unknown thing (God) exists. For if God does not exist, then it would be impossible to prove he did. But if he does exist, then it is foolish to try to prove it, in that I have assumed this existence is not doubtful the instant the proof begins, since an assumption, to the extent that it is an assumption, cannot be doubtful, otherwise I could not get started, understanding, as I would, that the whole thing would be impossible if there were no God. If, on the other hand what I intend by the expression 'prove God's existence' is to prove that the unknown, which exists, is God, then my expression is unfortunate, because then I would be proving nothing, least of all that something existed. I would merely be developing the content of a concept. It is generally very difficult to prove that something exists. And what is worse for those brave souls who nevertheless dare to undertake such a project, the difficulty is not one that will confer celebrity on those who preoccupy themselves with it. The whole proof is constantly in the process of becoming something completely other than a proof. It becomes merely a further development of the conclusion I drew from my assumption that the thing about which the question is asked exists. Thus my reasoning is never to the conclusion that something exists, but from the assumption that something exists, whether I am concerned with the tangible world of sense experience or the world of thought. Thus I do not prove that a stone exists, but that something that exists is a stone. A court does not prove that a thief exists, but proves that the accused, who certainly exists, is a thief. Whether he will call existence an

---

[1] [Kierkegaard's note.] I don't bother about such things, but accept the current beliefs about them, and direct my enquiries to myself, to discover whether I am really a more complex creature and more puffed up with pride than Typhon, or a simpler, gentler being whom heaven has blessed with a quiet un-Typhonic nature.

accessorium or an eternal *prius*,[1] it can never be proved. We are going to take our time here. There is, for us, certainly no reason to hurry, as there is for those who out of concern for themselves, or for God, or for something else, rush to get the proof that it exists. When such is the case, then there is certainly reason to be in a hurry, especially if the one concerned has rendered a sufficient account of the danger that he himself, or that of which we speak, did not exist before he got the proof and did not secretly nourish the thought that it did fundamentally exist independently of whether he proved it.

It would be strange if one of Napoleon's deeds were taken as proof of his existence. His existence does indeed explain his deeds, but [246] the deeds cannot prove *his* existence unless I have already assumed the word *'his'* in such a way that I have assumed he exists. Napoleon is, however, only an individual, and to this extent there is no absolute relation between him and his deeds, thus another could also have done the same things. Perhaps this is the reason I cannot conclude existence from works. If I call the deeds Napoleon's deeds, then the proof is superfluous in that I have already mentioned him. If I ignore this, then I can never prove from the deeds that they are Napoleon's, but only (purely abstractly) prove that such deeds are those of a great general, etc. But there is an absolute relationship between God and His works. 'God' is not a name, but a concept. Perhaps this is the reason that His *essentia involvit existentiam*.[2,3] God's works are thus things only

---

[1] *accessorium* is 'an additional attribute'; a *prius* is a presupposition.

[2] Essence involves existence.

[3] [Kierkegaard's note.] Thus Spinoza, who by immersing himself in the concept of God wants to bring forth being from it by means of thought. But, it should be noted, not as an accidental characteristic, but as a determination of essence. This is the profundity of Spinoza, but let us see how he conducts himself. *In Principia philosophiae Cartesianae, Pars I Propositio VII, Lemma I*, he says: *'quo res sua natura perfectior est, eo majorem existentiam et magis necessariam involvit; et contra, quo magis necessariam existentiam res sua natura involvit, eo perfectior'* ('The more perfect a thing is by its own nature, the more necessary is the existence. Conversely, the more a thing by its own nature involves necessary existence, the more perfect it is'). Therefore, the more perfect, the more being, the more being, the more perfect. This is, however, a tautology. This is made even clearer in a note, *nota II*: *'quod hic non loquimur de pulchritudine et aliis perfectionibus, quas homines ex superstitione et ignorantia perfectiones vocare voluerunt. Sed per perfectionem intelligo tantum realitatem sive esse'* ('We are not speaking here of beauty and other "perfections", which out of superstition and ignorance men have thought fit to call perfections. By perfection I understand only reality or being'). He explains *perfectio* [perfection] by *realitas* [reality], *esse* [being]. Thus the more perfect the thing is, the more it is. But its perfection is that it has more *esse* in itself. That is, the more it is, the more is it. So much for the tautology. There is more. What is missing here is a distinction between factual being and ideal being.

God can do. Quite right, but which are God's works? The works by means of which I would prove His existence do not exist immediately, or is the wisdom in nature, His benevolence, the wisdom of governance, [247] obvious? Do we not encounter here the most terrible temptations to doubt, and is it not impossible ever to be rid of these temptations? One cannot prove God's existence by the order of things. If I tried, I would never finish, but would have to live *in suspenso*,[1] in case something so terrible should happen that my little proof would be ruined. That is, through which works do I prove it? Through the works considered abstractly—i.e. not as they appear immediately. But then it is not through the works that I prove it. I simply develop abstractly what I have assumed. My confidence in *this assumption* allows me to defy all objections, even those that have not yet been made. In that I begin, I have assumed ideality and assumed I will succeed in accomplishing it, but what is this other than that I have assumed God exists and it is really through confidence in Him that I begin?

And how does God's existence emerge from the proof? Is this really so straightforward? Is the situation here not the same as with the Cartesian dolls?* As soon as I let go of the doll, it stands on its [248] head. As soon as I let go of it, and I have to let go of it. Thus it is also with the proof; as long as I am engaged with the proof (i.e. so long as I am in the process of proving it), being does not appear, if for no other reason, than because I am in the process of proving it. As soon as I let go of the proof though, existence is there. But that

---

This essentially opaque use of language, to speak of more or less being, that is, differences of degree in being, becomes even more confusing when this distinction is not made. In plain Danish, Spinoza does indeed speak profoundly, but does not first consider the difficulty. In relation to factual being, any discussion of more or less being is mean- [247] ingless. A fly, when it exists, has just as much being as God. The simple remark I write here has, in relation to factual being, as much being as Spinoza's profundity, because in relation to factual being Hamlet's dialectic: 'to be or not to be', applies. Factual being is indifferent to all the different determinations of essence. Everything that is, participates without the least jealousy in being, and participates equally.* Abstractly it is quite correct that the situation is different. *But as soon as I speak abstractly about being, I no longer speak about being but about essence.* The highest ideality has necessity, therefore it is. But this being is its essence which precisely precludes it from becoming dialectical with respect to the determinations of factual being, because it is; neither can it be said in relation' to anything else to have more or less being. This was expressed in olden days, though admittedly imperfectly, as when God is possible he is also *eo ipso* necessary (Leibniz). Spinoza's claim is thus correct and the tautology in order. It is also clear, however, that he completely avoids the difficulty, because the difficulty is to get hold of factual being and to somehow dialectically insert God's ideality into factual being.

[1] In a perpetual state of suspense.

I let go, this is also something, that is my *Zuthat*.[1] Should this not also be taken into account, this little moment, however brief it may be? It does not need to be long, because it is a *leap*. However brief this moment is, whether it is right now, this instant, it must also be taken into account. Just in case one forgets this, I will take a moment to tell a little anecdote. Chrysippus* experimented with a sorites* to see if he could establish a qualitative break in its progressive or retrogressive operation. Carneades* could not get into his head, when a new quality actually appeared. Then Chrysippus said to him that when counting, he could simply pause for a moment, and then, and then one could better understand it. But Carneades answered: 'Be my guest, you should not trouble yourself for my sake. You may not only pause, you may lie down and go to sleep, it will not be of any more help. When you wake we will begin again where you left off. And there you have it. You can no more sleep something away than you can sleep yourself to something.'

He who wants, therefore, to prove God's existence (in a different sense than simply to illuminate the concept of God, and without the *reservatio finalis*,[2] that we have pointed out, that existence emerges from the proof by means of a leap),* he proves something else instead, something that perhaps does not always need a proof, and in any case never something better, because the fool says in his heart that there is no God;* but he who says in his heart, or to others: wait a minute and I will prove it — is he not a rare sage![3] If it is not, in the moment when he must begin the proof, undecided whether God exists, then he does not prove it; and if it is like this at the beginning, then he will never really be able to begin, partly out of fear that he [249] might not succeed, because God may not exist, and partly because he has nothing with which to begin.— In ancient times one was hardly preoccupied with such things. At least Socrates, who is said to have produced the physico-teleological proof for God's existence, did not concern himself with such things. He constantly assumed God existed and, operating on this assumption, endeavoured to permeate existence with the idea of purpose. If one had asked him why he conducted himself in this way, then he would surely have explained that he did not have the courage to venture upon such a voyage of

---

[1] My contribution.
[2] Final or ultimate reservation.
[3] [Kierkegaard's note.] What an excellent subject for a madcap comedy.

discovery without having the security behind him that God existed. On the basis of God's word he, so to speak, casts the net in order to capture the idea of purpose; because nature finds many subterfuges and ways to frighten in order to disturb the inquirer.

The paradoxical passion of the understanding is constantly running into this unknown, which certainly exists, but is also unknown, and to this extent, does not exist. The understanding cannot come any further than this, but its paradoxical character cannot help but bring it to this point and preoccupy itself with this limit, because to want to express its relation to this limit in such a way that the unknown does not exist will not work, because this claim involves a relation. But what is this unknown; because that it is God can mean only that it is the unknown? To claim that it is the unknown because one cannot know it, and if one could actually know it, could not express it, does not satisfy this passion, though it has correctly grasped the unknown as the limit, but the limit is precisely passion's anguish even if it is also its incitement. And yet it cannot come any further even if it endeavours to get a result *via negationis* or *via eminentia*.*[1]

What is this unknown then? It is the limit that is constantly reached, and to this extent when the determinations of movement are exchanged for those of rest, the different, the absolutely different. But it is the absolutely different for which one has no distinguishing mark. Defined as the absolutely different, it would appear to be on the way to being revealed, but this is not so, because absolute difference cannot even be thought; because the understanding cannot absolutely negate itself, but uses itself in order to do this and thus thinks this difference in its own terms, that it thinks via itself; it cannot go beyond itself absolutely and thus conceives this thing [250] which transcends itself by means of itself. If the unknown (God) does not simply remain the limit, then this thought of the different becomes confused with the many thoughts of the different. The unknown is thus a διασπορά,[2] and the understanding has a pleasant selection of what is at hand and what the imagination can come up with (the monstrous, the laughable, etc., etc.).

But this difference cannot be pinned down. Each time one tries to do this, what one has is fundamentally arbitrary, and deep down

---

[1] The way of negation (subtracting), the way of eminence (perfecting).
[2] A dispersion.

in the heart of piety lurks an insane and lunatic arbitrariness that knows that it has itself produced its God. So the difference cannot be pinned down, because there is no distinguishing mark. Then it happens with difference and likeness as it does with all dialectical oppositions, that they become identical. The difference upon which the understanding focuses confuses it so it does not know itself, and thus consistently confuses itself with the difference. Paganism was sufficiently rich with respect to fantastical inventions. In relation to the last assumption, which is the self-ironizing of the understanding, I will present only a couple of points and without respect to whether this assumption is historical or not. There exists then an individual, he looks like other people, grows up like other people, marries, has a trade, endeavours, as one ought, to be prepared for the future, because it can indeed be lovely to desire to live as the birds of the air, but it is not allowed and can end very tragically: either, if one can endure to such a point, with that one starves to death, or with that one lives off others. This individual is also God. How do I know this? I cannot know this, because then I would have to know God and the difference, but I do not know the difference because the understanding has made it like that with respect to which it was supposed to be different. Thus God becomes the most terrible deceiver, in that the understanding has deceived itself. The understanding has got God as close as possible, and yet He remains as far away as ever.

*   *
*

[251] Perhaps someone will say:

'You are a character, I am well aware of that, but you cannot believe that it would occur to me to preoccupy myself with such a caprice? It is so strange, or so laughable, that it has not occurred to anyone, and most of all, so preposterous, that I have to exclude everything else from my consciousness in order to hit on it.'

Indeed you must do this, but is it defensible to keep all the presuppositions *you* have in your consciousness, and then believe that you are thinking about your consciousness without any presuppositions? You do not deny the consistency of the position already detailed, that the understanding errs in defining the unknown as the different, and simply confuses difference with likeness? But it would appear that something else follows from this, namely that the individual, if he is truly to come to know something about the unknown (God), must come to know that it is different from himself, absolutely different. The understanding cannot come to know this by itself (because, as we have seen, this is self-contradictory). If it is to come to know this, it must come to know this through God, and if it comes to know this, it cannot understand this knowledge and thus cannot come to know it; because how should it understand the absolutely different? If this is not immediately clear, it becomes clearer when viewed from the perspective of its consequences; because if God is absolutely different from human beings, then human beings are also absolutely different from God. But how can the understanding grasp this? It would appear we have arrived at a paradox. One needs God simply in order to come to know that God is the different, and now comes to know that God is absolutely different from himself. But if God is absolutely different from human beings, this cannot have its basis in what human beings owe to God (for to this extent they are related), but in what they are themselves responsible for, or what they have themselves earned. What then is the difference? What else could it be but sin, since the difference, the absolute difference, is something human beings have themselves earned? We expressed this above by saying that the human being was in error, and was such through his own fault, and we said this partly in jest, but were in serious agreement that it was too much to ask of a person that he discover this by himself. Now we have again arrived at the same position. The man most well versed in a knowledge of human nature was at a loss with respect to himself when he came up against the unknown, he no longer knew whether he was a stranger monster than Typhon, or whether there was something divine in him. So what was he missing? [252] The consciousness of sin, which he certainly could not have taught anyone else, nor learned from anyone else, but only from the god — if the god wanted to be a teacher. But he did want this, at least according to our story, and wanted, in order to be this, to be equal to the most lowly human being so that even such a one as this could understand him. So the paradox becomes even more terrible, or the same paradox has a double character through which it shows itself to be the absolute negatively by emphasizing the absolute difference of sin, and positively by wanting to annul this difference through absolute likeness.

Can such a paradox be conceived? We are in no hurry here; when the dispute concerns how a question is to be answered, then the dispute is not like that on a race-track. Victory belongs to the accurate, not to the swift. The understanding cannot think it, could not hit upon it, and when it is asserted, cannot understand it, but senses only that it must be its ruin. To this extent, the understanding has much to object to in the paradox, and yet, on the other hand the paradoxical passion of the understanding is to will its own annihilation. But the downfall of the understanding is precisely what the paradox also wishes, and thus they have an understanding, but this understanding is present only in the moment of passion. Let us look at the analogy of romantic love, even if this is a somewhat imperfect image. Self-love lies at the foundation of love, but the height of its paradoxical passion is precisely to will its own downfall. This is also what love desires, and thus these two forces understand each other in the moment of passion, and this passion is precisely love. Why then should the lover not be able to grasp this, even if he who in self-love writhes in the face of romantic love can neither grasp it nor venture upon it because it would be his ruin? Thus it is with the passion of romantic love. Self-love has indeed been conquered. Despite this, however, it is not destroyed, but rather taken hostage, and is romantic love's *spolia opima*.[1] It can come to life again though, and this is the temptation of romantic love. Thus it is also with the relation between the paradox and the understanding, only this passion has another name, or more correctly: we must find another name for it.

ADDENDUM

[253]

OFFENCE AT THE PARADOX
(AN ACOUSTIC ILLUSION)

If the paradox and the understanding come together in the mutual understanding of their difference, then the encounter is happy like romantic love's understanding, happy in the passion to which we have not yet given a name, and will not give a name until later. If the encounter is not one of mutual understanding, then the relationship is unhappy, and this, dare I say it, unhappy love of this understanding (which, it should be noted, is only like the unhappy love that

---

[1] Spoils of war.

has its foundation in misunderstood self-love; the analogy will not stretch any further than that, because the power of chance is capable of nothing here) we could refer to more specifically as: *offence*.

All offence is fundamentally passive.[1] It is here as with that form of unhappy love just mentioned. Even when self-love (and does it not already seem a contradiction to say that the love of oneself is passive?) proclaims itself in foolhardy exploits, in astonishing deeds, it is passive, it is injured, and the pain of the injury produces an illusory expression of power which looks active, but can easily disappoint, especially since self-love wants to hide its passivity. Even then, when it tramples upon the object of love, even when it masochistically disciplines itself to a state of hardened indifference and martyrs itself in order to show its indifference, even then when it surrenders itself in triumphant delirium that it succeeded (this is the most deceptive form), even then it is passive. Thus it is also with offence; it can express itself however it will, even when it arrogantly celebrates the triumph of spiritlessness, it is suffering independently of whether the offended one sits crushed and stares almost like a beggar at the para- [254] dox, paralysed by his suffering, or whether he arms himself with derision and aims the arrow of wit as if from a distance — he is passive and is not at a distance; even if offence came and took the last crumb of comfort and joy from the offended one or made him strong — offence is still passive, it has wrestled with the stronger and the agility of its apparent strength is, with respect to the body, like that of one whose back is broken, which does indeed give a kind of suppleness.

We would do well, meanwhile, to distinguish between passive, or suffering, offence and active offence, without forgetting, however, that the passive form is always active to the extent that it cannot allow itself to be annihilated (because offence is always an act, not an event), and the active always so weak that it is unable to tear itself from the cross to which it is nailed, or to remove the arrow with which it has been injured.[2]

---

[1] [Kierkegaard's note.] Our language correctly refers to emotion as mental *suffering*, while we, through the mention of the word 'emotion', think more of the convulsive assurance that astonishes and then forgets that it is a form of passivity. Thus it is, for example with arrogance, defiance, etc.

[2] [Kierkegaard's note.] Language also shows how all offence is passive. One speaks of 'being offended', which could almost be expressed as a condition, but this is considered synonymous with the expression to 'take offence' (a synthesis of the active and the passive). In Greek it is σκανδαλίζεσθαι. This word comes from σκάνδαλον (shock, offence), and means also to take offence. The direction here is clear; it is

But precisely because offence is thus passive, the discovery, if one wishes to use such an expression, does not belong to the understanding, but to the paradox, because just as the truth is *index sui et falsi*,[1] so also is the paradox, and offence does not understand itself,[2] but is understood by the paradox. While offence, however it expresses itself, sounds from somewhere else, yes from the opposite corner, so it is the paradox that echoes in it, and this is an acoustic illusion. But [255] if the paradox is *index* and *judex sui et falsi*,[3] offence can be viewed as an indirect test of the correctness of the paradox; because offence is the erroneous calculation, is the consequence of error, which the paradox thrusts away. One who is offended does not speak with his own voice, but with the voice of the paradox, like one who mimics another, who does not produce anything himself, but merely copies another. The more deeply passionate is the expression of offence (whether active or passive), the more it reveals how much it owes to the paradox. Offence is not then an invention of the understanding, far from it. If this were the case then the understanding would also have to have been able to invent the paradox. No, offence *comes to be* through the paradox; if it *comes to be*, then once again we have the moment, upon which everything hinges. Let us recapitulate. If we do not assume the moment, then we go back to Socrates, and it was precisely from him we wanted to depart in order to discover something. If we posit the moment, then we get the paradox, because, in its most abbreviated form, the paradox could be called the moment. It is with the moment that the learner comes to be in error. The person who knew himself becomes confused about himself, and instead of self-knowledge he receives sin-consciousness, etc., because as soon as we assert the moment the rest follows of itself.

Considered psychologically, offence will manifest itself in a variety of forms according to whether it is more active or more passive. To present a sketch of this is not in the interest of our present concerns.

not offence that presents an obstacle, but offence that presumes an obstacle, that is, it is passive, even if it is active to the extent that it takes offence. The understanding has therefore not invented the offence, because the paradoxical affront that the isolated understanding develops discovers neither the paradox nor offence.

[1] A mark of itself and of the false.

[2] [Kierkegaard's note.] Thus the Socratic view that all sin is ignorance is correct; it does not truly understand itself. It does not follow from this, however, that it cannot will itself in error.

[3] A mark and criterion of itself and of the false.

On the other hand, it is important to remember that the offence is essentially a misunderstanding of *the moment*, because it is offence at the paradox, and the paradox is, again, the moment.

The dialectic of the moment is not difficult. From the Socratic perspective, it cannot be seen or distinguished. It does not exist, has not been, and will not come. The learner is therefore himself the truth and the moment of the occasion is simply a jest, like an extra title-sheet that is not really an essential part of the book; and the moment of decision is *foolishness*; because if it is assumed there is a decision (cf. the preceding), then the learner is in error, but it is precisely this that makes a beginning in the moment necessary. The expression of offence is that the moment is foolishness, the paradox is foolishness, which is really the claim of the paradox that the understanding is the absurd, but which resonates within, and thus appears to come from, the offence. Or the moment is constantly approaching, one *regards* it, and the moment is supposed to be *highly regarded*, but since the paradox has made the understanding into the absurd, the [256] estimation of the understanding means nothing.

Offence remains outside the paradox, and the reason is *quia absurdum*.[1] It is not the understanding, however, that has discovered this; on the contrary, the paradox has discovered it and now testifies against offence. The understanding says that the paradox is the absurd, but this is only a distorted imitation because the paradox is the paradox *quia absurdum*. Offence remains outside the paradox holding onto probability, while the paradox is the most improbable. It is, again, not the understanding that discovers this; it merely repeats what the paradox says, strange as it may seem, because the paradox says itself: comedies and novels and lies may be probable, but how should I be probable? What wonder then that the understanding remains outside the paradox, what wonder when the paradox is the wonder? The understanding has not discovered this; on the contrary, it was the paradox that showed the understanding to the wonder stool* and asked: Now what are you puzzled about? It is just as you say, and the strange thing is that you believe this is an objection; but the truth in the mouth of a hypocrite is dearer to me than in the mouth of an angel or apostle. When the understanding celebrates its superiority relative to the paradox, then it is most wretched and contemptible. So the understanding has not invented

---

[1] Because it is absurd.

this. The paradox is itself the inventor who turns over the splendour, including the splendid sins (*vitia splendida*). When the understanding wants to pity the paradox and facilitate for it an explanation, the paradox will not have anything to do with this, but finds it in order that the understanding does this; because do our philosophers not exist precisely in order to transform the preternatural into the ordinary and trivial? When the understanding cannot get the paradox into its head, the understanding has not created this problem, but the paradox has, which was paradoxical enough not to be ashamed to declare the understanding a thick-headed simpleton, who at his best says both yes and no to the same things, which is not good theology. Thus it is with offence. Everything it says about the paradox, it has learned from the paradox, even if, through the means of an acoustic illusion, it claims to have created the problem itself.

*   *
*

[257] But then perhaps someone will say:

'You are really boring, you are, because now we have the same story again, all the claims you put in the mouth of the paradox do not belong to you.'

'How could they belong to me when they belong to the paradox?'

'Spare me your sophistry. You know what I mean. These expressions do not belong to you. They are familiar to everyone and everyone knows to whom they belong.'

'Oh dear, what you say does not hurt me in the way you perhaps think it might. No, it makes me deliriously happy, because I will confess that I trembled when I wrote them down. I did not know myself, that I, who am normally anxious and fearful, would dare say such things. If, however, the claims are not mine, will you not say to whom they do belong?'

'Nothing is easier. The first is from Tertullian, the second from Hamann, the third from Hamann, the fourth from Lactantius and oft-quoted, the fifth is from one of Shakespeare's comedies, *All's Well that Ends Well*, Act II, scene 5, the sixth from Luther, the seventh is a comment of King Lear.* You can see I know what I am talking about and have caught you with the goods.'

'Oh, I see this, but will you answer me now whether all these men have not spoken of the relation between a paradox and offence, and will you now acknowledge that they were not offended, but were precisely those who held onto the paradox, and yet they speak as if they were offended and offence can find no expression that is more telling than this. Is it not strange that the paradox takes the bread, so to speak, from the mouth of offence and turns it into an unprofitable pursuit that earns nothing for all its troubles, but is just as ludicrous as if a purported critic absentmindedly defended an author rather than attacked him? Does this not seem to you to be the case? Offence does profit in one sense, however, in that it more clearly shows the difference; because in this happy passion to which we have not yet given a name, the difference is on good terms with the understanding. The difference is to be united in some third thing. But the difference was precisely that the understanding surrenders itself and the paradox offers itself (*halb zog sie ihn, halb sank er hin*[1]), and understanding lies in this happy passion, that will certainly get a name, and this is the least of the matter, even if my happiness had no name—if I am only happy, I demand nothing more.'

CHAPTER IV [258]

THE SITUATION OF THE CONTEMPORARY DISCIPLE

So the god has appeared as a teacher (because now we are going to continue with our story); he has assumed the form of a servant; because to send another in his place, one highly trusted, could not satisfy him, just as it could not satisfy the king to send the most trusted man in his kingdom in his place. The god has an additional reason though; because between one human being and another the Socratic relationship is the highest, the truest. If the god did not come himself, then everything would be Socratic, we would not have the moment and would miss the paradox. The god's servant form, however, is not something put on; it is not a virtual, but an actual body, and the god has, from that hour when by means of his omnipotent love's omnipotent decision he became a servant, caught himself so to speak in his decision and must now remain there

---

[1] She half dragged him, he half sank down.*

(if we are to speak foolishly) whether he wants to or not. He cannot betray himself. It is not possible for him, as it was for the king, suddenly to reveal that he is actually the king, which, however, is not a perfection of the king's (to have this possibility), but shows only his feebleness and the impotence of his decision, that he is unable actually to become what he wishes to become. While the god would not be able to send another in his place, he could certainly send another in advance who could arouse the attention of the learner. This predecessor cannot, of course, know anything of what it is the god will teach, because the god's presence is not incidental to his teaching, but essential, and the god's presence in human form, yes, in the form of a lowly servant, is precisely the teaching, and the god must himself provide the condition (see Chapter I), or the learner will not be able to understand it. Such a predecessor can arouse the attention of the learner, but cannot do more than this.

The god did not take on the form of a servant, however, to ridicule human beings. His intention cannot thus be to go through the world in such a way that not a single person ever came to know it. He does indeed want something about himself to be understood, though [259] every attempt to make himself understandable will not essentially help anyone who does not receive the condition, which is why he only reluctantly makes such attempts, and why they can also just as well alienate the learner as draw him closer. He debased himself and took the form of a servant, but he did not come in order to live as a servant in the service of a single man, taking care through his works that neither his master nor his fellow servants would come to know who he was. We dare not attribute such rage to the god. That he appeared as a servant will then mean only that he was a lowly person, a poor man who neither through fine clothes nor through any other earthly advantage distinguished himself from the mass of humanity, indistinguishable from other people, even for the countless legions of angels he left behind when he debased himself. But even if he were this lowly man, his concerns would not be those that people generally have. He would go about his life unconcerned about the distribution of worldly goods, as he who owns nothing and wishes to own nothing, unconcerned about where his next meal will come from, just as are the birds of the air, unconcerned about house or home, as he who has no sanctuary nor place to rest* and seeks none. Unconcerned about burying the dead,* without taking any notice of things that ordinarily attract people's attention, not bound to any woman, captivated by her in such a way that he desires to please her, but seeking only the disciple's love. This all certainly appears beautiful, but is it also proper? Does he not in this way elevate himself above what is normally required of people; because is it right that a person should be as carefree as a bird, even less concerned than the bird that flies here and there in search of food, when he ought to be concerned about tomorrow?* Yet we cannot present the god in any other way, but what does a story prove; is it permissible to roam about in this way, and to put up wherever one is when it draws toward evening? The question is thus, dare a human being express the same thing; because if not, then the god has not realized the human. Yes, if he is able, then he may also dare to do it; if he can so lose himself this way in the service of spirit that it never occurs to him to be concerned about food and drink if he is certain that their lack will not distract him, that need will not distract him from his task and cause him to regret that he did not understand the teachings of childhood before he desired to understand more. Yes, he certainly can dare this, and his greatness is more glorious than the serenity of the lily.*

The teacher's elevated absorption in his work will immediately [260] draw the attention of the crowd, and in this crowd will be the learner, and this learner will again be likely to belong to the lowest rung of society; because the wise and learned, they will first put to him subtle questions, invite him to colloquia, or require him to take an exam, and then secure for him a tenured position and thus a living.

So let us allow the god to go about the city in which he has appeared (which city it is does not matter); to proclaim his teaching is the single necessity of his existence, his food and drink, to teach people is his work and to care about the learner is his rest from his work; he has no friends and no relatives, the learner is brother and sister to him. It is thus easy to see why a rumour is quickly woven about him that catches the curious mob in its net. Wherever the teacher appears, a crowd flocks around him, curious to see, curious to hear, greedy to be able to tell others that they have seen and heard him. Is this curious mob the learner? Not at all. Or if one of the city's appointed teachers came in secret to the god in order to match wits with him in a debate, would he be the learner? Not at all; if the mob, or if this teacher, learns something, then, in the purely Socratic sense, the god is only the occasion.

The appearance of the god is the news of the day on the square, in the homes, in the city council, in the ruler's palace, is the occasion of much foolish and idle talk, perhaps also the occasion of more serious reflections—but for the learner, the news of the day is not the occasion for anything else, not even for him to engage seriously in Socratic self-examination, no, it is the eternal, the beginning of eternity. The news of the day is the beginning of eternity!—Even if the god had allowed himself to be born in an inn, wrapped in swaddling-clothes, laid in a cradle, the contradiction could not be greater than that eternity is swaddled in the news of the day, yes, as in the case we have been considering, its actual form, in such a way that *the moment* is actually decisive for eternity! If the god does not give the condition for understanding this, how would the learner hit [261] upon it? But we deduced earlier that the logic of *the moment* required that the god must give the condition himself and showed that the moment is the paradox, and that without this we come no further, but go back to Socrates.

We will be careful to make it clear here immediately that the question of a historical point of departure exists also for the contemporary disciple; because if we are not careful here, the difficulty that will appear at a later point (Chapter V), when the discussion concerns the situation of the person we will call 'the disciple at second hand', will be insurmountable. The contemporary also gets a historical point of departure for his eternal consciousness; because he is precisely contemporary with the historical, that does not want to be merely an occasion, and this historical will interest him in another sense than purely historically, will determine his eternal blessedness (yes, let us turn the logic around). If this is not so, then this teacher is not the god, but only a Socrates, who, if he does not behave like Socrates, is not even a Socrates.

How does the learner come to an understanding with this paradox, because we do not say that he should understand the paradox, but understand only that it is the paradox? We have already shown how this happens. It happens when the understanding and the paradox meet happily in the moment; when the understanding sets itself aside and the paradox gives itself; and this third thing, in which this happens (because it happens neither through the understanding, which is excused, nor through the paradox which offers itself—but *in* something), is the happy passion we will now give a name, even if the name is not really important to us. We will call it: *faith*. This passion must thus be the condition we discussed, that the paradox gives. Let us not forget that if the paradox does not give this condition, then the learner must himself possess it, but if he possesses it, then he is *eo ipso*[1] himself the truth and the moment is only the occasion for his learning this (see Chapter I).

The contemporary learner can easily get all relevant historical information. We should not forget, however, that with respect to the birth of the god, he will be in the same position as the disciple at second hand, and in such a way that if we were to insist on the absolute accuracy of the historical knowledge, there would be only one person who would be completely informed, namely the woman through whom he allowed himself to be born. The contemporary learner can easily be a historical eyewitness. The difficulty, however, is that to know a historical fact, yes to know them all with the credibility of an eyewitness, does not in any sense make the eyewitness [262] a disciple, which can be seen from the fact that this knowledge has no more than historical significance for him. It very quickly becomes apparent that the historical, in the concrete sense, is unimportant here. We can allow ignorance to come into play and to destroy one piece of historical knowledge after another; if only the moment remains as the point of departure for the eternal, the paradox will be there. If there were a contemporary who had reduced his sleep to the absolute minimum in order to follow this teacher, whom he followed more closely than the little fish that follows the shark, if he employed a hundred spies who observed this teacher everywhere he went and with whom he conferred every evening so that he knew everything about this teacher down to the smallest detail, knew what he had said, where he had been every hour of the day—because his enthusiasm had led him to consider the most insignificant thing as important—would such a person be a disciple? By no means. He could defend himself against any charge that his information was historically inaccurate, but he could do no more than this. If another had been concerned only with the instruction this teacher occasionally gave, if every enlightening word that issued from his mouth had been more important to him than his daily bread, if he employed a hundred others who wrote down every letter in order not to

---

[1] By that fact.

miss anything; if he studiously conferred with them in order to produce the most trustworthy presentation of these teachings, would he thus be a disciple? By no means, no more, in any case, than Plato was a disciple of Socrates. If there were a contemporary who had been living in a foreign land and did not come home until the teacher had only a day or two left to live, if this contemporary was detained on business so that he was not able even to see the teacher until he was on his deathbed, could this historical ignorance prevent him from becoming a disciple when the moment was for him the decision of eternity? For the first contemporary, the teacher's life was merely a historical event; for the second, it was an occasion for an increase in his self-knowledge, and he would thus be able to forget the teacher (see Chapter I); for in relation to an eternal knowledge of oneself, knowledge of the teacher is only accidental and historical knowledge, a matter for memory. So long as the eternal and the historical are independent of each other, the historical is only an occasion. If this eager learner, who did not, however, become a disciple, should speak often and loudly about what he owed to this teacher, so that his speeches seemed never to end and their richness was almost incalculable, if he were to become angry with us when we tried to explain that this teacher had been merely an occasion, then neither his speeches nor his anger would be worth our consideration, because they would both have the same foundation, that he, without having the courage even to understand, did not want to let this lack prevent him from the rashness of going further. By trumpeting, like him, such incoherent nonsense, one only deceives oneself and others to the extent that one convinces oneself and others that one actually has thoughts—since one owes these thoughts to another. But despite the fact that politeness does not normally cost money, this politeness is bought very dearly; because the enthusiastic thanks, which is perhaps also not without tears, and which may perhaps move others to tears, is a misunderstanding; because the thoughts of such a person he certainly does not owe to anyone else, nor does he owe the talk to anyone else. Alas, there have been many who have been so polite as to have felt themselves indebted to Socrates a great deal, and this despite the fact that they did not owe him anything! Because he who understands Socrates best understands precisely that he owes Socrates nothing, which is what Socrates most desires and what it is lovely to be able to desire; and he who believes he owes Socrates much, he can be pretty confident that Socrates would be only too glad to forgive this debt, he will be disappointed to find that he was supposed to have given the person in question any sort of working capital with which he could gain an advantage in this way. If the whole thing is not Socratic, however, as we have assumed, then the disciple owes the teacher *everything* (which it would be impossible to owe Socrates, since he, as he says himself, was not able to *give birth*), and this relationship cannot be expressed through fanciful and non-sensical trumpeting, but only in this happy passion we call faith, the object of which is the paradox; but paradox precisely unites contra-dictories, is the eternalizing of the historical and the historicizing of the eternal. Anyone who understands the paradox in any other way may retain the honour of having explained it, which honour is won through an unwillingness to be content with understanding it.

It is easy to see (if what is implied in the view that the understand-ing has been excused needs to be pointed out) that belief is not a kind of knowledge; because all knowledge is either knowledge of the eter-nal that excludes the temporal and the historical as unimportant, or [264] it is purely historical knowledge. No knowledge can have as its object the absurdity that the eternal is the historical. If I know the teach-ings of Spinoza, then in that moment in which I know them, I am not concerned with Spinoza, but with his teachings, while at another time I may be concerned with him historically. The disciple, on the other hand, relates, through faith, to the teacher in such a way that he is eternally concerned with his historical existence.

If we accept now that the situation is as we have assumed it to be (and without this assumption we return to the Socratic), that this teacher gives the learner the condition for understanding the truth, then the object of faith is not *the teaching*, but *the teacher*; because the Socratic lies precisely in this, that because the learner is himself the truth and has the condition for understanding this, he can push the teacher away; yes, the Socratic art and heroism lay precisely in helping people to do this. Faith must hold firmly onto the teacher. But in order for the teacher to be able to give the condition, he must be the god, and in order to ensure that the learner receives the condition, he must be a human being. This contradiction is the object of faith and the paradox, the moment. That God gave the condition to human beings once and for all is the eternal Socratic presupposition, which does not collide antagonistically with time, but is incommensurable with temporal determinations. The contradiction is that one receives the condition in the moment, which, since it is the condition for understanding the eternal truth, is *eo ipso* an eternal condition. If this is not the case, then what we have is Socratic recollection.

It is easy to see (if what is implied in the view that the understanding has been excused needs to be pointed out) that faith is not an act of will, because all human willing is efficacious only within the condition. Thus if I have the courage to will it, I can understand the Socratic—i.e. understand myself, because viewed Socratically, I possess the condition and now can will it. But if I do not possess the condition (and we assume this in order not to go back to the Socratic), then my willing is no help, though as soon as the condition is given, that which was valid Socratically is again valid.

The contemporary learner does now have one advantage for which, alas, the one who comes later, if he wishes to take a position here, will greatly envy him. The contemporary can go out and [265] observe this teacher—but does he dare believe his eyes? Yes, why not; but dare he also therefore believe that he is a disciple? By no means. If he believes his eyes, then he is precisely deceived, because the god cannot be known immediately. So can he then close his eyes? Of course; but if he does this, what advantage does he have from being contemporary? And if he closes his eyes, then he will certainly imagine the god. But if he can do this by himself, then he has the condition. And what he imagines will be a form that shows itself to the soul's inner eye. If he sees this, then the servant form will definitely disturb him as soon as he opens his eyes. Let us take this a step further. This teacher dies. All right, so now he is dead, what does the contemporary then do? Perhaps he drew a portrait of the teacher, perhaps even a whole mass of portraits that precisely represent every change in his appearance brought on by age or mood. When he views these pictures and thus convinces himself that this was how the teacher looked, does he dare then to believe his eyes? Yes, why not; but is he therefore a disciple? By no means. He can imagine the god in this way, but the god cannot be imagined. This was the reason he appeared in the form of a servant and yet this form was no deception, because if it were, then this moment would not be the moment, but something accidental, an appearance, that would vanish infinitely as the occasion in comparison with the eternal. And if the learner could picture the god himself, then he would have the condition, and would need only to be reminded to picture the god as he was able to imagine him, even if he was unaware of this. But if this is the case, then the reminder instantly vanishes as an atom of the eternal possibility that was in his soul, which now becomes actual, but which again had eternally presupposed itself as an actuality.

How then does the learner become a believer or disciple? When the understanding is excused and he receives the condition. When does he receive it? In the moment. What does this condition determine—his understanding of the eternal. But such a condition must be an eternal condition.— Thus in the moment he receives the eternal condition, and he knows that he has received it in the moment because otherwise he merely recollects that he has had it from eternity. He receives the condition in the moment and receives it from this teacher himself. Any fantastical trumpeting to [266] the effect that he, despite the fact that he did not get the condition from the teacher, was, however, shrewd enough to discover the god's disguise: that he could see this for himself because he felt so strange every time he saw this teacher; that there was something in his voice, in his demeanour, etc., etc.—that is meaningless twaddle with which one does not become a disciple but only mocks the god.[1] This form was no disguise, and when the god, through his omnipotent decision, which is like his love, wants to be equal to the lowest, then neither an innkeeper nor a professor of philosophy need imagine that he is shrewd enough to notice anything if the god himself does not give the condition. And when the god in servant form stretches out his omnipotent hand, then he who gapes with astonishment at this should not imagine that he is therefore a disciple because he is astonished, and because he can gather others together who are in turn astonished by his account. If the god does not himself give the condition, then the learner would have known from the beginning what the situation was with the god, even if he did not know that

---

[1] [Kierkegaard's note.] Any determination of the god's nature that would suggest he could be known immediately is definitely a milestone on the road of approximation, but one of regress rather than progress, in that it leads away from the paradox rather than toward it, all the way back past Socrates and Socratic ignorance. One must be careful that it does not go with him in the realm of spirit as it went with that wanderer who asked the Englishman whether the road he was on went to London and was told that it did, and yet who despite this never reached London because the Englishman had not mentioned that he needed to turn around, that he was headed away from London.

he knew it, and this alternative is not the Socratic but something infinitely inferior.

But for the disciple, the god's external appearance (not its detail) is not unimportant. It is what the disciple has seen and touched with his own hands. But the appearance is not important in the sense that he would cease to be a believer if he saw the teacher on the street one day and did not immediately recognize him, or even walked a way with him without becoming aware that it was him. But the disciple was given the condition to see this, and thus had the eyes of faith opened for him by the god. But to see this external form was terrible: to go [267] about with him as one of us and at every moment when faith was not present, to see only the servant form. When then the teacher dies, memory can certainly reproduce his appearance. One does not believe, however, on the basis of such a memory. But because he has received the condition from the teacher, he sees the god in the trustworthy image produced by memory. Thus it is with the disciple who knows that without the condition he would have seen nothing, because the first thing he understood was that he was himself in error.

But then is faith just as paradoxical as the paradox? Absolutely; how else could it have the paradox as its object and be happy in relation to it? Faith is itself a wonder, and everything that is true of the paradox is also true of faith. But within this wonder everything is once again Socratic, but in such a way that the wonder that the eternal condition was given in time is never removed. Everything is Socratic, because the relation between one contemporary and another, to the extent that they are both believers, is completely Socratic; the one owes the other nothing, but both owe everything to the god.

*   *

*

Someone might perhaps say:

'So does a contemporary have no advantage whatever from being contemporary? And yet one is so inclined, if we accept what you have assumed concerning the god's appearance, to celebrate the blessedness of the contemporary generation which saw and heard.'

'Of course one is inclined to do this, so inclined, I believe, that this generation also thought itself blessed. Should we assume this? Because it was otherwise not blessed, and our praise would express only that under other circumstances, by having behaved otherwise, they could have been blessed. But if this is so, then the praise, if we reflect on it more carefully, could take many forms. Yes, it could, in the end, become completely ambiguous. Suppose what we read about in old histories, that an emperor celebrated his wedding for eight days with such display as had never been seen before, so that even the air one breathed was perfumed, while the ear was treated to the constant strains of stringed instruments and song, to increase the enjoyment of many edible delicacies that were offered in unimaginable abundance. Day and night the festivities continued, for the night was as light as the day due to the illumination of the many torches. But whether one saw her by the light of day or by torchlight, the queen was more beautiful and gracious than any earthly woman, and the whole thing was more enchanting than the most ambitious [268] wish's even more ambitious fulfilment.—Let us assume that this has happened and that we must be content with the abstemious report that this took place. Why should we not consider the contemporaries lucky? The contemporaries, that is to say, those who saw and heard and touched with their hands. Because how otherwise would it help to be contemporary? The magnificence of the imperial wedding and its abundant pleasures could be immediately seen and partaken of, so if someone was contemporary in the strict sense, then he would certainly have seen and allowed his heart to rejoice. But if the magnificence was of another sort so that it could not be seen immediately, how would it help one to be contemporary; one would not therefore be contemporary with the magnificence. One certainly could not call such a contemporary lucky, or envy his eyes and ears, because he was not contemporary with, and saw and heard nothing of, the magnificence, which is not to be explained by the fact that he was denied the time or opportunity (understood in an immediate sense), but by something else, that he could lack even if his position had been highly advantageous in terms of opportunities to see and hear, and even if he had not failed (in an immediate sense) to take advantage of this. But what does this mean? Can one be contemporary without being contemporary; that is, can one be contemporary and yet, despite using (in an immediate sense) this advantage, be non-contemporary? What else can this mean, but that one cannot be immediately contemporary with such a teacher and event, so that the actual contemporary is not the actual contemporary by virtue of immediate contemporaneousness, but by virtue of something else. Thus, the contemporary can despite this be a non-contemporary. The actual contemporary is such not by virtue of immediate contemporaneousness, but by virtue of something else, ergo the non-contemporary (in an immediate sense) must also be able to be a contemporary by virtue of this other thing through which the contemporary becomes the actual contemporary. But this non-contemporary (in the immediate sense) is someone who comes later, thus someone who comes later must also be able to be an actual contemporary. Or is this to be a contemporary, and the contemporary we celebrate, he who can say: "I ate and drank with this teacher. And he taught in our streets. I saw him many times. He was an insignificant-looking man of humble origins and only a few people believed they had found something extraordinary in him, which I could not see although I was, so far as [269] being contemporary is concerned, certainly a contemporary despite what anyone says." Or is this what it means to be contemporary, is this the contemporary, to whom the god might say, if they should meet each other in another life, and he would appeal to the fact that he had been contemporary: "I do not know you"? And thus it truly was, just as truly as that this contemporary had not known the teacher, which only the believer (i.e. the one who was not immediately contemporary) could who had received the condition from the teacher himself and thus knew him as he was known.'

'Wait now for a moment, if you continue to speak this way I will not be able to get a word in, because you speak as if you were defending your dissertation; yes, you speak like a book, and what is unfortunate for you is that you speak like a very specific book, because you have now, either wittingly or unwittingly, mixed in some words that do not belong to you, and were not placed by you in the mouth of the speaker, but which are known to everyone, except that you use *singularis*[1] instead of *pluralis*.[2] The biblical passage (for it is a biblical passage) reads as follows: "We have eaten and drunk in thy presence, and thou hast taught in our streets — I know you not whence ye are."* Never mind. But do you not conclude too much when you conclude from the fact that this teacher says "I know you not", that this person was not contemporary with the teacher and did not know him? If the emperor, of whom you spoke, would answer someone who claimed

---

[1] The singular.   [2] The plural.

to have been present at his magnificent wedding: "I know you not",
did he thus show that the other had not been present?'

'The emperor in no way showed this. The most he showed was
that he was a fool who was not even, as Mithridates,* satisfied to
know the name of every soldier in his army, but who wants to know
all those who had been present, and through this acquaintance
determine whether a particular individual had been present or not.
The emperor could be known immediately. An individual could,
therefore, certainly have known the emperor even if the emperor had
not known him. But this teacher, of whom we speak, could not be
known immediately, but only after he had himself given the condition. He who received the condition received it from the god himself,
and thus this teacher must know everyone who knows him, and an
individual can know the teacher only by being known by him. Is this
not the case, and do you not see immediately what is implied by what
we have said? When the believer is the believer and knows the god by
having received the condition from the god himself, then the one who
comes later must, in absolutely the same sense, receives the condition [270]
from the god himself and cannot receive it second hand, because if he
should do this, then the second hand would have to be that of the god
himself, and in this case then we are not speaking at all of anything
second hand. But if the one who comes later receives the condition
from the god himself, then he is a contemporary, an actual contemporary, which only the believer is, and which every believer is.'

'I see this clearly now that you have explained it, and already
glimpse the far-reaching consequences, even though I am surprised
that I did not think of it myself and would give a lot to have been the
one to have discovered it.'

'I would give even more though to have fully understood it,
because I am more concerned with this than with who it was who
discovered it. But I have not yet entirely understood it, as I will soon
have the opportunity to show. I will then rely on your help, you who
have immediately understood the whole thing. If you will allow me,
however, I will give here what those who are learned in the law call a
brief that will summarize what I have up to this point developed and
understood. As I present this brief you must take care to assert your
right to voice objections, because I herewith summon you *sub poena*

praeclusi et perpetui silentii.[1] Immediate contemporaneousness can be only an occasion. (*a*) It can be an occasion for the acquisition of historical knowledge. In this respect, the contemporary at the imperial wedding is happier than the contemporary of the teacher, because the latter has only the opportunity to see the servant form, and at most one or two curious works, with respect to which he cannot be certain whether he should marvel at them or become indignant that he is being duped, because he certainly will not move the teacher to repeat them, the way a magician does and by which he gives the spectators the opportunity to better understand how the trick was done; or (*b*) it can be the occasion for the contemporary to focus Socratically on himself, through which focus contemporaneousness disappears as nothing in comparison with the eternal that he discovers in himself. (*c*) Finally (and this was our assumption in order not to return to the Socratic), it may become the occasion for the contemporary, as one who is in error, to receive the condition for understanding the truth from the god and thus to see his magnificence with the eyes of faith. Yes, blessed is such a contemporary! But such a contemporary is not an eyewitness (in an immediate sense), but as a believer is contemporary [271] in the autopsy of faith. But in this autopsy, all non-contemporaries (in the immediate sense) are, again, contemporary. If someone who comes later, perhaps moved by his own enthusiasm, wishes to be contemporary (in the immediate sense), he shows by this that he is a fraud, recognizable as the false Smerdis* by the fact that he has no ears — namely the ears of faith, even if he had ears as long as an ass's with which one, despite being contemporary (in an immediate sense) listens, but does not become contemporary. If someone who comes later persists in speaking nonsensically about the glory of being contemporary (in the immediate sense), and constantly wants to take off, then one should certainly let him go; but if you watch him, then you will easily see from his gait, as well as from the way he takes off, that he does not go toward the horror of the paradox, but bounds away like a dance-instructor to arrive in time for the royal wedding. And even if he gives his expedition a hallowed name and preaches community with others so that multitudes join the expedition, he will hardly discover the holy land (in an immediate sense), because it is found neither on maps nor on this earth. His journey is sport like the game: to follow another to grandmother's door.* Even if he

---

[1] Under penalty of not being able to give further testimony.

allows himself no rest, neither day nor night, and if he runs faster than a horse can gallop, or a man can lie, he merely runs with a limed branch,* mistaking himself for the bird-catcher; because if the birds will not come to him, to chase after them with a limed branch will not help at all. — In only one sense would I be tempted to praise the contemporary (in an immediate sense) as more fortunate than those who come later. If we assume that centuries have passed between this event and the life of one who comes later, then there will have been much talk among people concerning this event, so much nonsensical talk that the false and confusing rumours, which the contemporary (in the immediate sense) had to put up with, did not make the correct relationship nearly so difficult as the human probability of the echo of the centuries, that like the echo in some of our churches, does not simply want to gossip about faith, but to reduce it to gossip, which could not happen to the first generation, where faith must have appeared in its pristine form, with its opposite easy to distinguish from everything else.'

INTERLUDE

Is the past more necessary than the future?
or
Has the possible, by having become actual,
become more necessary than it was?

* * *

Dear reader! Let us assume now that this teacher has appeared, that he is dead and buried, and that some time passes between Chapters IV and V.

It can happen in a comedy that there will be a space of several years between two acts. In order to allude to the passing of these years, the orchestra will sometimes play a symphony, or something like that, in order to foreshorten the time by filling it up. I have in a similar fashion decided that I would like to fill up the time between Chapters IV and V with a consideration of the above question. How long the time should be is something you can decide for yourself, if you think it is suitable; however, both for the sake of seriousness and jest, we will assume that exactly eighteen hundred and forty-three years have passed. You can see that, for the sake of the illusion, I ought to give myself ample time, because eighteen hundred and forty-three years is an extraordinarily generous amount of time that could swiftly place me in a predicament opposite to that in which our philosophers find themselves, whom time generally allows no more than an intimation, as well as opposite to that in which historians find themselves, whom not the material but [273] time leaves in the lurch. If you find me a little long-winded, repeating the same thing, note well, 'on the same thing',* you must keep in mind that it is for the sake of the illusion, and then you will certainly forgive me my prolixity, and interpret it in a completely different and more satisfactory way than by supposing I allowed myself to believe this situation required consideration, even by you, because I had suspected you of not having completely understood yourself in this respect. And this despite the fact that I do not doubt at all that you have completely understood and approved the most recent philosophy, which like the most recent times, is thought to suffer from a strange absent-mindedness, that confuses the heading with the text; because what is so astonishing and so astonishingly great as the most recent philosophy and the most recent times—in headings?

*   *
*

§ 1

BECOMING

How is that which comes to be changed, or what is the change (κίνησις)[1] of becoming? All other change (ἀλλοίωσις)[2] presupposes that the thing that undergoes the change exists, even if the change is that of ceasing to exist. Such is not the case with becoming, because if the thing that comes into existence does not remain unchanged in the change of becoming, then the thing that comes into existence is not this becoming, but another, and the question is one of a μετάβασις εἰσ ἀλλὸ γένος,[3] in that the inquirer, in this case, will either see something different come to be, which would confuse the question for him, or he would not see the change correctly and thus not be in a position to ask the question. If a plan is altered in its realization, then it is not this plan that is realized. If, on the other hand, it is realized without alteration, then what is this change? This change is not in essence, but in being. It is a change from not being to being. But this non-being, which the thing that comes to be leaves behind must also have some sort of being, otherwise 'that which comes to be would not remain unchanged in this coming to be', unless it had not existed at all, in which case the change of becoming would again for another reason be absolutely different from every other change, [274] because it would not be a change at all, because every change always presupposes a something. But the sort of being that is nevertheless non-being is precisely possibility, and a being that is being is precisely actual being, or actuality, and the change of becoming is thus the transition from possibility to actuality.

---

[1] Motion, tumult, disturbance.
[2] Change, transformation.
[3] Transition from one kind, or genus, to another.

Can the necessary come to be? Becoming is a change, but the necessary can in no way be changed because it always relates to itself and relates to itself in the same way. All becoming is a *suffering*, and the necessary cannot suffer, cannot suffer the suffering of actuality, which is that the possible (not only the possibility that is excluded, but also the possibility that is accepted) shows itself to be nothing the instant it is actualized, because possibility is *annihilated* by actuality. Everything that comes to be shows precisely with this becoming that it was not necessary, because the only thing that cannot come to be is the necessary, because the necessary *is*.

Is necessity then not the unity of possibility and actuality? — What would that mean? Possibility and actuality are not different in essence, but in being. How could necessity be the unification of such a difference, necessity which is not a determination of being but of essence, in that it is the essence of the necessary to be? If that were the case, then possibility and actuality, by becoming necessity, would become absolutely different in essence from what they had been, which, as we saw, is not the case with any change, and would by becoming necessity, or the necessary, become the only thing that excludes becoming, which is as impossible as a self-contradiction. (The Aristotelian inference 'it is possible', 'it is possible that it is not', 'it is not possible' — the doctrine of true and false propositions (Epicurus*) is only confusing here, in that it concerns essence and not being, and thus as a consequence nothing can be learned with respect to the determination of becoming by proceeding in this way.)

Necessity stands completely alone; nothing at all comes to be with necessity, just as little as necessity comes to be, or that something by coming to be becomes necessary. Nothing is because it is necessary, but the necessary is because it is necessary, or because the necessary is. The actual is no more necessary than the possible, because that which is necessary is absolutely different from both. (Aristotle's [275] teaching (is) that there are two types of possibility in relation to the necessary. The mistake is that he starts with the claim that: everything that is necessary is possible. In order to avoid making a contradictory claim, yes the self-contradictory claim concerning the necessary, he aids himself by creating two kinds of possibility, rather than discovering that his first assertion was false because possibility cannot be predicated of the necessary.)

The change of becoming is actuality, the transition takes place with freedom. No becoming is necessary, not before it came to be, because then it could not come to be; and not after it has come to be, because then it has not come to be.

All becoming occurs freely, not necessarily; nothing that becomes comes to be from a logical ground, but everything because of a cause. Every cause terminates in a freely acting cause. The illusion created by the intervening causes is that the becoming appears necessary; their truth is that, as having themselves come to be, they definitively point back to a freely acting cause. Even the logic of a natural law does not explain the necessity of any becoming so soon as one reflects definitively on the becoming. But the expressions of freedom are like this. So long as one does not allow oneself to be deceived by its expression but reflects on the becoming.

§ 2

THE HISTORICAL

Everything that has come to be *eo ipso* historical; because even if nothing else historical could be applied to it, the decisive predicate of the historical can be predicated of it: it has come to be. That thing, the becoming of which is a simultaneous becoming (*Nebeneinander*, Space*), has no other history than this, but even seen in this way (*en masse*), independently of what an ingenious consideration in a more specific sense calls the history of nature, nature has a history.

But the historical is the past (because the pressure of the present upon the confines of the future has not yet become historical). How can one say that nature, despite being immediately present, is historical, if one does not view it from this ingenious perspective? The [276] difficulty comes from the fact that nature is too abstract to have a dialectical relationship, in the stricter sense, with time. Nature's imperfection is that it has no history in any other sense, and its perfection is that it has the intimation of a history (namely that it has come to be, which is the past; and that it is, the present). But it is the perfection of the eternal not to have a history, to be the only thing that is and yet absolutely without a history.

Becoming can, however, contain a redoubling—i.e. the possibility of another becoming within its original becoming. Here is the historical in the stricter sense which is dialectical with respect to time. The becoming that is here the same as the becoming of nature is a possibility, a possibility that is nature's whole actuality. But this genuine historical becoming takes place within a becoming, this must be remembered. The more specific historical becoming comes to be through a relatively freely acting cause, which always definitively points back to an absolutely freely acting cause.

§ 3

THE PAST

What has happened has happened and cannot be undone; thus it cannot be changed (Chrysippus the Stoic* — Diodorus the Megarian*). Is this the immutability of necessity? The immutability of the past is brought about by a change, by the change of becoming, but such immutability does not exclude all change, because it has not excluded this. All change is excluded (dialectically with respect to time) only by being excluded at every moment. If one wants to consider the past as necessary, this can be done only by forgetting that it has come to be, but should such forgetfulness also be necessary?

What has happened has happened as it happened, thus it is immutable, but is this the immutability of necessity? The immutability of the past is that its actual 'thus' cannot be otherwise, but does it [277] follow from this that its possible 'how' could not have been other than it was? The immutability of the necessary, on the other hand, is that it constantly relates to itself and relates to itself in the same way, excluding every change. It is not content with the immutability of the past, which is not simply, as has already been shown, dialectical with respect to an earlier change, from which it proceeds, but which must also be dialectical with respect to a higher change that repeals it (e.g. repentance that wants to repeal an actuality).

The future has not happened yet; but it is not *therefore* less necessary than the past, because the past did not become necessary by having happened, but on the contrary, by having happened showed that it was not necessary. If the past became necessary, then one could not from this infer the opposite with respect to the future, but would have to conclude as a consequence that the future was also necessary. If it were possible at any point to speak of the appearance of necessity, then it would no longer be possible to speak of 'the past' and 'the future'. To want to predict the future (prophesy) and to want to understand the necessity of the past are the same thing, and only fashion makes the one seem more plausible than the other. The past has come to be; becoming is the change in actuality brought about by freedom. If the past had become necessary, then it would no longer belong to freedom—i.e. belong to that through which it came to be. Freedom would then be ill-served by the transition and would be something both to laugh at and to weep over, in that it would bear the responsibility for something that did not belong to it, would produce what necessity then devoured, and freedom itself, no less than becoming, would be an illusion; freedom would be witchcraft, becoming a false alarm.[1]

§ 4   [278]

THE APPREHENSION OF THE PAST

Nature, as a determination of space, has only an immediate existence. What is dialectical with respect to time has an internal duplicity in that, after having been present, it can exist as past. The genuinely

[1] [Kierkegaard's note.] The prophesying generation is contemptuous of the past, will not listen to the witness of the Scriptures; the generation that is busy understanding the necessity of the past does not like to be asked about the future. Both attitudes are completely consistent; because each will, in its opposite, get an opportunity to see how bad its behaviour is. The absolute method, which is Hegel's invention, is already problematic in terms of its logic, yes, a brilliant tautology, which has served scholarly superstition with many signs and strange works. In historical scholarship it is a fixed idea. The fact that the method begins immediately to become concrete, since history is the concretion of the idea, has certainly provided Hegel with an opportunity to display a rare erudition, and a rare ability to master the material, which through him was certainly given life. But this has also occasioned a certain distraction in the reader, so that he perhaps precisely from respect and admiration for China and Persia, the minds of the Middle Ages, the philosophers of Greece, the four world-historical monarchies (a discovery which did not escape Geert Westphaler* and also started many later Hegelian Geert Westphalers gabbing), forgot to check whether it became apparent in the end, at the conclusion of this fascinating excursion, what was constantly promised at the beginning, what was the whole point, for which no amount of worldly glory could compensate, and what could alone make up for the unnatural tension, in which one was held—the correctness of the method. Why did one immediately become concrete, why did one immediately begin to experiment *in concreto* [in actual circumstances]? Or is this question unanswerable in the dispassionate concision of abstraction, which has no means of charming or diverting this question of what it means for the idea to become concrete, what becoming is, how one relates to that which has come to be, etc.? Just as he ought to have explained, in the *Logic*,* what transition was before he undertook to write three books in which he demonstrated transition in categorical determinations and astonished the superstitious, making so precarious the position of him who would gladly be greatly in the debt of a superior intellect and grateful for this debt, but cannot for this reason forget what Hegel himself must consider to be the main point.

[279] historical is always the past (it is over, whether a year ago or only days makes no difference), and has actuality as the past, because it is certain and dependable that it happened. But that it happened is again precisely its uncertainty, which will constantly prevent apprehension from taking the past as something that had been that way from eternity. Only in this contradiction between certainty and uncertainty, which is the *discrimen*[1] of that which has come to be and thus also of the past, is the past understood. If it is understood in any other way, then apprehension has misunderstood itself (that it is apprehension) and its object (that such a thing could become an object of apprehension). Any apprehension of the past, that wishes to understand the past thoroughly by constructing it, has thoroughly misunderstood it. (A manifestation theory instead of a construction theory is initially deceptive, but one soon sees a secondary construction and a necessary manifestation.) The past is not necessary, because it came to be; it did not become necessary by coming to be (a contradiction), and still less does it become necessary through any apprehension. (Distance in time occasions an intellectual deception, just as distance in space occasions a sense deception. The contemporary does not see the necessity of what comes to be, but when centuries lie between the becoming and the observer — then he sees the necessity, like him, who from a distance, sees a square tower as round.) If the past could become necessary through apprehension, then the past would win what apprehension had lost because it would have apprehended something else, which is a flawed apprehension. If that which is apprehended is altered in the apprehension, then apprehension is transformed into misapprehension. Knowledge of the present confers no necessity (Boethius*), a knowledge of the past confers no necessity, because all apprehension, like all knowledge, has nothing to give.

He who grasps the past, *historico-philosophus*,[2] is therefore a retrospective prophet (Daub*). That he is a prophet comes from the fact that at the basis of the certainty of the past is an uncertainty, in precisely the same sense as there is uncertainty with respect to the future, the possibility (Leibniz's possible worlds*) from which it is impossible for it to *issue* necessarily, *nam necessarium se ipso prius sit,*

---

[1] The distinguishing mark.   [2] As a philosopher of history.

necesse est.[1] The historian thus stands again at the past, moved by the passion, which is the passionate sense for becoming — i.e. wonder.*
If the philosopher marvels at nothing (and how could one, without [280] some new form of contradiction, marvel at a necessary construction?), then he is *eo ipso* not concerned with the historical; because wherever there is becoming (which there is with respect to the past), there the uncertainty (which is that of becoming) of the most certain thing that has come to be can be expressed only in this passion, which is both worthy of and necessary to a philosopher (Plato–Aristotle). Even if that which has come to be is now most certain, even if wonder would give its approval in advance by saying that if this had not happened, then one would have to have made it up (Baader*), even there the passion of wonder is self-contradictory if it wants to ascribe necessity to what has come to be and thus to dupe itself.—Both the word, and the concept: 'Method', show sufficiently that the progress one can speak of here is teleological; but in all such progress there is at every moment a pause (here wonder stands in *pausa*[2] and waits for becoming), which is the pause of becoming and possibility, precisely because its τέλος[3] lies outside itself. If only one way is possible, then the τέλος is not outside, but in the progress itself, indeed behind it, as in the case of the progress of immanence.

So much for the apprehension of the past. It is assumed, however, that there is knowledge of the past; how is this attained? The historical cannot be sensed immediately because it has within it becoming's *duplicity*. The immediate impression of a natural phenomenon or of an event is not an impression of the historical, because *becoming* cannot be immediately sensed, but only presence. But the presence of the historical has becoming within it, otherwise it is not the presence of the historical.

Immediate sensation and immediate cognition cannot deceive. This in itself shows that the historical cannot be the object of either, because the historical has within it the duplicity that is becoming's. In relation to the immediate, becoming is namely a duplicity through which that which is most certain is made doubtful. Thus when an observer sees a star, the star becomes dubious to him the moment he desires to become certain that it has come to be. It is as if reflection

---

[1] The necessary necessarily presupposes itself.
[2] Pause, short rest, expectation.
[3] Purpose, end.

removed the star from the senses. This much is clear: the organ for the historical must be made in likeness to the historical itself, it must have something within it through which it constantly in its cer-
[281] tainty cancels the uncertainty that corresponds to the uncertainty of becoming, which is twofold: the nothingness of non-being, and the annihilated possibility, which is, in addition, the annihilation of every other possibility. Such is precisely the nature of belief; because in the certainty of belief* there is constantly present as cancelled the uncertainty that in every way corresponds to the uncertainty of becoming. Belief thus believes what it does not see; it does not believe that the star is; it sees that; but it believes that the star has come to be. The same thing is true in relation to an event. What has happened can be immediately known, but that it has happened cannot. It cannot even be known that it is happening, not even if it is happening, as they say, right under one's nose. The duplicity of what has happened is that it has happened, wherein lies a transition from nothing, from non-being and from the manifold possible 'how'. Immediate sensation and immediate cognition have no suspicion of the uncertainty with which belief approaches its object, but neither have they any suspicion of the certainty that develops from this uncertainty.

Immediate sensation and cognition cannot deceive. This is impor-
tant to understand if one is to understand doubt, and through this to assign belief its place. This thought, strange as it seems, lies at the basis of Greek scepticism. It is not too difficult, however, to understand, or to understand the light this casts on belief, if one is not completely disturbed by the Hegelian doubt about everything, against which one truly need not preach; because what the Hegelians say about this is of such a nature that it could almost be thought to favour a modest reservation concerning to what extent it is consistent with their having doubted anything. Greek scepticism was retiring (ἐποχή[1]). The sceptics doubted not by virtue of knowledge, but by virtue of will (withheld assent — μετριοπαθεῖν[2]). From this it follows that doubt can be cancelled only through freedom, through an act of will, which every Greek sceptic would understand, in that he has understood himself. But he did not want to do away with his scepticism, precisely because he *wanted to* doubt. That is his prerogative.

---

[1] Suspending judgement.   [2] Moderate feeling.

But one should not attribute to him the stupidity that he believed one doubted with necessity, or by the same token what is even dumber, that if such were the case, doubt could be abolished. The Greek sceptic does not deny the correctness of sensation and immediate cognition. Error, he says, has a completely different source; it comes from the inferences I draw. If I can just refrain from drawing any inferences, then I will never be deceived. If, for example, my senses present to me some object that appears round at a distance but which [282] appears square when viewed more closely, or shows me a stick that appears bent in water despite the fact that it is straight when it is taken out of the water, the senses have not in any way deceived me, but I am deceived only when I infer something about the stick or the object. Therefore, the sceptic remains constantly in *suspenso*,[1] and this condition was precisely what he willed. To the extent that Greek scepticism is called φιλοσοφία ζητητική ἀπορητική, σκεπτική,[2] these predicates do not express what is peculiar to Greek scepticism, that it constantly used cognition to achieve peace of mind, which was the main objective and thus would not even assert cognition's negative result θετικῶς[3] in order to avoid being caught drawing a conclusion. Disposition was the main thing (τέλος δὲ οἱ σκεπτικοί φασι τὴν ἐποχήν, ᾗ σκιᾶς τρόπον ἐπακολουθεῖ ἡ ἀταραξία,[4] Diogenes Laertius, IX §107).[5]

In contrast to this, it is easy to see that belief is not a type of knowledge, but a free act, an expression of will. It believes becoming and has thus in itself cancelled the uncertainty that corresponds to the nothingness of non-being. It believes the 'thus' of that which has come to be and has therefore in itself cancelled the possible 'how', without denying the possibility of another 'thus', and yet the 'thus' of that which has come to be is the most certain for faith.

[1] Suspended, undecided.
[2] Inquiring, doubting, sceptical philosophy.
[3] Categorically.
[4] The end to be realized they hold to be suspension of judgement, which brings with it tranquillity like a shadow.
[5] [Kierkegaard's note.] That immediate sensation and immediate cognition cannot deceive is emphasized by both Plato and Aristotle. Later Descartes says, precisely as the Greek sceptics said, that error comes from the will that is too eager to draw conclusions. This also casts a light on faith; in deciding to believe it runs the risk that it was mistaken, but it wants to believe anyway. There is no other way to believe; if one wants to avoid the risk, then one wants to know with certainty whether one can swim before getting in the water.

To the extent that what becomes historical through belief and as historical becomes an object of faith (the one corresponds to the other) exists immediately and is apprehended immediately, it does not deceive. The contemporary certainly uses his eyes, etc., but he is careful about drawing any inferences. He cannot know immediately that it has come to be, but neither can he know with necessity that it has come to be, because the first expression of becoming is precisely a break in continuity. The moment faith believes something has [283] come to be, has happened, it makes that which has happened and come to be doubtful and its 'thus' doubtful in becoming's possible 'how'. The conclusion of belief is not an inference but a decision, thus doubt is excluded. One might think, when faith decides: this exists, ergo it has come to be, that this is an inference from effect to cause. This is, however, not exactly the case, and even if it were, one must remember that the inference of knowledge is from cause to effect, or more correctly, from ground to consequent (Jacobi*). But this is not exactly the case, because I cannot immediately sense, or know, that that which I immediately sense and know is an effect. Immediately, it simply is. That it is an effect is something I believe, because in order to predicate of it that it is an effect, I must already have made it doubtful through the uncertainty of becoming. But if belief decides this, then doubt is removed; in the same moment the equilibrium and indifference of doubt is removed, not by knowledge, but by the will. Thus, from the perspective of approximation, faith is supremely disputable (because the uncertainty of doubt contains an equivocation* that is strong and insurmountable—*disputare*[1] is fundamental to it), and yet indisputable by virtue of its new quality. Belief is the opposite of doubt. Belief and doubt are not two different types of knowledge that can be determined in continuity with each other, because neither of them is a cognitive act; they are opposite passions. Belief is a sense for becoming and doubt is a protest against any conclusion that goes beyond immediate sensation and immediate cognition. The doubter does not, for example, doubt his own existence, but he infers nothing, because he does not want to be deceived. He uses dialectic to make the opposite equally probable. It is not, however, by virtue of this that he is a sceptic; that is just an external expression, an accommodation for others. He has no result, not even a negative one (because this would be to admit knowledge), but by

[1] Openness to disputation, doubly vulnerable.

virtue of the will he decides to restrain himself (φιλοσοφία ἐφεκτική[1]) from drawing any conclusions.

He who is not contemporary with the historical, has, instead of sensation's and cognition's immediacy (which cannot, however, apprehend the historical), the report of contemporaries, with respect to which he is related in the same manner as the contemporaries were related to immediacy; because even if what is said in this report has been changed, he cannot consider it as if he does not himself accept that it is historical without changing it into something that is not historical for himself. The immediacy of the report—i.e. that there is a report—is what is immediately present, but the historicity of the present is that it has come to be, of the past that it was present by having come to be. As soon as someone who comes later believes the past (not its truth; because that is an object of knowledge, that concerns essence, not being; but believes that it was present by having come to be), then the uncertainty of becoming is there; and this uncertainty of becoming (the nothingness of non-being—the possible 'how' of the actual 'thus') must be for him just as it was for the contemporary, his mind must remain *in suspenso* just as was the case with the contemporary. Thus he no longer has any immediacy to deal with, but neither does he have any necessary becoming, but only *becoming's* thus. The one who comes later believes by virtue of the contemporary's statement, but only in the same sense that the contemporary believes by virtue of immediate sensation and cognition; but the contemporary cannot believe by virtue of this, and thus the one who comes later cannot believe by virtue of the report. [284]

* *
*

The past is thus never for a moment necessary, just as little as it was necessary when it came to be, or showed itself to be necessary for the contemporary who believed it, i.e. believed that it had come to be; because belief and becoming correspond to each other and relate to the abrogated determinations of being: the past and the future, and to the present only to the extent that it is viewed from the perspective of the abrogated determination of that which has come to be. Necessity relates to essence, and in such a way that the determinations of

---

[1] In aporetic suspension.

essence precisely exclude becoming. The possibility from which the possible that becomes the actual issued constantly accompanies that which has come to be and remains with it as past, even if centuries lie between. As soon as one who comes later repeats that it has come to be (which one does by believing it), one repeats its possibility, independently of whether we can speak here of a more specific conception of this possibility, or not.

SUPPLEMENT

APPLICATION

What has been said here is valid for the straightforwardly historical, whose contradiction[1] is only that it has come to be, whose contradiction is only that of becoming; because, again, one must not be deceived here, as if it were easier to understand that something has come to be after it has come to be, than before it came to be. He who believes this does not yet understand that it has come to be; he has only the immediate sensation and cognition of that which is present, wherein becoming is not contained.

We will return now to our story and to our presupposition that the god has been. The straightforwardly historical cannot become historical for immediate sensation or cognition, no more for the contemporary than for one who comes later. But this historical fact (which is the content of our story) has a unique quality in that it is not a straightforwardly historical fact, but a fact that is based on a self-contradiction (which is sufficient to show that there is no difference between the immediate contemporary and one who comes later; because when confronted with a self-contradiction, and the risk bound up with giving assent to it, immediate contemporaneousness is not in any way advantageous). Yet it is a historical fact, and for faith alone. Faith is taken here first in its straightforward and ordinary sense of the relation to the historical; but then it must also be taken in an absolutely eminent sense, in such a way as it can be used only once, i.e. many times, but only in one relationship.

---

[1] [Kierkegaard's note.] The word 'contradiction' must not be taken here in the weak sense in which Hegel has convinced himself and others and contradiction, that it had the power to produce something. So long as nothing has come to be, contradiction is only the dynamic power in wonder, its *nisus* [pressing, straining, effort] not the *nisus* of becoming. When it has come to be, the contradiction is again present as the *nisus* of wonder in the passion that reproduces becoming.

Eternally understood, one does not *believe* that there is a God, even though one assumes that there is. This is a misuse of language. [286] Socrates did not have faith that there was a God. What he knew about God he achieved through recollection, and God's existence was, for him, in no way historical. We are not concerned here with whether his knowledge of God was very imperfect in relation to that of one who, according to our hypothesis, has received the condition for understanding the truth from the god himself. Belief is not concerned with essence, but with being, and the acceptance that there is a God determines him eternally, not historically. The historical is that the god came to be (for the contemporary), that he has been present in that he has come to be (for one who comes later). But precisely herein lies the contradiction. No one can be immediately contemporary with this historical fact (cf. the preceding). It is an object of faith because it concerns becoming. The issue here is not the truth of the assertion that the god has come to be, but whether one will accept this, accept that the eternal being of God is inflected in the dialectical determinations of becoming.

Thus it stands with this historical fact. It has no immediate contemporary because it is historical in the first sense (belief in the ordinary sense) and it has no immediate contemporary in another sense in that it is based on a contradiction (faith in the eminent sense). But the egalitarian nature of this second sense as concerns the most extreme temporal distinctions swallows up these distinctions as they exist in the first sense. Every time the believer allows this fact to be an object of belief, allows it to become historical in itself, he repeats the dialectical determinations of becoming. Even if thousands of years passed, even if this fact produced myriad consequences, it would not therefore become more necessary (and, from the definitive perspective, the consequences themselves become only relatively necessary, because they rest on a freely acting cause), not to mention the most backward assertion of all, that the event could become necessary because of its consequences, since consequences normally have their basis in something else and cannot provide a foundation for this. Even if the contemporary, or perhaps a predecessor, saw the preparations, or an intimation of such, or an indication to that effect, this fact would still not be necessary, in that it came to be, i.e. this fact is no more necessary when considered as future than it is necessary when considered as past.

CHAPTER V

THE DISCIPLE AT SECOND HAND

'Dear reader! Since, according to our assumption, eighteen hundred and forty-three years lie between the contemporary disciple and this discussion, that would seem to provide sufficient occasion to inquire about a disciple at second hand, as there will certainly have been many cases of such a thing. The question appears inescapable, as does the demand for an explanation of the difficulties that might possibly be associated with defining the disciple at second hand in continuity with and yet also discontinuous with the contemporary. Despite this, however, should we not first consider whether the question is really so legitimate as it immediately appears to be? If it should become apparent that the question is not legitimate, or that one cannot ask such a thing without inquiring like a fool and thus without being entitled to charge him with foolishness who is so sensible that he is unable to answer it—then the difficulties would appear to be removed.'

'Undeniably; because when one cannot ask a question, then the question cannot cause any trouble, and the difficulties become unusually easy.'

'But this does not follow, for supppose the difficulty lay in the realization that one could not ask in this way. Or have you perhaps already appreciated this; was this perhaps the point of what you said in our last conversation (Chapter IV): that you had understood me and all the implications of my assertion, while I have not yet completely understood myself?'

'Not at all. That was not my view, just as little as it is my view that the question can be dismissed, even less so because it contains a new question of whether there is not a difference between the many who are subsumed under the category "disciple at second hand". In other words, is it correct to divide such a monstrously large chunk of time into two such unequal parts: the contemporary/the one who comes later?'

'Do you mean you think one could speak of a disciple at 5th, at 7th hand, etc.? But if, in order to accommodate you, one spoke of such things, would it not follow that the discussion of such differences, if it were not to be incoherent, should not allow them to be grouped under one heading in contrast to the determination: the contempor- [288] ary disciple? Or would the discussion be conducted correctly if it conducted itself as you did, so that it was simple enough to do what you were cunning enough to do, to cause the question of the disciple at second hand to be transformed into an entirely different question, through which, instead of either accepting or rejecting my proposal, you found the opportunity to dupe me with a new question? But since you presumably do not wish to continue this discussion, out of fear that it will degenerate into sophistry and squabbling, I will break it off. You will see, however, from what develops from what I plan to present here, that I have taken the views exchanged between us into account.'

§ 1

DIFFERENCES AMONG DISCIPLES AT SECOND HAND

We reflect here not on the secondary disciple's relation to the contemporary. The internal differences under consideration here are such that, despite them, the similarity of the former remains in contrast to the latter, because the variations that are only variations within a class are subordinate to the likeness that constitutes the class. Neither, for this reason, is it capricious to stop wherever one wants to, because the relative difference is here no sorites,* from which a quality appears through a *coup de mains*,[1] when it is within a specific quality. A sorites would arise only if one made being contemporary dialectical in a negative sense by, for example, showing that in a certain sense no one was contemporary, because no one could be contemporary with all the stages; or by asking when contemporaneousness ceased, where non-contemporaneousness began, whether there was not a haggling *confinium*[2] about which the jabbering understanding could say: to a certain extent, etc., etc. All such superhuman profundity leads to nothing, or perhaps in our day to becoming respected as a genuine speculative philosopher, because the despised sophistry, the devil knows how it happened, has become

---

[1] Blow of the hand, snap of the fingers, sudden action.
[2] Boundary zone.

the wretched secret of genuine speculation, and what was in ancient times viewed negatively, 'to-a-certain-extent' thinking (the para-
[289] doxical indulgence that, without trifling, mediates everything), has become positive, and what the ancients called positive, the passion for making distinctions, has become silliness.

Opposites show themselves most clearly by being placed next to each other, and therefore we choose here the first generation of secondary disciples, and the latest generation (those that form the boundaries of the given *spatium*,[1] the eighteen hundred and forty-three years) and will be as brief as possible, because we are not speaking historically, but algebraically, and do not wish to be diffuse, or to dazzle anyone with the magic of multiplicity. On the contrary, we never forget the common likeness, in relation to the contemporary, that lies at the basis of the differences (only in the next § will we clearly see that the question of the disciple at second hand, properly understood, is a pseudo-question), as well as that the difference must never expand to such an extent that it confuses everything.

(a) *The First Generation of Secondary Disciples*

This generation has the (relative) advantage of being closer to the immediate certainty, of being closer to acquiring an exact and reliable account of what happened from men, whose reliability one can check in other ways. We have already calculated this immediate certainty in Chapter IV. To be closer to it is surely a deception, because he who is not so close to an immediate certainty as to be immediately certain, is absolutely distanced from it. Suppose, however, that we bring this relative difference (which the first generation of secondary disciples has in relation to the later ones) into consideration; how high should we estimate it? We can estimate it only in relation to the advantage of the contemporary; but his advantage (immediate certainty in the strict sense) we showed already in Chapter IV to be dubious (*anceps* — dangerous) and will show in more detail in the next §. — If, in the immediately succeeding generation, there lived a person who, with the power and passion of an absolute ruler, had decided to concern himself with nothing other than to get to the truth on this point, would he thus become a disciple? Assume he
[290] seized all the contemporary witnesses and those who were closest to

---

[1] Interval.

them, who were still living, had each independently interrogated as thoroughly as possible, shut them all up like the seventy interpreters,* starved them as a means of getting them to tell the truth, cunningly confronted them with one another, simply to ensure in every way possible the most reliable account — would such a person, with the help of this account, be a disciple? Would not the god rather smile at him, that he wished in this way to procure for himself what can neither be bought for money, nor seized by force? Even if the fact of which we speak were a simple, historical fact, the difficulty would not disappear, if he wished to establish an absolute agreement in all the small details, which would be of enormous significance for him, because the passion of faith, i.e. the passion that is as intense as faith, had been misdirected out to the purely historical. It is well known that the most upright and honest people are easily entangled in contradictions when they become the objects of interrogation and of the inquisitor's fixed idea, while it is reserved for only a depraved criminal, because of the exactness enforced by an evil conscience, not to contradict himself in his lie. Be that as it may, this fact, about which we speak is not a simple historical fact. How then did all this precision help him? If he procured a detailed account, consistent down to every letter and minute, then he would beyond a doubt be deceived. He would have gained a greater degree of certainty than the contemporary who saw and heard, because the latter would easily have discovered that sometimes he did not see, and other times he saw incorrectly, and so with hearing, and he would have to be constantly reminded that he did not see or hear the god immediately, but saw a person in a lowly form, who said of himself that he was the god; in other words, he would have to be constantly reminded that this fact was based on a contradiction. Was this person served by the credibility of his account? Yes, from a historical perspective, but in no other way because all talk of the god's worldly splendour (when, however, he was in only a servant's form — an individual human being, like one of us — an object of offence), of his immediate divinity (when, however, divinity is not an immediate determination, and the teacher would first have to develop in the learner the most profound self-reflection, sin-consciousness, as the condition for understanding), of the immediate wondrousness of his works (when, however, the wonder is *not* immediate, but only for faith, if it is true that he who does not believe does not see the wonder), is here [291] as everywhere a galimatias,* an attempt to stave off serious consideration of the situation through idle chatter.

This generation has the relative advantage of being nearer to the tremor produced by this fact. This tremor and its aftershocks serve to arouse attention. The significance of such attention (which can also easily become offence) was already evaluated in Chapter IV. Let us allow that to be a little closer to this (in relation to those who come later) is an advantage, the advantage consists only in its relation to the dubious advantage had by the contemporaries. The advantage is thoroughly dialectical, just as is attention itself. The advantage is that one becomes aware, whether one is offended or believes. Attention is in no way partial to faith, as if faith followed as a simple consequence of attention. The advantage is that one is placed in a state where the decision confronting one shows itself more clearly. This is an advantage, and this advantage is the only one that means anything, means so much, in fact, that it is terrible and in no way an easy convenience. If this fact had not through stupid senselessness found its way into meaningless human convention, then every generation would exhibit the same relation of offence as did the first, because no immediacy will bring one closer to this fact. One can be brought up with this fact as thoroughly as you like, it does not help. On the contrary, if the one doing the upbringing is himself thoroughly versed in the fact, it can even incline one to become a well-trained windbag in whose mind there is neither any intimation of offence, nor place for faith.

(b) *The Latest Generation*

This generation is far from the initial shock, but has, on the other hand, the consequences to hold onto, has the proof of probability provided by the results; has the consequences immediately before it, with which this fact may well have encompassed everything; has the demonstration of probability close at hand, from which, however, there is no immediate transition to faith, since, as was shown, faith is in no way partial to probability, and to say that it was would be to [292] defame it.¹ If this fact came into the world as the absolute paradox,

---

¹ [Kierkegaard's note.] The ambition (however it can actually be understood *in concreto* [in actual circumstances]) to connect a probability proof to the improbable (in order to prove — that it is probable? But then the concept has been altered; or to prove — that it is improbable? But it is a contradiction to use probability for this purpose), is, when taken seriously, so stupid that one has to view it as impossible for anyone to have; as a joke or

then nothing that happens later can be of any help, because the consequences would for all eternity be consequences of a paradox, and thus definitively just as improbable as the paradox itself, unless one assumed that the consequences had retroactive power to transform the paradox, which would be as acceptable as that a son could have the retroactive power to transform his father. Even if one views the consequences purely logically, that is, under the determination of immanence, it remains true that the consequences can be determined only as homogeneous with, and identical to, their cause; they could least of all have the power to transform their cause. To have the consequences before one is thus just as dubious an advantage as to have immediate certainty, and he who takes the consequences immediately is deceived just as much as is he who takes immediate certainty for faith.

The advantage of the consequences is thought to lie in that they gradually make the fact seem more natural. If this is the case (i.e. allow that this is conceivable), then the later generation is plainly at an advantage in relation to the contemporary generation (and the

---

a bit of fun, on the other hand, it is hysterically funny and, according to my opinion, very entertaining to employ in this narrow sense — A magnanimous gentleman wishes to do humanity a service by producing a probability proof to help it accept the improbable. It is a wild success. He is moved by all the thanks and congratulations he receives, not simply from dignitaries, who really know how to appreciate the proof, but also the community — Alas, this magnanimous gentleman has precisely ruined everything. — Or a man has a conviction; the content of this conviction is absurd, improbable. This same man is very vain. One does the following. In as calm and friendly a manner as possible, one entices him to expound on the substance of his conviction. Because he suspects no mischief, he presents it in sharp outline. When he is finished, one pounces on him in a manner that is calculated to be maximally irritating to his vanity. He becomes confused, embarrassed, ashamed, 'that he should accept something so preposterous'. Instead of [293] calmly replying: 'Honourable sir, you are a fool; it is preposterous and cannot help but remain so despite all objections, which I have contemplated myself much more thoroughly than anyone else who might hope to embarrass me with them, and yet I have still chosen the improbable', instead of replying in this way, he seeks to produce a probability proof. Now one helps him. One allows oneself to be defeated, and ends something like this: 'Oh, now I see it, it is more probable than anything.' One embraces him. If one really wishes to push the joke, one kisses him and thanks him *ob meliorem informationem* [for the superior grasp], looks once more, in parting, into his romantic eyes, and departs from him as from a friend and sworn brother in life and death, as from a kindred spirit one has understood from eternity. — Such fun is justified because if the man had not been vain, then I would have been the fool in contrast to the sincerity of his conviction. — What Epicurus says on the relation of the individual to death (even if his view provides little comfort) is valid for the relation between probability and improbability: when I am there, it (death) is not, and when it (death) is there, I am not.

person who spoke of the consequences in this sense would have to
[293] be very stupid to fantasize about the joy of being contemporary with
this fact), and can appropriate this fact untroubled by any notice of
the dubiousness of attention, from which offence can issue just as
easily as faith. This fact cannot, however, be tamed, is too proud
to desire a disciple who wants to come along because of the event's
fortunate results; it is contemptuous of any attempt through the
protection of a ruler or a professor to naturalize it. It is and remains
a paradox, and admits of no approach through speculation. This
fact is only for faith. Faith can certainly become second nature in a
person, but the person whose second nature it becomes must actually
have had a first nature, since faith became the second. If this fact is
to be made a natural one, then, in relation to the individual, it can be
expressed by saying that the individual is born with faith, i.e. with
his second nature. If we begin our discussion this way, then we allow
at the same time the rejoicing of all sorts of galimatias, because now
it has been let loose and there is no way to stop it. This galimatias
must naturally have been invented as the result of going further;
[294] because Socrates' view made good sense, even if we did depart from
it in order to explore what we had earlier postulated, and such a galimatias would take it as a deep offence that it should not be viewed
as having gone way beyond the Socratic. Even in the transmigration
of souls there is meaning, but to be born with one's second nature,
a nature that refers back in time to a given historical fact, that is a
real *non plus ultra*[1] of insanity. From the Socratic perspective, the
individual had been before he came to be, and recollects himself, so
recollection is pre-existence (not recollection of pre-existence); the
individual's nature (the only one; because here there is no talk of
a first and a second nature) is determined in continuity with itself.
Here, on the other hand, everything is forward-looking and historical, in such a way that to be born with faith is fundamentally just as
plausible as to be born twenty-four years old. If one were really able
to point to a person who had been born with faith, then that would
be a monstrosity more worth seeing than the one the barber in *The
Busy Man* relates as having been born in the *neuen Buden*,* even if
it seems to barbers and busy men to be the sweetest little being, the
greatest triumph of speculation. —Or is a person perhaps born with

---

[1] Epitome.

both natures at once, but not, note well, two such natures as belong together to form the substance of ordinary human nature, but with two complete human natures, one of which assumes the intermediation of a historical event. If this were the case, everything that we had hypothesized in Chapter I would become confused. Neither, though, would our situation be Socratic. It would be merely a confusion that not even Socrates would be in a position to remove. It would be a prospective confusion that would have a lot in common with the one Apollonius of Tyana* invented retrospectively. He was, namely, not content to recollect, like Socrates, that he had been before he came to be (the eternity and continuity of consciousness is the thought behind, and the profundity of, the Socratic), but quickly went further, and recollected, namely, who he had been before he became himself. If this fact is naturalized, then birth is not merely birth but is, in addition, rebirth, in such a way that he who never was, is born again—in being born.—This is expressed in an individual life in the following way, that the person is born with faith; the same thing is expressed in the race by saying that the race, after the introduction of this fact, becomes a completely different race, and yet despite this is determined in continuity with the first. In this case, the race ought to take a new name, because faith, as we have postulated it, is not something inhuman such as a birth within a birth (rebirth), but would, on the other hand, become a fantastical [295] monstrosity, if it were as the objection would have it.

The advantage of the consequences is also dubious for another reason, to the extent that they are not a simple consequence of this fact. Let us estimate the greatest possible advantage of the consequences, assume this fact has completely transformed the world, that its omnipresence has permeated through to even the most insignificant thing   how has this happened? It did not happen all at once, but through successive steps; still, how were these steps made? Through each individual generation again coming into relation to this fact? This intermediate determination must also be checked so the full force of the consequences can benefit a person only through a conversion. Or is it not possible for a misunderstanding also to have consequences, possible for a lie also to be powerful? And has it not happened this way with every generation? Even if all the earlier generations would simply hand over to the last generation the whole magnificent array of the consequences—the consequences are a misunderstanding. Or is Venice not built upon the ocean, even though it was built in such a way that there finally came a generation that did not even notice it, and would it not be tragic if this generation persisted in this misunderstanding until the pilings began to rot and the city sank? But consequences that are built on a paradox are, humanly speaking, built upon an abyss, and the total worth is transferred to the individual only upon the agreement that it is by virtue of a paradox. It is not to be passed down like real estate because the whole thing hovers in suspension.

(c) *Comparison*

We will not pursue any further what has been developed here, but leave it to each person individually to practise coming back, from various angles, to this thought, to use his imagination to discover the strangest cases of relative differences and relative situations, to do the calculations himself. Thus the quantitative is circumscribed [296] but has unrestricted space to move about within these confines. The quantitative is the variety of life. It is constantly weaving its multicoloured tapestry; it is like the goddess of fate who spun, but then thought, as the second fate, takes care of clipping the thread, which, independently of the picture, ought to be done, any time quantity wants to determine quality.

The first generation of secondary disciples has then the advantage that the difficulty is there, because it is always an advantage, a relief, when it is the difficult I have to appropriate, that it is made difficult for me. If the latest generation, when it considers the first generation and sees it almost collapsing under the burden of the horror, should hit upon saying: 'That is incomprehensible; because the whole thing is no heavier than that one can take it and run with it', then there would certainly be someone who would answer: 'Be my guest, run with it, but you should make sure that what you are running with is actually that of which we speak; because we are certainly in agreement that it is easy enough to run with the wind.'

The latest generation has the advantage of ease, but as soon as it discovers that this ease is precisely a danger that creates a difficulty, then this difficulty will correspond to the difficulty of the horror, and the horror will grip the latest generation of secondary disciples just as primitively as it did the first generation.

§ 2

THE QUESTION OF THE DISCIPLE AT SECOND HAND

Before we look at the situation of the disciple at second hand, we will present a couple of considerations by way of orientation. (*a*) If one considers this fact as a simple historical fact, then there is something to being contemporary, and it is an advantage to be contemporary (this understood in the specific sense presented in Chapter IV), or to be as close as possible, or to be able to assure oneself of the reliability of the contemporaries, etc. Every historical fact is only a relative fact and it is therefore appropriate that the relative power of time determines the relative fate of human beings with respect to contemporaneousness. No historical fact can be more than this, and only childishness or stupidity can elevate it to the absolute. (*b*) If this fact is an eternal fact, then every period is equally near to it; but, it should be noted, not in faith, because faith and the historical [297] correspond to each other completely, and it is thus only a concession to an imprecise use of language that I use the word 'fact', which is taken from the historical. (*c*) If this fact is an absolute fact, or to put it even more precisely, is that which we have proposed, then it would be a contradiction to suppose that time could determine the relation of individuals to it, that is to say, determine such relations in a decisive sense; because what is essentially divisible by time is *eo ipso* not the absolute, because it would follow from that that the absolute was itself a *casus*,[1] in life, a particular state in relation to something else, while, despite being declinable according to all of life's *casibus*,[2] the absolute remains constantly the same and, though perpetually related to other things, continues to enjoy the status of the absolute. But the absolute fact is also a historical fact. If we are not careful about this, then our entire hypothesis is destroyed, because then we would speak only of an eternal fact. The absolute fact is a historical fact, and as such an object of faith. The historical aspect should certainly be accentuated, but not in such a way that it becomes absolutely decisive for individuals, because then we would be in position (*a*) (despite the fact that, understood in this way, it is a contradiction, because a simple historical fact is not an absolute fact and has no

---

[1] A (grammatical) case indicating how something is inflected or declined.
[2] (Grammatical) cases.

power to force an absolute decision); but neither can the historical be removed, because then we would have only an eternal fact. — Just as the historical becomes the occasion for the contemporary to become a disciple, it should be noted, by having received the condition from the god himself (because otherwise we speak Socratically), so the account of the contemporaries becomes the occasion for everyone who comes later to become a disciple, though only, it must be noted, by having received the condition from the god himself.

Now we begin. He who, by having received the condition, becomes a disciple, receives the condition from the god himself. If this is the case (and this is what we developed above, where it was shown that immediate contemporaneousness is only an occasion, though note well, not in such a way that the condition was straightforwardly in the occasioned), where then is there a place for the question of a disciple at second hand? Because he who has what he has from the god himself, he obviously has it at first hand; and he who does not have it from the god himself, he is not a disciple.

Let us assume that this is not the case, that the contemporary generation of disciples had received the condition from the god, and that [298] now the succeeding generations would receive the condition from these contemporaries. What would follow from this? We do not want to distract attention by reflecting on the historical pusillanimity with which one, presumably with a new contradiction and therefore new confusion (because if one starts here, then the chaos is inexhaustible), would covet the accounts of these contemporaries as if they were decisive. No, if the contemporary gives the condition to the one who comes later, then the latter will come to believe in him. He receives the condition from the contemporary, and in this way the contemporary becomes the object of faith for the one who comes later; because he, from whom the individual receives the condition, he is *eo ipso* (cf. the preceding) the object of faith and is thus the god.

Such meaninglessness will be sufficient, however, to frighten thought away from accepting this assumption. If, on the contrary, the later generation also receives the condition from the god, then we return to the Socratic, though it must be noted, within the complete difference which is this fact and the individual's (both the contemporary and the one who comes later) relation to the god. The meaninglessness described above, on the other hand, is inconceivable in a different sense from the one we use when we say that this fact and the individual's relation to the God is inconceivable. Our hypothetical assumption of this fact and the individual's relation to the god contains no self-contradiction, and thought can thus engage with it as with the strangest of all assumptions. But the meaningless logic developed above, on the other hand, contains a self-contradiction: it is not content to make the absurd claim that is our hypothetical assumption, but produces from within this absurdity the self-contradiction that the god is the god for the contemporary, but that the contemporary is the god for the third person. Only by placing the god in relation to the individual did our project go beyond the Socratic; but who would dare approach Socrates with such a claim as that a human being can be a god in relation to another human being? No, Socrates had such a heroic grasp of how one person relates to another that it in itself requires fearlessness to understand. And yet what is required here is an appropriation of this same understanding from within the assumption that the one person, to the extent he is a believer, owes the other nothing, but owes the god everything. It takes no effort to see that it is not easy to understand this and, in particular, to maintain this understanding (because to understand it once and for all without considering the concrete objections, i.e. to delude oneself that one has understood it, is not difficult); and [200] he who wishes to drill himself in this understanding will certainly often catch himself in various misunderstandings; and if he wishes to involve others, then he must be careful. But if one has understood it, then one will also understand that there is not and cannot be any talk of a disciple at second hand, because the believer (and only he is a disciple) constantly has the autopsy of faith and does not see through others' eyes, but sees the same thing every believer sees — with the eyes of faith.

What then can the contemporary do for the one who comes later? (*a*) He can tell him that he has himself believed this fact, which is not actually a communication at all (this is expressed by the fact that there is no immediate contemporaneousness, and that the fact is based on a contradiction), but only an occasion. When I say: this or that has happened, then I am recounting something historical; but when I say 'I believe and have believed, that this has happened, *despite the fact that it is foolishness to the understanding and an offence*

to the human heart', then I have in the same instant precisely done
everything possible to inhibit others from determining their own
views in immediate continuity with mine, to decline any companion-
ship, in that each individual must conduct himself in precisely the
same way. (*b*) He can in this form give the content of the fact, which
content is, however, only for faith in precisely the same sense that
colours are for sight, and sounds are for hearing. He can do it in this
form; in any other form he will be speaking to the wind and will
perhaps mislead the one who comes later into determining his views
in continuity with this idle chatter.

   *In what sense can the credibility of the contemporary be significant for
the one who comes later?* It cannot be significant with respect to the
question of whether he has actually had faith in the manner he has
claimed. This is of no concern to the one who comes later, does not
help him, is of no help one way or the other in terms of his coming
to believe. Only he who receives the condition himself from the god
(which corresponds to what is required of a person, that he surrender
his understanding, and yet on the other hand is the only authority
that corresponds to faith), only he believes. If he wishes to believe
(i.e. delude himself that he believes), because many righteous people
on the hill have believed (i.e. have said they believed; because no one
can prove of anyone else that he believes; even if the other endured,
suffered everything, for the sake of this belief, an outsider can come
[300]   no further than to what the other says about himself, because a lie
can stretch just exactly as far as truth—for human eyes, not for
God's), then he is a fool, and whether he believes by virtue of his
own opinion and a perhaps pervasive assessment of the views of
righteous folk, or whether he believes a Münchhausen,* is purely
arbitrary. If the credibility of the contemporary is of any interest to
him (alas, one can be confident that this is an issue that will become
a huge sensation and provide an occasion for the writing of folios,
because this deceptive appearance of earnestness which contemplates
whether this person or that person is credible, instead of whether
one has faith oneself, is an excellent way to cloak intellectual laziness
and European town gossip), if the credibility of the contemporary
is to be of any interest to him, then it must be with respect to some
historical fact. But what historical fact? The fact that can become
an object only for faith, and which one person cannot communicate

to another—i.e. which one person can certainly communicate to another, but, it must be noted, not in the sense that the other believes it, while he, if he communicates it in the form of faith, precisely does what he can to prevent the other from accepting it immediately. If the fact of which we speak were a simple historical fact, then the precision of the historian would be very important. But this is not the case here, because one cannot distil faith from even the finest detail. The historical fact that the god appeared in human form is the central thing. The other historical details are even less important than they would be if, instead of speaking about the god, we were speaking about a human being. Jurists say that a capital crime absorbs all lesser crimes—thus it is with faith, its absurdity completely consumes all other trivial details.

Inconsistencies that would otherwise be troubling are not troubling here and have no effect on the issue. On the other hand, it can be very important that someone, through some sort of petty calculation, wishes to auction off faith to the highest bidder, because that can have the effect that he will never come to have faith. Even if the contemporary generation had left nothing more than these words: 'We believed that the god, *anno* this or that, appeared in the lowly form of a servant, lived and taught among us, and then died'—that would be more than enough. The contemporary generation would have done what was necessary, because this little advertisement, this world-historical *NB*,[1] is sufficient to provide the occasion for someone who comes later. The most prolix eyewitness account could never do more.

If we wish to express the relation of the one who comes later to the contemporary as briefly as possible, without, however, sacrific- [301] ing accuracy to brevity, then one would say that: the one who comes later believes *on account of* (through the occasion of) the contemporary's report by virtue of the condition he has himself received from the god. The contemporary's report is the occasion for the one who comes later, just as immediate contemporaneousness was the occasion for the contemporary. And if the report is what it ought to be (the report of a believer), then it will give rise to precisely the same ambiguous attention to which immediate contemporaneousness with the god gave rise. If the report is not of this sort, then it is

---

[1] *Note Bene* (Note well).

either that of a historian and thus not concerned with the object of faith (as would be the case if a contemporary historian who was not a believer described this or that); *or* that of a philosopher and thus not concerned with the object of faith. The believer, on the other hand, presents his report in such a way that it cannot be immediately accepted, because the phrase: I believe it (in spite of reason and my own capacity to invent objections) is a very significant *aber*.[1]

There is no disciple at second hand. The first and the last are essentially equal, except that the later generation has its occasion in the report of the contemporaries, while the contemporaries have their occasion in immediate contemporaneousness and thus are not beholden to any other generation for anything. But this immediate contemporaneousness is merely the occasion, and this cannot be expressed more emphatically than by saying that the disciple, if he understood himself, must wish precisely that his contemporaneousness ceased through the god's once again departing from the earth.

*   *
*

Someone may well say:

'That is strange; I have read the development of your thesis, and not without a certain interest, all the way to the end and have been pleased to see that there were no cues, nothing written between the lines. But no matter how you twist and turn, like Saft* always ends up in the pantry, you always end up mixing in a few words that are not your own and which arouse disturbing recollections. Your claim that the god's departure is beneficial to the disciple is from the New Testament, in the Gospel of John. Whether it was done intentionally or not, whether you wished to give this remark a special effect by clothing it in this form, according to your presentation, the
[302] advantage of the contemporary, which I was originally inclined to consider very great, appears to be significantly reduced, since there can be no questions of a disciple at second hand, which, in ordinary Danish, is to say the same thing as that everyone is essentially equal. But not only this; according to your last remark, immediate contemporaneousness would appear, considered from the perspective of advantageousness, to be so dubious that the most one can say

[1] 'But (German).

about it is that it is beneficial for it to cease. This is to say that it is an intermediate condition which is important, cannot be omitted without, as you say, returning to the Socratic, but which does not, however, have absolute significance for the contemporary so that he would be robbed of what is essential when it ceased, but on the contrary would gain something, even though if he had not had it, he would have lost everything and returned to the Socratic.'

'Well said,' I would have to respond, if modesty did not prevent me. 'I could not have said it better myself. That is absolutely correct, immediate contemporaneousness is by no means a decisive advantage when one thinks about it, is not curious, is not hasty, does not wish to, indeed is not already poised to, leap forth like that barber in ancient Greece who put his life on the line to be the first to bring news of the extraordinary; is not foolish enough to see such a death as that of a martyr. Immediate contemporaneousness is so far from being an advantage that the contemporary must wish precisely for it to cease so that he will not be tempted to run out and look with his physical eyes and hear with his earthly ears; which inconvenience and trouble is not simply a waste but, sadly, dangerous. This you have, however, figured out yourself, belongs in another treatise, when the issue would be what advantage a contemporary believer would have, after becoming a believer, from his contemporaneousness, whereas here we speak only of to what extent immediate contemporaneousness makes it easier for one to become a believer. One who comes later cannot be tempted in this way because he has only the report of the contemporaries, which, to the extent that it is a report, is in the prohibitive form of faith. If, therefore, the one who comes later understands himself, then he must wish that the report of the contemporary is not too wordy, and most importantly, not presented in so many volumes that the world could barely contain them. There is a restlessness in the immediate contemporary that ceases only when it can be said: it is fulfilled, without, however, the rest having the effect of whisking the historical away, because then everything would be Socratic.'

'Equality is established then in this way and the incompatibility of [303] the two generations removed.'

'This is also my opinion, but you must remember that it is the god himself who brings about the reconciliation. Would he enter into an agreement with a group of people to this effect that their agreement with him set them apart in a striking manner from all other human beings? That would create discord. Would the god allow time the power to determine whom he would benefit, or would it not be worthy of the god to make the agreement such that it would be equally difficult for everyone in every age and in every place; equally difficult because no human being is able to give himself the condition for understanding the truth, but neither, through a new contentiousness, can he receive it from another human being; equally difficult, but also equally effortless, to the extent that the god gives it? For this reason, you see, I viewed my project from the beginning (that is, to the extent that a hypothesis can be viewed this way) as a pious one, and still view it in that way, without, however, being insensible to any human objection. On the contrary, I invite you again to come forward with any legitimate objections you may have.'

'How festive you have suddenly become! Even though the situation does not require it, one might decide to come forward with an objection just for the fun of it, unless it is more fun not to, and your solemn challenge was designed indirectly to enjoin silence. In order that the nature of my objection shall at least not disturb the festive atmosphere, I will draw my objection from the festiveness with which, it seems to me, a later generation comes to distinguish itself from the contemporary one. I certainly see how the contemporary generation must have a deep sense of, and must suffer through, the pains that lie in the coming to be of such a paradox, or in, as you have expressed it, the god's planting himself in a human life. This new order of things must, however, gradually become victorious and then, finally, the fortunate generation will come and harvest, with joyful singing, the fruit of the seed that was sown with the tears of the first generation. Is this triumphant generation that goes singing through life not distinguished from the first and from the earlier generations?'

'Yes, it is undeniably different, so different perhaps that it does not have the resemblance to those earlier generations that was the condition for our speaking about it; so different that its difference disturbs my efforts to establish equality. But should such a trium-
[304] phant generation that marches singing and celebrating through life, as you say, and with which you, if I remember correctly, remind me of a well-known wit's jaunty ale-Norse* translation of a scriptural passage, actually be one of believers? Indeed, if faith should ever get

the idea of coming forward triumphantly en masse, then it would
not need to give permission to anyone to sing satirical songs, because
it would not help if it forbade this of everyone. Even if people were
struck dumb, one would hear, above this crazy procession, the ring-
ing of laughter, like the mocking sounds that are an acoustical curiosity of Ceylon, because a triumphant faith is incomparably ridiculous.
If the contemporary generation of believers did not have time to
declare victory, then no generation does; because the task is the same
and faith is always a struggle. But so long as there is still a struggle,
then there is still the possibility of defeat. With respect, therefore, to
faith one ought never to celebrate victory prematurely—i.e. never
in time, because when is there time to write victory songs or the
opportunity to sing them? If this happens, then it is as if an army
that was ready to advance on the field of battle would instead march
triumphantly home to the town barracks—even if no one laughed
at this, even if the entire contemporary generation sympathized
with this abracadabra—would not existence's own stifled laughter
break forth when one least expected it? What did the later so-called
believers do here other than what was even worse than that which
the contemporaries did in vainly entreating the god not to expose
himself to humiliation and contempt (Chapter II)? Because the later
so-called believers were not content with humiliation and contempt,
not content to be militant in what the world considered foolishness,
but were more than willing to believe when it involved singing and
celebration. The god could not say to such a person, as to his contemporaries: So you love only the omnipotence that performs miracles, not the one who lowered himself to be equal to you.

'I will stop here. Even if I were a better dialectician than I am, I
would still have my limits. It is fundamentally an unwavering insist-
ence on what is absolute and on absolute distinctions that makes one
a good dialectician, something we have failed completely to appreciate in our day when we are so keen to abolish this and that and, in
particular, to abolish the law of contradiction, without appreciating
what Aristotle emphasized, that this assertion that the law of contradiction has been abolished is itself based on the law of contradiction,
for otherwise the opposite claim, that it was not abolished, would be
equally true.

'There is only one last remark I will make now with respect to [305]
your many allusions that were all directed at the fact that I mixed

many borrowed expressions in with what I said. I do not deny that
this is the case. Nor will I conceal that I did so deliberately, and that
the next instalment of this piece, if I ever write another instalment,*
will refer to the matter by its proper name and clothe it in its historical costume. If I ever write a next instalment, because an author
of pamphlets, such as myself, lacks, as you will certainly come to
hear about me, seriousness, so how could I here, at the conclusion,
pretend to seriousness in order to please people by making such a
significant promise? Pamphlet-writing is a flighty endeavour—but
to promise a system, that is seriousness, and it has made many a
man into a very serious man, both in his own eyes and in the eyes of
others. It is not difficult, however, to see what that historical costume
will be in the next instalment. It is well known that Christianity is
the only historical phenomenon that despite the historical, yes, precisely with the historical, has wished to be the point of departure for
the individual's eternal consciousness, has wished to interest him in
another way than purely historically, has wished to base his eternal
happiness on his relation to something historical. No philosophy
(because it concerns only the intellect), no mythology (because it
concerns only the imagination), no historical knowledge (which concerns only memory) has ever got such an idea, which suggests that
in this connection one can make the ambiguous claim that it did not
arise in any human heart. This, on the other hand, I have wished, to
a certain extent, to forget. I thus made deliberate and unrestricted
use of a hypothesis, supposed the whole thing was my own bizarre
idea which I did not want to discard until I had thought it through
to its conclusion. The monks never finished relating the history of
the world because they kept beginning with creation. If, in describing the relation between Christianity and philosophy, one began by
describing what had already been said—how then could one—not
finish, but ever get started, because the material continues to grow?
If one should begin with "this great thinker and wise man, *executor
Novi Testamenti*, Pontius Pilate",* who in his way has done various
services to Christianity and philosophy, even though he did not
invent mediation, and if one, before beginning with him, waited for
[306] one or another decisive work (perhaps the system), for which there
have already been several proclamations *ex cathedra*,*[1] how would
one then ever come to begin?

---

[1] From the chair.

THE MORAL

This hypothesis indisputably goes beyond the Socratic, as is apparent at every point. Whether it is therefore truer than the Socratic is an entirely different question that cannot be answered in the same breath, in that here we have assumed a new organ: faith, and a new presupposition: the consciousness of sin; a new decision: the moment, and a new teacher: the god in time. Without these I truly would not have dared to present myself before the ironist admired for millennia and whom I approach with an enthusiasm so ardent it is surpassed by none. But to go further than Socrates, when one essentially says the same thing he says only not nearly so well — that at least is not Socratic.

EXPLANATORY NOTES

In compiling these notes we have benefited from the work of previous editors, and in particular from *Philosophical Fragments*, tr. and ed. David F. Swenson, Niels Thulstrup, and Howard V. Hong (Princeton: Princeton University Press, 1962); '*Philosophical Fragments*' and '*Johannes Climacus*', tr. and ed. Howard V. and Edna H. Hong (Princeton: Princeton University Press, 1985); '*Fear and Trembling*' and '*Repetition*', tr. and ed. Howard V. and Edna H. Hong (Princeton: Princeton University Press, 1983); and *Søren Kierkegaards Skrifter* (hereafter referred to as *SKS*), ed. Niels Jørgen Cappelørn, Joakim Garff, Johnny Kondrup, Alastair McKinnon, and Fin Hauberg Mortensen (G. E. C. Gads Forlag, 1997–).

REPETITION

TITLE PAGE: earlier subtitles to the text included 'A Fruitless Venture' and 'A Venture (or Essay) in Experimental Philosophy'. Kierkegaard used pseudonyms to distance himself from his writing, and to frustrate any attempt to discover the meaning of a text by looking into his biography. He is playfully revealing in his choice of pseudonyms. The name Constantine Constantius, or 'Constant Constant', affirms repetition (a kind of change) *and* constancy.

2 *epigraph:* from the *Heroicus* ('On Heroes') of the Greek writer Flavius Philostratus, born *c*.AD 170. Kierkegaard refers to his *Life of Appolonius of Tyana* in *Philosophical Crumbs* (see note to p.161).

3 *Eleatics*: school of Greek philosophers associated with Zeno of Elea (born *c*.490 BC), who was famous for such constructed abstract paradoxes as that motion is impossible. The paradox is 'refuted' here by the founder of the Cynics, Diogenes (*c*.400–*c*.325 BC).

Leibniz: the eighteenth century German philosopher claimed that the present contained the future within itself: the future, then, is a 'replay' or 'repetition' of (some aspect of) the present.

one author: the author is Kierkegaard himself. Against the view that a love that has gone by is therefore 'unhappy', Constantine alludes to a view contained in the first volume of *Either/Or*, in the 'Diapsalmata', to the effect that in this sad life the *only* happiness comes through memory— nothing stays with us long enough in the present to give happiness.

5 *Farinelli*: the famous *castrato* singer (1705–82); the reference here is to the opera *Farinelli*, by the Danish composer J. L. Heiberg (1837), in which he is portrayed as the only person able to distract the Spanish king Philip V from his depression.

7 *Møller*: Poul Martin Møller (1794–1838) was Kierkegaard's friend and professor.

There comes a dream ... golden hair: from Møller's poem 'Den gamle Elsker' (The Old Lover). The last line literally translates as: 'You sun of women!' I have taken the liberty of changing the line in order to preserve the rhyme of the original.

8 *Strandveien*: a coastal road near Copenhagen.

11 *Stadsgraven*: the moat around Copenhagen.

12 *Lessing giving ... birth*: in the *Concluding Unscientific Postscript* Climacus praises the eighteenth-century German writer G. E. Lessing for always seeking the truth, and having less interest in available finished truths (as if truth were best as it is being born) and as a Socrates might seek to bring it to birth in his interlocutors. Climacus quotes Lessing as saying: 'If I had to choose between the truth in God's right hand, and the search for truth in His left hand, I'd choose the left hand.' (*Concluding Unscientific Postscript*, ed. and trans. Howard V. Hong and Edna H. Hong (Princeton: Princeton University Press, 1992), 106.)

14 *Elvira*: in Mozart's opera *Don Giovanni*, Donna Elvira is abandoned by the great seducer, yet she never gives up hope that he might reform and return to her. Kierkegaard loved the opera, attending a Copenhagen production several times, and wrote a long essay on it in the first volume of *Either/Or*.

16 *disappearance*: this was originally his 'death'. Kierkegaard apparently changed 'death' (*Død*) to 'disappearance' (*Forsvinden*) after learning of his former fiancée's engagement. *SKS* has *Forvinden* ('recovery') rather than *Forsvinden*. As there is no editorial explanation for the change from the 1843 first-edition printing of *Forsvinden*, this appears to be an error in *SKS*.

18 *Heraclitus*: Presocratic Greek philosopher, known for his view that everything is flux, nothing eludes change. For the Eleatics see note to p. 3 above.

Mediation: a term common among Hegelian philosophers, referring to the view that a reconciliation or negotiation (mediation) among opposite forces is the engine of change, whether in debates or in personal development or in historical transitions. Constantine will suggest that neither mediation nor Greek recollection captures the essence of the sort of movement or change he calls 'repetition'.

19 *ethnic view*: Constantine needs a general contrast to 'modern', and uses 'ethnic' for a 'pre-Christian view, a viewpoint that we might call 'traditional' or 'historically-conventional' or even 'tribal' (in some very broad sense).

mit mancherlei ... argumentire: [I] express myself in various tongues, chattering away in the language of sophists, the puns of Cretans and Arabs, of whites, Moors and Creoles, a combination of criticism, mythology, *rebus*, and axioms, arguing now in a human, now in an extraordinary way.' From a letter of the German philosopher J. G. Hamann (1730–88) to J. G. Linder.

Professor Ussing: Tage Algreen Ussing (1797–1872) was a liberal politician and a professor of law at the University of Copenhagen.

28th of May Society: society formed to commemorate the introduction, on 28 May 1831, of the new ordinances on the Estates of the Realm.

20 *Molbos*: inhabitants of the Jutland peninsula of Mols, just north of Zealand. The Molbos are the butt of many Danish jokes.

coupé: a small section of a carriage, usually seating only two persons.

postillion: a coachman who rides the lead horse.

22 *marriage*: Kierkegaard discusses 'the aesthetic validity of marriage'— roughly, the question whether, apart from any moral or religious validity to marriage, there might be a beautiful or pleasing aspect to it, in his *Either/Or*, published a few months earlier.

23 *Tunnel*: a rail tunnel under the Thames had just been completed in 1843.

for amusement: the Royal Theatre in Copenhagen had a banner over the stage reading 'Not for Pleasure Only'.

Lars . . . Kehlet: two popular Copenhagen restaurants.

der Talisman: famous farce by the Viennese playwright Johann Nepomuk Nestroy that opened in 1843.

27 *Nüremberg print*: popular coloured woodcuts, produced in Germany. There are allusions to such prints in Kierkegaard's later works, *Practice in Christianity* and *Sickness Unto Death*.

entrechat: a ballet leap in which the dancer 'flutters' her (or his) feet while aloft. In *Fear and Trembling* Kierkegaard's pseudonym Johannes de Silentio contrasts 'the knight of faith' and 'the knight of infinite resignation' in terms of the capacity of each to complete a ballet leap gracefully.

28 *The orchestra and the first balcony*: these were the most expensive seats, and would generally have been occupied by a more cultured audience than one would find in the cheaper seats.

Cimbrian-Teutonic: Celtic or Germanic peoples, in this context, crude and 'uncivilized'.

30 *Chodowiecki*: the German illustrator Daniel Chodowiecki (1726–1801) produced engravings for a satirical version of Virgil's *Aeneid* that Kierkegaard owned. One depicted the founding of Rome.

31 *Socrates . . . nature*: in Plato's *Phaedrus* (229e–230a), Socrates wonders (perhaps ironically) whether he is a human being (with a more or less stable essence) or instead a changeable sea-monster like Typhon. The wording here is from *The Collected Dialogues of Plato*, ed. Edith Hamilton and Huntington Cairns (Princeton: Princeton University Press, 1961).

Beckmann and Grobecker: Friederich Beckmann (1803–66) and Phillipe Grobecker (1815–83) were leading actors at the Konigstädter in the early 1840s.

31 *Baggesen. . . . Sara Nickles*: Jens Immanuel Baggesen (1764–1826) was a
     Danish poet and literary figure. Baggesen is considered important in the
     transition from the Enlightenment to the Romantic period. Sara Nickles
     is a character who appears in Act 5 of *Ludlams Hule*, an opera by the
     Danish poet and literary figure Adam Ochlenschlager (1779–1850). This
     remark was made by Baggesen in a review of Oehlenschläger's opera.

32 *Even Dr Ryge . . . an effect*: allusion to two actors well-known at the time,
     and to J. L. Heiberg's vaudeville, *King Solomon and Jörgen the Hatter*.

     Münchhausen-like: Baron von Münchhausen, notorious for his tall tales,
     claimed that once when he fell in a bog he rescued himself by hauling
     himself up by his own coat collar (or hair, or bootstraps).

     Dyrhavesbakken: a popular amusement park just outside of Copenhagen.

37 *friendship*: the poet in question, who writes on coffee and friendship, is
     Johannes Ewald, referring to his '*Paaskrift paa en Kaffeekande*' (Recipe on
     a Coffeepot).

38 *every head*: for Proserpina's plucking hair, see Virgil, *Aeneid*, 4. 698–9.

     woman . . . dripping: Proverbs 19: 13.

     Unter den Linden: Berlin's main thoroughfare.

     beadle: sexton or church officer charged with keeping order.

     Kerner tells somewhere: the story comes from the German poet and medi-
     cal writer Justinus Kerner, *Eine Erscheinung aus dem Nachtgebiete der
     Natur* (An Apparition from Nature's Nocturnal Realms) (1836).

39 *Grønmeyer the businessman*: character in a play by J. L Heiberg, *Kjøge
     Huuskors* (Domestic Troubles in Kjøge).

     faithlessly . . . repetition: Kierkegaard makes a word-play here. The Danish
     for repetition is '*gjentagelse*', or to 'take again', so the first two italicized
     words are *tage* and *igjen*. The italics are Kierkegaard's.

41 *summing up*: Kierkegaard quotes Shakespeare from his Danish version of
     Schegel and Tieck's German translation: 'en Øltappers Regnekunst var
     tilstrækkelig for at opsummere dem'. Shakespeare's words are 'a tapster's
     arithmetic may soon bring his particulars therein to a total'. *Troilus and
     Cressida*, I. ii.

     passed: here in the sense in which it is used in card games.

     life is a stream: another allusion to Heraclitus' view of life as flux (see note
     to p. 18 above).

42 *The little nun . . . heart*: this poem appears in the original text in German:

> Das Nönnlein kam gegangen
> In einem schneeweißen Kleid;
> Ihr Häärl war abgeschnitten,
> Ihr rother Mund war bleich.
>
> Der Knab, er setzt sich nieder,
> Er saß auf einem Stein;
> Er weint die hellen Thränen,
> Brach ihm sein Herz entzwei.

post-horn: the driver of a mail coach would announce the mail's arrival by blowing a flourish on his horn.

everything . . . passes away: Ecclesiastes 1.

post-chaise: A horse-drawn carriage for carrying mail. Constantine is intrigued by the fact that a postal carriage is always on the move, but that it also predictably (and boringly) returns.

43 πεισιθάνατος: the philosopher Hegesias of Cyrene *c.*300 BC (nicknamed *Peisithanatos*, 'The Death-Persuader'), believed that no complete happiness exists, and thus counselled suicide. In one book, he suggests self-starvation.

44 *Domitian*: emperor of Rome, AD 81–96.

45 *Eleusinian mysteries*: rites of initiation held in Ancient Greece from *c.*1700 BC on into the Hellenistic era, performed in honour of Demeter and Persephone, and of great cultural-religious significance.

Demonax . . . defence: according to the dialogue on him by Lucian, the Greek philosopher Demonax (*c.*AD 70–170) defended his failure to be initiated into the Eleusinian mysteries by saying that if the mysteries were of no value then no one needed them, but if they were true then everyone should know them.

47 *eschatologist . . . Lucian*: an eschatologist writes about 'first and last things', for instance, about the afterlife. Aristophanes, the Greek comic playwright, wrote about the land of the dead in *The Frogs*, and the Roman-Syrian satirist Lucian (*c.*AD 125–80) wrote a series of *Dialogues of the Dead*. *Doctores cerei* is a medieval term referring to scholars given an honorary degree by papal dispensation ('with a wax seal'), without having to defend a thesis, i.e. second-rate or spurious scholars.

50 *Archimedean point*: Archimedes, (*c.*250 BC), the Greek mathematician and physicist, proposed that if he had a long enough lever, and a steady 'point' or fulcrum to rest it on, he could lift the world.

scrapes himself with potsherds: Job 2:8.

51 *Job . . . Greek symposium*: the most famous Greek symposium ('drinking-party') is the one related in Plato's dialogue of that name, in which Socrates and others give speeches on the nature of love. Constantine is contrasting the young man's attraction to the model of insight found in the Book of Job to a Greek model.

55 *Don Juan . . . Commandatore*: in Mozart's opera *Don Giovanni*, the statue of the Commandatore, murdered by Don Giovanni, appears in the last act in order to drag him to hell. The Don tears himself away from the cold hand of the Commandatore with a defiant 'No!'

57 *Adresseavisen*: newspaper composed of classified advertisements.

blue boys: orphans in the Royal Orphanage established in 1753 in Copenhagen, so called because of the blue outfits they received at confirmation.

Because of what value . . . from a young girl's breast: from the poem 'Elskovsbaalet' (Love's Fire) by the Danish poet Schak von Staffeldt.

I have taken some liberties here in order to preserve the rhyme of the original. A more literal translation would be: 'What is the adulation that comes with a famous fame, compared to a sigh of love from a young girl's breast?' Even this is not as faithful to the original as is possible though, because a faithful translation of *Navnkundighed* (i.e. 'renown', 'celebrity', or 'fame') would lose the allusion to 'name' (i.e. the *Navn* of *Navnkundighed*).

57 *The clouds . . . grave*: from the poem 'Der ewige Jude,' (The Wandering Jew), by the German poet Wilhelm Müller. This poem appears in the original text in German:

> Die Wolken treiben hin und her,
> Sie sind so matt, sie sind so schwer;
> Da stürzen rauschend sie herab,
> Der Schoos der Erde wird ihr Grab.

no pleasure in them: Ecclesiastes 12: 1.

58 *name of the Lord*: Job 1: 21.

days of your youth: Job 29.

60 *salt*: Mark 9: 50.

Pierrot: sad clown, a stock figure of the Commedia dell'Arte.

Seelenverkopper: 'soul-seller', the colloquial name for an innkeeper who served sailors so much drink that they passed out; they were then sold to a ship's captain needing a crew.

62 *Balle's Catechism*: *Lærebog i den Evangelisk-christelig Religion, indrettet til brug i de danske Skoler* (Textbook of the Evangelical-Christian Religion, designed for use in Danish schools), by Nicolai Edinger Balle (1791). Kierkegaard read *Balle's Catechism* as a child; it made a lasting impression on him.

Per Degn: an earthy character in the comedy *Erasmus Montanus* by the Danish playwright Ludvig Holberg (1684–1754), who puts Latin scholars to shame.

64 *Philoctetes*: the central character of the tragedy of that title by Sophocles (performed 409 BC). Bitten by a snake while on the way to attack Troy, Philoctetes is abandoned on an island by the rest of the Greek army, who were unable to endure the stench of his wound. Philoctetes' agonized lamentations are prominent in the play.

65 *his neighbour*: Job 16: 21.

66 *Eliphas . . . Elihu*: the first three are his neighbours who argue with Job, pressing his putative guilt, since otherwise he would not be suffering (Elihu arrives later in the book, and shows a somewhat different attitude).

pity on me: Job 19: 221.

67 *with lies*: Job: 13: 4.

   does the wild ass . . . grass: Job 6: 5.

   The Lord gave the Lord: Job 1: 21.

69 *days of his youth*: Job 29: 4.

   earring of gold: Job 42: 11.

   had before: Job 42: 10.

72 *marriage*: the Danish term for 'married': *gift*, also means 'poison'.

74 *off the street*: Luke 10: 29–37.

75 *Ilithyia*: the Greek goddess of childbirth.

76 *Clemens Alexandrinus*: Clement of Alexandria, *c*.AD 200, was one of the first thinkers to blend biblical thinking with Greek philosophy.

77 *1. 2. 3. development*: a Hegelian 'development' of ideas was taken as a three-step dialectic, an idea or claim countered by its opposite, and that conflict resolved by a mediating or reconciling step.

79 *see only darkly in him*: cf. 'we see through a glass darkly', 1 Corinthians 13: 12.

81 *fear and trembling . . . something strange*: Constantine here describes the condition of *Fear and Trembling*'s 'Knight of Faith'.

PHILOSOPHICAL CRUMBS

TITLE PAGE: the Danish title, *Philosophiske Smuler*, was first translated into English by David Swenson as *Philosophical Fragments* (Princeton: Princeton University Press, 1936). The revised version of Swenson's translation by Howard and Edna Hong, as well as the Hongs' own later translation (Princeton: Princeton University Press, 1985), retained this title. The present translation uses 'crumbs' instead of 'fragments', for two reasons. First, there was a Danish cognate of the English 'fragments' in Kierkegaard's time (see Meyer's *Fremmedordbog* (Copenhagen, 1853), s.v. *Fragment*), which Kierkegaard could easily have chosen but did not. Second, Kierkegaard may well have chosen *Smuler* over *Fragmenter* (the plural of the Danish *Fragment*) because it alludes to the well-known Danish saying, *Smulerne er også Brød* (The crumbs are also bread), which in turn alludes to Matthew 15: 21–8. For Kierkegaard's adoption as a pseudonym 'John Climacus' (John the Ladder'), the name of a seventh-century theologian, See Introduction, p. xvii.

84 *Epigraph*: Shakespeare, *Twelfth Night*, I. v. (See Introduction, p. xvii.)

85 *Holberg's . . . deo*: in the comedy by the Danish-Norwegian playwright Ludvig Holberg, *Jacob von Tyboe eller den stortalende Soldat* (Jacob von Tyboe, or the Grandiloquent Soldier) (1725), a Magister Stygotius declares that 'God willing (*volente deo*), I will defend my thesis day after tomorrow'. Kierkegaard did write a sequel to *Philosophical Crumbs* entitled *Conluding Unscientific Postscript*, published in 1846.

85 *crime against the state*: in Athens under Solon, there was a legal requirement to serve in public affairs. To fail to do so would be to commit the
crime of 'refusal to participate in civic life'(*apragmosyné*).

Archimedes: Greek mathematician and physicist (287–212 BC).

Diogenes: founder of the Cynic school of Greek philosophy. Anecdotes
about his distain for cultural refinements abound, collected mainly in
Diogenes Laertius' *Lives of Eminent Philosophers*, written in the third century AD. Kierkegaard owned both Greek and Danish editions. He is also
referred to at the start of *Repetition* (see note to p. 3). The anecdote cited
here, however, comes from Lucian (see *Lucian, Selected Dialogues*, translated with an introduction and notes by Desmond Costa, Oxford World's
Classics (Oxford: Oxford University Press, 2005), 182.

86 *world-historical significance*: in many texts, Kierkegaard mocked the pre-
tentions of Hegelians to know that history was bringing us closer and
closer to an ideal, with the help of 'world-historical' figures, for example
Alexander the Great or Napoleon.. This optimism about the march of
history, in Kierkegaard's opinion, distracted individuals from the sort of
personal, existential significance essential to the lives of everyday individuals.

Goldkalb: a character in a popular play by J. L. Heiberg. *King Salomon
and Jörgen The Hatter* (1825). There is a mix-up of identities, and the
citizens of Copenhagen greet with celebratory parades and speeches a
person they take to be the illustrious Baron Goldkalb. The person in fact
is an insignificant merchant, Salomon Goldkalb. For another reference to
this play see note to *Repetition*, p. 32.

falls over: Hegel speaks of antinomies, concepts that are opposed (for
example, freedom and bondage). Historical motion takes place when the
freedom of a master (for example) is challenged by a slave, the slave
subsequently becoming free. This exchange of positions can be seen
abstractly, Hegel believed, as a 'dialectical advance' in history, since
the newly free slave will have a different freedom than his master
possessed, and the unfree former master will not be precisely in the
bondage formerly suffered by the slave. Climacus mocks this so-called
'dialectical progress' with the image of a 'concept' that 'flips over' in
undergoing a 'dialectical reversal'. One can follow up the sort of
scenario that is mocked here in Hegel's account of 'the master–slave relationship' in *The Phenomenology of Spirit*, trans. A. V. Miller (Oxford,
1977), 111–19.

87 *Cratylus*: in Plato's dialogue *Cratylus*, Socrates says (ironically) that he
would have taken the more expensive course in logic and philosophy
offered by the sophist Prodicus, if only he had had the money. See
Cratylus, 384b. Prodicus (*c*.465–415 (BC) was among the first of the free-
lance teachers later called sophists.

88 *be taught*: Danish has only one word, *'lære'* for both 'teach' and 'learn'. Both the earlier translations of this work have 'learned' 'here. It is impossible to know definitely which Kierkegaard intended; 'teach' and 'instruct' actually precede 'learn,' however, in Vinterberg and Bodelsen's *Dansk-Engelsk Ordbog* (Danish–English Dictionary). Given that either 'learned' or 'taught' will work here and that the former has been tried twice already, it seemed time to try the latter.

Protagoras . . . Euthydemus: Platonic dialogues in which the question of knowledge and virtue is discussed.

89 *the positive*: Socrates did not offer 'positive knowledge' but instead used questioning to show what others did not know, while pleading ignorance himself (thus remaining, so some thought, 'negative'). Kierkegaard disputes this view, holding that Socrates had a 'most positive' relationship to his 'voice', to 'the god', and to his philosophical vocation. And he understood that being a midwife, helping to bring others into the world, was the highest relation anyone could have to another.

Diogenes Laertius: the wording is from the Loeb Classical Library edn.: *Diogenes Laertius, Lives of Eminent Philosophers*, trans. R. D. Hicks (Cambridge, Mass.: Harvard University Press, 1972), i.151.

90 *Prodicus*: see note to p. 87 above, on *Cratylus*.

Common shipwreck: alludes to the Latin saying: *commune naufragium dulce* (common shipwreck is sweet).

91 *Clitophon*: Clitophon is a dialogue sometimes attributed to Plato. Its authenticity is uncertain.

94 *Aristotle*: this is Kierkegaard's summary paraphrase of Aristotle's *Nicomachean Ethics*, book 3 ch. 5.

95 *fullness of time*: cf. Galatians 4: 4: 'But when the time had fully come, God sent forth His Son.'

97 *Minos . . . Rhadamanthus*: Socrates names these as the judges of the underworld (*Apology*, 41a).

99 *go to the next house*: phrase in a parlour game, which is equivalent to 'go fish' in the card-game fish. That is, it means: I do not have the card (or in this case, I am not the one) you want.

autopathetic: sympathy is feeling for others, and autopathy is feeling for oneself.

100 *Alcibiades*: in Plato's *Symposium* (212c–223d), the young Alcibiades complains of how Socrates has rejected his amorous advances.

Corybantic mystic: Corybantes were worshippers of the Phrygian goddess Cybele. Kierkegaard's readers would think of them as noisy, frenzied, intoxicated singers.

102 *Gorgias*: in the Platonic dialogue named after the sophist Gorgias, this complaint about Socrates is actually made by the Athenian Callicles rather than Gorgias pupil Polos.

Themistocles' lovely words: Themistocles (*c*.524–*c*.460 BC) was an Athenian politician. Plutarch writes that Themistocles said to the Persian king Xerxes (486–465 BC) that 'the speech of man was like embroidered tapestries, since like them this too had to be extended in order to display its patterns, but when it was rolled up it concealed and distorted them' (*Plutarch's Lives*, trans. Bernadotte Perrin, Loeb Classical Library [Cambridge, Mass.: Harvard University Press, 1914], ii. 79).

104 *out of grief's house*: at the start of the *Symposium* Socrates asks the flute-player to leave (176e); during his last hours he asks his wife to leave, so as not to be distracted by the noise of her weeping (*Phaedo*, 60b).

106 *summer robe*: Socrates is said to have marched in snow wearing only a light cloak (*Symposium*, 22b).

harvest of philosophy: the wording here is taken from *The Collected Dialogues of Plato*, ed. Edith Hamilton and Huntington Cairns (Princeton: Princeton University Press, 1961).

107 *lay his head*: cf. Luke 9: 58.

behold the man: cf. John 19: 5.

108 *the woman whose sins were forgiven*: Luke 7: 37.

what have you to do with me: John 2: 4, 'what have I to do with thee'.

get thee behind me: Luke 4: 8.

pierces her heart: Luke 2: 35.

111 *stranger monster than Typhon*: see note to *Repetition* p. 31 above.

Democritus: Presocratic Greek philosopher.

112 *Sextus Empiricus*: a second- (possibly third-) century AD philosopher who provides the oldest surviving account of the many schools of ancient Greek and Roman scepticism; see *Outlines of Pyrrhonism*, trans. R. G. Bury, Loeb Classical Library (London: Heinemann, 1933).

man the measure of all things: saying attributed to the fifth-century BC philosopher and sophist Protagoras.

as did Socrates: on the way to the symposium, Socrates mysteriously 'halts' in a doorway, apparently lost in thought (*Symposium*, 174e). Later, towards the end of the party, Alcibiades tells the story of Socrates remaining trans-fixed for a day while on a military campaign (*Symposium*, 220c–d).

love the neighbour as himself: Matt. 22: 36–40; Mark 12: 31.

115 *Cartesian dolls*: toys that right themselves when pushed over.

participates equally: Plato and medieval philosophers generally distin-guished *degrees* of being: a grain of sand had less being than a child, and a child had less being than an angel, etc. Climacus is holding an 'equality' of being: things just are (or are not), whether angels or grains of sand.

116 *Chrysippus*: leading Stoic philosopher, (*c.*280–*c.*207 BC), reputed author of 700 texts, none of which survives intact. We know his views from fragments and from Diogenes Laertes (see note above, 'Diogenes', for p. 3). He performed thought experiments that stressed the continuity between quantity (23 or 25 beans) and quality (100 beans is a heap).

sorites: a chain of argument than can lead to paradox. For example, one might argue that a given number of grains of sand does not make a heap and that an additional grain does not either, and conclude that therefore no additional grains will make a heap. Climacus might say that a conceptual 'leap' is involved in such shift from quantity (grains of sand) to quality (heaps).

Carneades: (*c.*214–129 BC), an academic sceptic and eventualy head of the Academy.

leap: see note on *sorites*, above.

there is no God: Psalms 14: 1 and 53: 2.

117 *via eminentia*: getting a result *via negationis* is attaining to an idea of God by removing (negating) all attributes: God is not powerful (as we know that term), not loving (as we know that term), etc. Getting a result *via eminentia* is attaining to an idea of God by adding on all possible attributes, to a 'high or highest degree': God is powerful (in excess of what we usually mean by that term); loving (in excess of what we usually mean by that term), etc.

123 *wonder stool*: a parlour-game in which one person sat on a stool while another person asked each of the other players, in a whisper, what he or she wondered about or wished to know about the person on the stool. The latter then had to guess which questions had come from which player.

124 *Tertullian . . . King Lear*: the passage includes allusions to the African Church Father Tertullian (*c.*160–*c.*225); the German religious thinker Johann Georg Hamann (1730–88); the Christian apologist Lactantius (*c.*240–*c.*320); the German Reformer Martin Luther (1483–1546); and Shakespeare's *King Lear*, IV. vi.

125 *She half dragged him, he half sank down*: from Goethe, 'Der Fischer', (The Fisherman).

126 *nor place to rest*: cf. 'The son of man hath no place to rest his head' (Luke 9: 58; Matt. 8: 5).

126 *burying the dead*: cf. 'Let the dead bury their dead' (Luke 9: 60).

127 *concerned about tomorrow*: cf. Matt. 6: 31.

the lily: cf. Matt. 6: 25–33.

136 *We have eaten . . . whence ye are*: Luke 13: 26–7.

137 *Mithridates*: Mithridates VI, king of Pontus (132–63 BC).

138 *Smerdis*: in Book 3 of his *Histories* Herodotus tells how the Persian throne was usurped by a Magian claiming to be Smerdis, brother of the dead king Cambyses.

to grandmother's door: a move in a game, as in 'advance to the jackpot'.

139 *limed branch*: i.e. 'go on a wild-goose chase'; to run after birds with a limed branch, hoping that they will settle and stick on it.

140 *on the same thing*: in Plato's *Gorgias* Callicles accuses Socrates of endlessly 'saying the same old thing' (*Gorgias*, 490).

142 *Epicurus*: Greek philosopher (341–270 BC).

143 *Nebeneinander, Space*: Hegel calls space an 'ideal' wherein the idea 'becomes external', or manifests itself as nature unfolding (*Hegel's Philosophy of Nature*, trans. A. V. Miller (Oxford: Oxford University Press, 1970), 28). *Nebeneinander* can mean 'simultaneous', in which case Hegel is claiming that 'Nature' and 'The Idea' unfold simultaneously.

144 *Chrysippus*: see note to p. 116.

Diodorus: Diodorus Cronus (fl. *c*.300 BC), Greek logician and philosopher, who argued that since everything that is is necessary, then the future is as fixed as the past.

145 *Geert Westphaler*: character in the comedy *Master Geer Westphaler, or The Very Talkative Barber* by Ludvig Holberg.

in the Logic: Hegel's *Science of Logic*.

146 *Boethius*: Christian philosopher (*c*.AD 480–*c*.525), author of the *Consolation of Philosophy* and of translations of some of Aristotle's logical works.

Daub: Karl Daub, German theologian–historian (1765–1836), whose writing Kierkegaard admired.

Leibniz: Gottfried Leibniz (1646–1716), German logician, mathematician, and philosopher known for his theory of 'logically possible worlds' and discussion of God's foreknowledge. He argued in his *Théodicée* (1710) that God has created the best of all possible worlds, a view Voltaire would mock in *Candide*.

147 *wonder*: Plato has Socrates claim that philosophy begins in wonder (*Theaetetus*, 155).

Baader: Franz Baader, German philosopher (1765–1841). The source of this claim attributed to Baader is unknown.

148 *belief*: there is only one Danish expression, *Tro*, for both 'faith' and 'belief'.

150 *Jacobi*: Friedrich Heinrich Jacobi (1743–1819), German philosopher notable for coining the term 'nihilism'. He held that every move from effect to cause is a matter of 'belief' or 'faith', since we have no certain knowledge that the causal principle itself is true.

equivocation: the Danish term here is *tvetyde*, which literally means, 'to suggest two things'. Kierkegaard has italicized the *tve* portion of the word, apparently to emphasize, in line with the Pyrrhonist sceptics, that doubt contrasts two opposing possibilities.

155 *sorites*: see note to p. 116, above.

157 *the seventy interpreters*: according to tradition, seventy scholars each produced a translation of the Pentateuch from Hebrew into Greek, for
Ptolemy II (287–247 BC). When the translations were compared they were
found to be identical. The Greek version became known as the *Septuagint*,
from the Greek word for 'seventy'.

158 *galimatias*: gibberish, nonsense.

160 *neuen Buden*: Ludvig Holberg's comedy *The Busy Man* has a character who
was born in 'Neuen-Buden', a housing development near Østerport in
Copenhagen, who tells of a woman who gave birth to '32 children'. 'Is this
possible?' a character asks in disbelief? The (darkly) humorous answer is yes,
that all immediately died.

161 *Apollonius of Tyana*: neo-Pythagorean philosopher (*c*.AD40–*c*.120) who
claimed to have been a sailor in a previous life. The story (perhaps fictional)
is told in a biography written by the sophist Philostratus, who completed
his *Life of Apollonius of Tyana* sometime between AD217 and 238.

166 *Münchhausen*: cf. note to *Repetition*, p. 32.

168 *Saft*: character in the play *Sovedrikken* (The Sleeping Draught) by
Oehlenschlager, who is interested only in eating.

170 *ale-Norse*: the Danish here is *ølnordisk*, which literally means 'ale-Norse'.
This is a play on the Danish *oldnordisk*, which means 'old Norse', and is
very likely a satirical reference to Nikolaj Frederik Severin Grundtvig
(1783–1872). Grundtving was a Danish pastor, writer, and cultural figure
who, among other things, wrote many Scandinavian-themed hymns.
Gruntvig emphasized the Scandinavian roots of Danish culture, and is
considered by many to be the father of modern Danish nationalism.
Kierkegaard tended, however, to disparage both the substance of
Grundtvig's thought and the aesthetic quality of his literary output. He is
the butt of the rather extended joke in the *Postscript* on 'the new
hymnal'.

172 *another instalment*: he did, called: *Concluding Unscientific Postscript*.

Pilate: Pontius Pilate was perhaps the 'executor of the will' of the
New Testament insofar as he brought the plot of those books to fruition.
Cf. Luke 24: 44.

ex cathedra: this expression is normally used to signify authoritative
statements on doctrinal issues made by the pope.

The Oxford World's Classics Website

www.worldsclassics.co.uk

- Browse the full range of Oxford World's Classics online

- Sign up for our monthly e-alert to receive information on new titles

- Read extracts from the Introductions

- Listen to our editors and translators talk about the world's greatest literature with our Oxford World's Classics audio guides

- Join the conversation, follow us on Twitter at OWC_Oxford

- Teachers and lecturers can order inspection copies quickly and simply via our website

www.worldsclassics.co.uk

American Literature

British and Irish Literature

Children's Literature

Classics and Ancient Literature

Colonial Literature

Eastern Literature

European Literature

Gothic Literature

History

Medieval Literature

Oxford English Drama

Poetry

Philosophy

Politics

Religion

The Oxford Shakespeare

A complete list of Oxford World's Classics, including Authors in Context, Oxford English Drama, and the Oxford Shakespeare, is available in the UK from the Marketing Services Department, Oxford University Press, Great Clarendon Street, Oxford OX2 6DP, or visit the website at www.oup.com/uk/worldsclassics.

In the USA, visit www.oup.com/us/owc for a complete title list.

Oxford World's Classics are available from all good bookshops. In case of difficulty, customers in the UK should contact Oxford University Press Bookshop, 116 High Street, Oxford OX1 4BR.

A SELECTION OF   OXFORD WORLD'S CLASSICS

HORACE	The Complete Odes and Epodes
JUVENAL	The Satires
LIVY	The Dawn of the Roman Empire
	Hannibal's War
	The Rise of Rome
MARCUS AURELIUS	The Meditations
OVID	The Love Poems
	Metamorphoses
PETRONIUS	The Satyricon
PLATO	Defence of Socrates, Euthyphro, and Crito
	Gorgias
	Meno and Other Dialogues
	Phaedo
	Republic
	Selected Myths
	Symposium
PLAUTUS	Four Comedies
PLUTARCH	Greek Lives
	Roman Lives
	Selected Essays and Dialogues
PROPERTIUS	The Poems
SOPHOCLES	Antigone, Oedipus the King, and Electra
STATIUS	Thebaid
SUETONIUS	Lives of the Caesars
TACITUS	Agricola and Germany
	The Histories
VIRGIL	The Aeneid
	The Eclogues and Georgics
XENOPHON	The Expedition of Cyrus

	Late Victorian Gothic Tales
JANE AUSTEN	Emma
	Mansfield Park
	Persuasion
	Pride and Prejudice
	Selected Letters
	Sense and Sensibility
MRS BEETON	Book of Household Management
MARY ELIZABETH BRADDON	Lady Audley's Secret
ANNE BRONTË	The Tenant of Wildfell Hall
CHARLOTTE BRONTË	Jane Eyre
	Shirley
	Villette
EMILY BRONTË	Wuthering Heights
ROBERT BROWNING	The Major Works
JOHN CLARE	The Major Works
SAMUEL TAYLOR COLERIDGE	The Major Works
WILKIE COLLINS	The Moonstone
	No Name
	The Woman in White
CHARLES DARWIN	The Origin of Species
THOMAS DE QUINCEY	The Confessions of an English Opium-Eater
	On Murder
CHARLES DICKENS	The Adventures of Oliver Twist
	Barnaby Rudge
	Bleak House
	David Copperfield
	Great Expectations
	Nicholas Nickleby
	The Old Curiosity Shop
	Our Mutual Friend
	The Pickwick Papers

CHARLES DICKENS	A Tale of Two Cities
GEORGE DU MAURIER	Trilby
MARIA EDGEWORTH	Castle Rackrent
GEORGE ELIOT	Daniel Deronda
	The Lifted Veil and Brother Jacob
	Middlemarch
	The Mill on the Floss
	Silas Marner
SUSAN FERRIER	Marriage
ELIZABETH GASKELL	Cranford
	The Life of Charlotte Brontë
	Mary Barton
	North and South
	Wives and Daughters
GEORGE GISSING	New Grub Street
	The Odd Women
EDMUND GOSSE	Father and Son
THOMAS HARDY	Far from the Madding Crowd
	Jude the Obscure
	The Mayor of Casterbridge
	The Return of the Native
	Tess of the d'Urbervilles
	The Woodlanders
WILLIAM HAZLITT	Selected Writings
JAMES HOGG	The Private Memoirs and Confessions of a Justified Sinner
JOHN KEATS	The Major Works
	Selected Letters
CHARLES MATURIN	Melmoth the Wanderer
JOHN RUSKIN	Selected Writings
WALTER SCOTT	The Antiquary
	Ivanhoe

	Travel Writing 1700–1830
	Women's Writing 1778–1838
WILLIAM BECKFORD	Vathek
JAMES BOSWELL	Life of Johnson
FRANCES BURNEY	Camilla
	Cecilia
	Evelina
	The Wanderer
LORD CHESTERFIELD	Lord Chesterfield's Letters
JOHN CLELAND	Memoirs of a Woman of Pleasure
DANIEL DEFOE	A Journal of the Plague Year
	Moll Flanders
	Robinson Crusoe
	Roxana
HENRY FIELDING	Jonathan Wild
	Joseph Andrews and Shamela
	Tom Jones
WILLIAM GODWIN	Caleb Williams
OLIVER GOLDSMITH	The Vicar of Wakefield
MARY HAYS	Memoirs of Emma Courtney
ELIZABETH INCHBALD	A Simple Story
SAMUEL JOHNSON	The History of Rasselas
	The Major Works
CHARLOTTE LENNOX	The Female Quixote
MATTHEW LEWIS	Journal of a West India Proprietor
	The Monk
HENRY MACKENZIE	The Man of Feeling

ÉMILE ZOLA
L'Assommoir
The Attack on the Mill
La Bête humaine
La Débâcle
Germinal
The Kill
The Ladies' Paradise
The Masterpiece
Nana
Pot Luck
Thérèse Raquin